Manufacturing Renaissance

The Harvard Business Review Book Series

Manufacturing Renaissance

Edited with
an Introduction by
Gary P. Pisano and
Robert H. Hayes

A Harvard Business Review Book

Copyright © 1974, 1983, 1984, 1985, 1986, 1988, 1989, 1990, 1993, 1994, 1995 by the President and Fellows of Harvard College.
All rights reserved.
Printed in the United States of America
99 98 97 96 95 94   5 4 3 2 1

Editor's Note: Some articles in this book have been written before authors and editors began to take into consideration the role of women in management. We hope the archaic usage representing all managers as male does not detract from the usefulness of the collection.

The *Harvard Business Review* articles in this collection are available as individual reprints. Discounts apply to quantity purchases. For information and ordering contact Customer Service, Harvard Business School Publishing, Boston, MA 02163. Telephone: (617) 495-6192, 9 a.m. to 5 p.m. Eastern Time, Monday through Friday. Fax: (617) 495-6985, 24 hours a day.

The paper used in this publication meets the requirements of the American National Standard for Permanence of Paper for Printed Library Materials Z39.48-1984

Library of Congress Cataloging-in-Publication Data

Manufacturing renaissance / edited with an introduction by Gary P. Pisano and Robert H. Hayes.
    p.   cm. — (A Harvard business review book)
ISBN 0-87584-610-6
1. United States—Manufactures—Management.   2. Industrial management—United States.   I. Pisano, Gary P.   II. Hayes, Robert H.
III. Series
HD9725.M363   1995
658.5—dc20   94-43320
                                                                   CIP

Contents

Part III   Improving Competitiveness through Systems and Procedures

Before managers can take steps to boost productivity, they must have accurate performance-measurement systems. While managers have many tools to improve productivity at the structural level (such as investing in new equipment, eliminating waste, and cutting inventories), greater productivity gains can be achieved through streamlining operational processes, introducing change gradually, and promoting learning throughout the organization.

A comprehensive comparison of Japanese and U.S. room air conditioning plants reveals underlying determinants of product performance. This study suggests that sound management practices and careful attention to activities outside the manufacturing process are the keys to Japan's quality advantage.

The authors argue that the "robustness" of products is more a function of good design than of on-line control. Critiquing the traditional quality principle of "zero defects," they offer an alternative methodology for creating product designs that are less likely to experience defects during manufacture, even when the production process or component parts are slightly off-target.

Part IV   Creating the New Manufacturing Organization

Appropriate measurement systems must include more nonfinancial indicators of performance.

manufacturing function may require a fundamental reassessment of goals, capabilities, and organizational design.

Introduction

Gary P. Pisano
Robert H. Hayes

The past two decades have been a period of ferment for both managers and students of manufacturing. From the cauldron of steadily intensifying global competition have emerged aggressive and highly competent competitors, rapid technological change, and increasingly demanding (and, in some countries, environmentally conscious) consumers. This heightened intensity of industrial competition has forced managers and academics alike to reconsider many long-held beliefs about manufacturing, its role in the modern enterprise, and the way it should be managed. Many traditional ideas have been reexamined in light of a changing world and cast aside, while other, older (some almost forgotten—or even discredited) practices and approaches have been resurrected, sometimes with new labels. Managers have found themselves barraged with new concepts and approaches: JIT (just-in-time), TQM (total quality management), DFM (design for manufacturability), and other TLAs (three letter acronyms), not to mention lean manufacturing, process reengineering, benchmarking, empowerment, and the ubiquitous team approach.

This situation has led to widespread experimentation with a variety of new ideas about manufacturing strategy and management. Inevitably, some ideas were discarded quickly; they simply could not be implemented, proved ineffective, or were useful only in special circumstances. Others enjoyed a brief, almost faddish popularity before fading from view. Still others, however, not only have stood the test of time and practice but have helped change the way scholars and managers think about the very nature of industrial competition and manufacturing management.

In this volume, we have brought together some of these important ideas as conveyed in articles published in the *Harvard Business Review* over the past decade or so. Our motivations in selecting and organizing the articles for this book have both historical and practical roots. We attempted to capture some of the major new streams of thought that have been evolving since the end of fixed exchange rates in the early 1970s (which fundamentally changed the ground rules for international competition), while highlighting those that we believe will continue to influence practice over at least the next decade. Given space limits, we could not include all of the many excellent and influential articles on manufacturing published in the *Review*, but we believe this collection is representative of those with the greatest potential to shape future thinking and practice.

We have organized the articles into five major parts, each of which focuses on a different theme. To put them into context, we begin with a look at how the thinking about what constitutes "good manufacturing practice" has evolved over the past century.

A Brief Historical Background

Until the early 1980s, most American managers thought about manufacturing in terms of a paradigm whose roots extended back well over one hundred years. The "American system of manufacturing," with its emphasis on mass markets, standard designs, and mass production using interchangeable parts, revolutionized manufacturing in the mid-nineteenth century. Modified and elaborated by the principles of "Scientific Management," as promulgated by Frederick Taylor and his disciples, as well as by such great industrialists as Andrew Carnegie, Isaac Singer, and Henry Ford, this new paradigm was the foundation upon which the United States built itself into an industrial powerhouse in the early years of this century. By the 1960s, most U.S. managers accepted its basic principles: work is most efficiently done when divided and assigned to specialists, managers and staff experts should do the thinking for workers (so workers could concentrate on "doing"), every process is characterized by an innate amount of variation (and hence an irreducible rate of defects), and communication in an organization should be tightly controlled and should proceed through a hierarchical chain of command. The best manufacturing process is one based on long runs, and it uses inventories to buffer different stages both from each other and from the erratic behavior of suppliers and customers.

One challenger of the notion that there was "one best way" (to use Frederick Taylor's phrase) to organize and operate the manufacturing function was Professor John McLean, who, during the late 1940s, developed a course at Harvard Business School called Advanced Production Problems. Embedded in that course was the germ of a "contingency theory" for manufacturing—that companies, even within the same industry, often follow different competitive strategies and adopt different policies about such important issues as the location of facilities, methods of production control, internal vs. external production of materials, and the administrative structure of plants. Thus, while the "mass production" approach might be appropriate in some competitive contexts, McLean argued that different approaches to manufacturing would be required in others. That course, and the message it carried, had a powerful impact on the students who took it—among them a young Wickham Skinner.

A dozen years later, Skinner found himself teaching the same course (which he renamed Manufacturing Policy). The U.S. manufacturing environment, as he saw it, had changed dramatically since he was a student. Whereas the United States dominated world industry in the 1950s, when foreign managers came to America in droves to study the latest manufacturing equipment and methods, by the mid-1960s Skinner sensed that U.S. companies were no longer managing their manufacturing resources as effectively as they had. Rather than providing competitive advantage, manufacturing organizations were increasingly seen as sources of problems and constraints. In a prophetic article entitled "Production Under Pressure," published in the *Harvard Business Review* in 1966, he wrote:

> In many industries we appear to be losing ground to foreign competition. . . . As I examine the U.S. manufacturing scene, it appears to me that these obvious and immediate concerns are symptomatic of an underlying process of change which is of major significance. The fact is, we have begun the painful process of replacing the techniques, skills, facilities, and even the managers of an already outdated concept of production, which I shall call, for want of a better name, "mass production." (139)

Few scholars or practitioners took Skinner's warnings to heart. By the early 1970s, he saw little change in the way manufacturing was managed in the United States or in how senior managers in most companies viewed its role. In his 1971 *Harvard Business Review* article

"The Anachronistic Factory," Skinner once again warned that U.S. manufacturing badly needed an overhaul:

> The conventional factory is fast becoming an anachronism. . . . Like it or not, we are being forced to challenge from the ground up all pieces of conventional wisdom concerning every facet of industrial management from individual job definition, work force management, the foreman's job, and equipment and process design to scheduling and inventory control. (62)

In this and other articles[1], Skinner laid out the basic principles of a framework that would have a remarkable impact on the way scholars and practitioners thought about manufacturing. The core tenets of that framework were that (1) different companies within the same industry compete in different ways (in terms of their relative emphases on such aspects as price, quality, product innovation, rapid delivery and customer service) and therefore adopt different yardsticks of success; (2) and similarly, different production systems (the composite of decisions in a number of key decision areas) have different operating characteristics—no single system of production can do all things equally well. Therefore, rather than adopting a "one size fits all," or even an "industry-standard" production system; (3) the "task" for a company's manufacturing function is to create a production system that, through a series of interrelated and internally consistent choices, reflects the priorities and trade-offs implicit in its specific competitive situation and strategy.

Unfortunately, Skinner's warnings went largely unheeded until the mid-1970s, when American companies began losing market share in such visible industries as automobiles, steel, and consumer electronics. Initially, the managers in those industries attributed their competitive difficulties to "lower wages" or to the inevitable flight of "mature" industries to less developed countries and the shifting patterns of comparative advantage within the global economy. It became an article of faith that the U.S. economy's comparative advantage lay in R&D-intensive industries (i.e., "high technology").

In the late 1970s and early 1980s, however, U.S. companies in such high-technology industries as semiconductors, computers, and advanced machining systems also began losing out to Japanese competitors. It became clear that the problems of American (and European) manufacturers were much deeper and broader than they had previously appeared. While recognizing that lower wages alone did not account for the success of Japanese companies, managers and observers began arguing that the real secret weapon the Japanese companies wielded was government assistance, in the form of protectionism combined with subsidies under the overall direction of an "industrial policy" that coordinated attacks on targeted industries. But as westerners took a closer look at Japanese management practices, and realized how vulnerable many U.S. industries had become, they came to understand that Japan's success was primarily a triumph of sheer manufacturing virtuosity. Studies indicated that Japanese productivity growth and quality levels significantly exceeded those of American companies competing in similar industries with similar products. The profound differences between Japan's and America's manufacturing performance were rooted in the way managers viewed the role of manufacturing in their companies and in the specific actions they took to nurture (or destroy) certain organizational capabilities.

The articles presented in this book contain many of the observations, ideas, and suggestions that initiated the process of transforming the "anachronistic" manufacturing organizations that Skinner had criticized many years earlier. That transformation is in no sense complete today. Indeed, in many respects, it has only just begun. Though a number of companies have experienced significant improvements in their manufacturing performance (measured in terms of productivity, quality, and other competitive dimensions), too few have been able to turn their manufacturing functions into sources of real competitive advantage.

A central theme of this collection is that improving manufacturing (and competitive) performance requires making changes at several levels in the organization and across the whole production system. We have thus organized the book into five parts, each of which focuses on a specific aspect of operations and discusses the kind of changes required in it, as discussed below.

Part I, New Visions of Manufacturing

A company will find it difficult to improve its manufacturing capabilities significantly if its senior management regards manufacturing as capable of making only a limited contribution to the company's competitive advantage. Equally dysfunctional is the view that the manufacturing function is being managed effectively as long as production costs are kept low and sufficient capacity is made available to meet demand. Thus, the first five articles in this book propose various approaches for expanding managers' views about the potential strategic role that manufacturing can play, and for elevating managers' thinking beyond the mass production-based dogma that reducing manufacturing cost should always have top priority.

In "Competing through Manufacturing," Steven Wheelwright and Robert Hayes describe a framework for helping managers calibrate the way they (and the rest of their organization) view the role of manufacturing in their company. The "Four Stages of Manufacturing Effectiveness" framework reflects the increasing importance of manufacturing as a company's competitive environment becomes more demanding. In "Stage One" companies, very little is required of manufacturing other than to "get the job (as defined by others) done" without creating problems for other functions, such as R&D and marketing. As competition intensifies, companies are forced into "Stage Two," where they must improve their manufacturing competence at least to the level of their major competitors. In "Stage Three," companies begin to adopt the Skinner framework—linking specific manufacturing choices (capacity, facilities, technology, work force practices, performance measurement, and so on) to their specific competitive strategy. But the best companies go even further. They encourage their manufacturing organizations to become so good that they generate new opportunities for other functional groups. In the process of identifying and exploiting such opportunities, these elite "Stage Four" manufacturing groups influence the reformulation of their company's competitive strategy. Whereas the role of Stage One manufacturing is almost entirely *reactive*, that of Stage Four manufacturing is largely *proactive*.

A widespread misconception about manufacturing is that improvement efforts should be directed primarily toward cost reduction. The next two articles in Part I, Wickham Skinner's "The Productivity Paradox" and Richard Chase and David Garvin's "The Service Factory," urge managers to consider more than cost in assessing manufacturing performance and its potential strategic role.

In "The Productivity Paradox" Skinner observes that, in their attempt to "get serious" about manufacturing, many companies have focused on productivity improvement—often making massive investments of capital as well as organizational energy. He offers two explanations for the shortfalls of many of these efforts. First, most companies opted for the "chipping away at productivity" approach, attempting to cut costs (e.g., through tighter discipline and improved worker attitudes) without addressing the fundamental structural problems in their operations, including the location, size, and scope of their plants, and their basic approaches to materials and work force management. Disappointment and frustration then set in as productivity improvements fell far short of their initial ambitious targets. Second, Skinner states, a narrow emphasis on improving productivity tends to blind managers to other ways of competing. "Quality, reliable delivery, short lead times, customer service, rapid product introduction, flexible capacity, and efficient capital deployment—these, not cost reduction, are the primary operational sources of advantage in today's environment," he argues.

Factories have traditionally been considered as places where workers physically transform raw materials and components into some tangible output—a car or a batch of chemicals or a television set. In "The Service Factory," Richard Chase and David Garvin urge managers to go beyond this traditional view. They suggest that in today's environment, where quick response, short product development lead times, and superior product quality are more important to many customers than cost alone, the role of the factory must be expanded. Increasingly, the value-added of a factory lies in the ancillary services it provides. These services can take a variety of different forms and address the needs of different customers. At one level, highly flexible factories enable companies to offer superior customer service through quick response or product customization. At another level, factories act as pilot plants, providing feedback to the R&D function about the quality and manufacturability of a product's design. At still another level, they can function as showrooms, places to demonstrate to customers the high quality of the company's production process.

Expanding the factory's role beyond the goal of low-cost production requires fundamental changes in the way companies approach manufacturing. In "The Emerging Theory of Manufacturing," Peter Drucker argues that the factory of the future will be "the product of four principles and practices that together constitute a new approach to manufacturing." These include: (1) Statistical Quality Control, which is changing the social organization of the plant; (2) new accounting practices that allow production decisions to be based more firmly on actual costs and revenues, rather than masked by averages and variances against expected outcomes; (3) the modular approach, which affords a high degree of flexibility while retaining the advantages of standardization; and (4) the "systems approach," whereby "the factory is not a place at all; it is a stage in a process that adds economic value. . . ." The rest of the manufacturing system, as Drucker sees it, includes everything from the purchase of raw materials through distribution to the final customer. He argues that companies need to link all these elements to customer demands.

In "Making Mass Customization Work," B. Joseph Pine, Bart Victor, and Andrew Boynton also tackle the problem of how to survive in a competitive environment that increasingly requires flexibility, while retaining at least some of the advantages of standardization. They, too, see competition shifting toward an emphasis on providing whatever customers want, whenever they want it, wherever they want it. The only way to achieve such service, they argue, is to create an organization in which people, processes, operating units, and technology are continuously reconfigured. They note that this view fundamentally differs from both the traditional mass production approach (which emphasizes repetition, tight control, and vertical communications) and continuous improvement practices (which emphasize the improvement of existing processes to produce standard products, rather than the creation and reconfiguration of new processes and the introduction of radically new products).

Two themes run throughout the articles in Part I. First, the role of manufacturing, far from merely supplying low-cost products, is also to provide competitive flexibility, responsiveness, innovation, and customer service. Second, in order to thrive in today's competitive environment, an organization must harness three levers of change and improvement: (1) investing in new facilities and technology, (2) creating new organizational processes and systems, and (3) restructuring the traditional form of organization. The articles in Part II, III and IV look in turn at each lever for improving the competitiveness of an enterprise.

Part II, Improving Competitiveness through Investments in Technology and Facilities

Three ideas influenced the manufacturing practices and strategies pursued by American companies through the 1980s. One of these, which originated in the nineteenth century, was that economies of scale were the key to manufacturing performance. *Bigger* was generally seen as *better.* The second idea, one that became salient after World War II, was that the only way companies in high-wage countries (like the United States and Europe) could survive was through extensive automation. Finally, if a company could neither be big nor automated, then its only hope was to move production to low-wage environments such as Mexico or South East Asia. The power of these ideas is evident in the wave of manufacturing consolidations, the billions of dollars spent on automation, and the exodus of manufacturing overseas during the past two decades. Each article in Part II challenges these three principles and offers new insights into the role of scale economies, factory automation, and offshore manufacturing strategies.

Wickham Skinner's "The Focused Factory" argues that when it comes to manufacturing operations, bigger is not necessarily better. Based on many field observations, Skinner concludes that smaller operating units with limited and well-defined missions could be much more potent competitors than large, unfocused plants. Rather than consolidate, therefore, he argues that most companies might benefit from splitting up such big plants into smaller, more focused factories.

In "Postindustrial Manufacturing," Ramachandran Jaikumar considers why investments in new manufacturing technology have so often led to disappointing results. He notes that despite massive investments in new forms of flexible automation (intended to help companies adapt to the new demands of customers described in Part I), the experience with them—in America, at least—generally has been disappointing. Based on his study of 65 flexible manufacturing systems (FMS) in both the United States and Japan, Jaikumar concludes that the problems lie primarily in the way the new technology is managed. While Japanese companies used FMS to efficiently produce a broad range of products and parts in small batches, American companies used them for high-volume production of a limited range of parts. Thus, even though many U.S. companies made the capital investments necessary to pursue a more flexible strategy, their performance was hobbled by the powerful, deeply embedded and unproductive logic of mass production.

Finally, the idea that to remain competitive U.S. companies must move production to low-wage environments is challenged by Constantinos Markides and Norman Berg in "Manufacturing Offshore Is Bad Business." They argue that companies usually badly underestimate the true costs and risks of moving production offshore. In addition, with labor costs comprising an ever diminishing share of total costs (less than 15% for the typical company), it makes less and less sense for most companies to chase low-wage labor. While offshore production makes sense in certain circumstances (e.g., when it provides access to raw materials or local markets), many companies would be better off redirecting their efforts toward improving their domestic operations.

Effectively debunking three different manufacturing myths, the articles in Part II share a common theme: investments in new plant and equipment may be necessary for improving competitiveness, but investments are only part of the story. Complementary changes in the infrastructure of manufacturing—the operating policies and procedures, measurement and control systems, and the management of a company's human resources—must be made to develop a world-class manufacturing organization. The creation of this manufacturing infrastructure, the "software" that drives the "hardware," is the focus of Part III.

Part III, Improving Competitiveness through Systems and Procedures

Over the past 20 years many industries have seen a profound shift in the terms of competition. Initially, companies generally competed primarily on price; then, the emphasis shifted gradually to product reliability and defect reduction. More recently the emphasis has shifted again to flexibility and speed. The underpinnings of these competitive capabilities—productivity, quality, and responsiveness—are examined in Part III.

In "Why Some Factories Are More Productive Than Others," Robert Hayes and Kim Clark present evidence from their multiyear, multiplant statistical study of the sources of productivity improvement in companies. They found that while structural factors, such as the size, age, and location of a plant, had important (and predictable) effects on productivity, far more important were such mundane details as bringing processes under control, carefully managing engineering change orders, reducing the number of changes in production schedules, and managing other controllable sources of confusion and complexity.

By the mid-1980s, just as many companies were catching up with their competitors on the productivity front, it had become apparent in many industries that Japanese companies held a quality advantage over their U.S. and European counterparts. A comparison of the management practices and philosophies underlying these differences was only natural. David Garvin's "Quality on the Line" presents evidence on the determinants of quality, based on his study of 17 room air conditioning plants in the United States and Japan. This study was one of the first to pinpoint the specific differences in U.S. and Japanese management practices that had important implications for the incidence of defects. Interestingly, the results of this study echoed the theme of Hayes and Clark's work on productivity: while physical structure has some effect, high quality is much more dependent on the policies and practices embedded in the plant's infrastructure. Garvin's study also revealed that what goes on outside the factory, during product design, is also critical to quality performance.

This is the central theme of "Robust Quality," in which Genichi Taguchi and Don Clausing go so far as to assert that "quality is a virtue of design." They describe a methodology for creating product designs that are less likely to experience defects during manufacture, even when the production process or component parts are slightly off target.

While Garvin's study identifies specific differences in practices and policies that could explain the lower rate of defects in Japanese factories, it raises two interesting questions: why do Japanese companies, on average, adopt such practices more frequently than their American counterparts? and why did they begin emphasizing defect reduction long before the "quality movement" swept the United States? Joseph Juran is uniquely positioned to lend insight to this issue. In "Made in U.S.A." he provides a firsthand historical description of the Japanese quality movement that emerged after World War II.

Juran identifies two major reasons why Japanese companies were so much quicker to look to superior quality as a source of competitive advantage. One was organizational. "To give top priority to quality, they [the Japanese] virtually redesigned their companies. . . . They broke down organizational barriers. . . ." The second concerned performance measures. In explaining why U.S. companies were slow to perceive superior Japanese quality as a competitive threat, Juran writes: "[They] lacked the proper instruments on their corporate dashboards. The indicators they were watching didn't measure quality. The Japanese indicators did." The importance of organizational structure and measurement systems in driving long-term improvements in manufacturing performance is the focus of Part IV.

By the early 1990s, many managers recognized that high productivity and high quality were not enough. The very best competitors in the world in many industries had developed the ability to respond quickly to rapidly changing and unpredictable consumer demands. Moreover, they did so without keeping large amounts of costly inventory. Once again, the key to their success appears to lie in the systems they used to control the flow of materials through the production chain, from suppliers all the way to end customers. The final two articles of Part III—"Getting Control of Just-in-Time" by Uday Karmarkar, and "Making Supply Meet Demand in an Uncertain World" by Marshall Fisher, Janice Hammond, Walter Obermeyer, and Ananth Raman—examine the production control systems and approaches that are required to support improved market responsiveness.

Both articles caution managers not to rush blindly into just-in-time production, an approach many hailed in the 1980s as a panacea. Karmarkar provides a framework for tailoring the design of a company's production control system to the specific requirements of its manufacturing and market environments. Fisher et al. urge managers to think beyond JIT and quick response, to *accurate* response. They describe an approach to forecasting and production scheduling that is designed to ensure a better match between demand and production for products with relatively short product lives. Whereas manufacturing effectiveness historically has been viewed in terms of physical flows of *materials*, these articles bring to the fore the way *information* is generated and utilized. Viewing manufacturing in terms of information flows, we believe, will be a central theme in the study and practice of operations management over the next decade.

Part IV, Creating the New Manufacturing Organization

The articles in Part II and III provide concrete suggestions for improving a company's competitiveness through investments in its operations structure and infrastructure. Together, they provide a road map for manufacturing reform. Yet, as many managers can attest, the road from Stage 1 to Stage 4 is too often disrupted by barriers and detours. When an implementation failure occurs blame is usually placed on a "lack of commitment" by senior management (a virtual mantra intoned by middle managers). While such a lack may often be the problem, the articles in Part IV suggest that the real causes extend far deeper.

Years of following the traditional approach to manufacturing have led to the erection and interweaving of a nearly impenetrable array of organizational structures, human resource policies, measurement and control systems, and functional roles. Not only is this infrastructure difficult to change, but it resists the kind of changes required to advance to Stage 4 manufacturing. In "Manufacturing's Crisis: New Technologies, Obsolete Organizations," Robert Hayes and Ramachandran Jaikumar focus on how traditional performance measurement and capital budgeting processes bias organizations away from investments in new production technologies. In particular, they note the failure of capital budgeting processes to take into account the value of organizational learning and skill creation, and of how the isolation of marketing, product design, and manufacturing groups prevents companies from exploiting the full competitive potential of programmable automation.

Two articles in Part IV examine the distorting effects of traditional cost accounting systems. In "The Hidden Factory," Jeffrey Miller and Thomas Vollman argue that with manufacturing overhead accounting for approximately 35% of total production costs across all U.S. industries (and as high as 75% in some), cost systems that focus primarily on the utilization and cost of direct labor are no longer appropriate. Worse, they prevent companies from understanding the causes behind (and thus from taking effective action to control) the growth in this manufacturing overhead.

Robert Kaplan, in "Yesterday's Accounting Undermines Production," similarly argues that outdated cost accounting and management control systems distort actual manufacturing performance. By failing to give managers the information they need to exploit the full benefits of computer-aided manufacturing processes and other advanced technologies, they are obstacles to manufacturing improvement. He makes the case that measurement systems in an evolving manufacturing environment must include more nonfinancial indicators of performance, such as quality and inventory levels, productivity improvement, and the skills and morale of the workforce.

Janice Klein, in "The Human Costs of Manufacturing Reform," focuses her attention specifically on this last point. She emphasizes the critical role that employees play in implementing manufacturing reforms, and the profound yet subtle tensions that arise when the imperatives of tighter process control collide with the trends toward decentralization and toward giving more responsibility and autonomy to factory workers.

Together, the articles in Part IV highlight the need for substantial changes in a company's control systems and fundamental management philosophies—encompassing both management control and human resource management—if it is to implement successfully most of the new manufacturing approaches.

Part V, Strategic Manufacturing: Competing through Superior Capabilities

A theme of several articles in this book is that a company's manufacturing organization if designed and managed properly, can be a source of great strategic value. This value springs directly from the variety of its organizational capabilities and is enhanced by the fact that they are embedded in people, systems, and organizational relationships, making them difficult for competitors to acquire or imitate. However, as the articles also make clear, such capabilities do not arise of their own volition but from careful choices about facilities, technology, operating procedures, and organizational structure. Moreover, they must be carefully nurtured and continuously renewed. The articles in this final part focus on the challenges of selecting, building, and exploiting the manufacturing capabilities that can provide a basis for sustained competitive advantage. They echo, in a sense, the growing literature about the critical role played by a firm's "core competencies."

In "Strategic Planning—Forward in Reverse?" Robert Hayes argues that the logic behind many companies' strategic planning focuses on financial and marketing goals and strategies and on buying or selling assets, an approach that undermines the creation of the kind of manufacturing capabilities that have the most strategic value. He then proposes a "reverse logic" that focuses on building such capabilities.

In "Beyond World-Class: The New Manufacturing Strategy," Robert Hayes and Gary Pisano further develop the notion that the manufacturing function can become a primary vehicle for building critical competitive capabilities. They argue that initiating a process of manufacturing improvement—by, for example, adopting one or more of the methodologies (such as JIT and TQM) discussed in this volume—does not constitute a manufacturing *strategy*. Rather than being ends in themselves, as many companies seem to believe, such methodologies should be viewed primarily as *means* for building strategically valuable manufacturing capabilities. Different improvement strategies create different kinds of capabilities and open up new strategic options. Although such issues began receiving attention only a few years ago, they have triggered a growing debate about the fundamental purposes of corporate planning and manufacturing strategy. Indeed, we anticipate that over the next ten years, managers and scholars alike will turn their full attention to the intellectual and practical challenges associated with identifying and cultivating strategically valuable manufacturing capabilities.

Notes

1. Wickham Skinner, "Manufacturing—Missing Link in Corporate Strategy," *Harvard Business Review* (May–June 1969): 136–145; "The Decline, Fall, and Renewal of Manufacturing Plants," *Industrial Engineering* (October 1974).

Manufacturing Renaissance

PART

I

New Visions of
Manufacturing

1
Competing through Manufacturing

Steven C. Wheelwright and Robert H. Hayes

Manufacturing companies, particularly those in the United States, are today facing intensified competition. For many, it is a case of simple survival. What makes this challenge so difficult is that the "secret weapon" of their fiercest competitors is based not so much on better product design, marketing ingenuity, or financial strength as on something much harder to duplicate: superior overall manufacturing capability. For a long time, however, many of these companies have systematically neglected their manufacturing organizations. Now, as the cost of that neglect grows ever clearer, they are not finding it easy to rebuild their lost excellence in production.

In most of these companies, the bulk of their labor force and assets are tied to the manufacturing function. The attitudes, expectations, and traditions that have developed over time in and around that function will be difficult to change. Companies cannot atone for years of neglect simply by throwing large chunks of investment dollars at the problem. Indeed, it normally takes several years of disciplined effort to transform manufacturing weakness into strength. In fact, it can take several years for a company to break the habit of "working around" the limitations of a manufacturing operation and to look on it as a source of competitive advantage.

In practice, of course, the challenge for managers is far more complex than is suggested by the simple dichotomy between "weakness" and "strength." There is no single end that every manufacturing function must serve—and serve well. There are, instead, several generic kinds of roles that the function can play in a company and—as Exhibit I suggests—these roles can be viewed as stages of development

Exhibit I. Stages in manufacturing's strategic role

Stage 1	Minimize manufacturing's negative potential: "internally neutral"	Outside experts are called in to make decisions about strategic manufacturing issues
		Internal, detailed management control systems are the primary means for monitoring manufacturing performance
		Manufacturing is kept flexible and reactive
Stage 2	Achieve parity with competitors: "externally neutral"	"Industry practice" is followed
		The planning horizon for manufacturing investment decisions is extended to incorporate a single-business cycle
		Capital investment is the primary means for catching up with competition or achieving a competitive edge
Stage 3	Provide credible support to the business strategy: "internally supportive"	Manufacturing investments are screened for consistency with the business strategy
		A manufacturing strategy is formulated and pursued
		Longer-term manufacturing developments and trends are addressed systematically
Stage 4	Pursue a manufacturing-base competitive advantage: "externally supportive"	Efforts are made to anticipate the potential of new manufacturing practices and technologies
		Manufacturing is involved "up front" in major marketing and engineering decisions (and vice versa)
		Long-range programs are pursued in order to acquire capabilities in advance of needs

along a continuum. At one extreme, production can offer little contribution to a company's market success; at the other, it provides a major source of competitive advantage.

Understanding the possibilities along this continuum can help managers identify both their company's current position and the transformations in attitude and approach that will be necessary if it is to advance to a higher stage of competitive effectiveness. Such understanding is also useful in judging how quickly a company may reasonably be expected to progress from stage to stage. It is useful, too, in

Exhibit II. Major types of manufacturing choices

Capacity	Amount, timing, type
Facilities	Size, location, specialization
Equipment and process technologies	Scale, flexibility, interconnectedness
Vertical integration	Direction, extent, balance
Vendors	Number, structure, relationship
New products	Hand-off, start-up, modification
Human resources	Selection and training, compensation, security
Quality	Definition, role, responsibility
Systems	Organization, schedules, control.

pointing out the changes that must be made in other parts of the company in order to sustain each higher level of manufacturing's contribution.

Stages of Manufacturing Effectiveness

Before describing each of these generic roles (or stages) in detail and outlining the problems that can arise when trying to move from one to the next, we must say a few things about the kind of framework we are proposing. First, the stages are not mutually exclusive. Every manufacturing operation embodies a set of important choices about such factors as capacity, vertical integration, human resource policies, and the like. (See Exhibit II for a listing of these.) A given operation may be—and often is—composed of factors that are themselves at different levels of development. What determines the overall level of the operation is where the balance among these factors falls—that is, where in the developmental scheme the operation's center of gravity rests.

Second, it is difficult, if not impossible, for a company to skip a stage. A new business can, of course, attempt to begin operations at any level it chooses, but a manufacturing function that is already up and running has far less freedom of choice. Attitudes and established modes of doing things are well entrenched, and it takes a tremendous effort just to move things along from one level to the next. Hence, the organizational strain imposed by an effort to leapfrog a stage makes the probability of failure uncomfortably high. In addition, it is the mastery of activities at one·stage that usually provides the underpinnings for a successful transition to the next.

It is possible, however, for a given operation to contain factors of the sort already mentioned that are well separated on the developmental continuum. But here, too, the forces of organizational gravity are remorselessly at work. Over time, the less advanced part of the operation will tend to draw the more advanced part back to its own level. The production group responsible for Apple's Macintosh computer has, for example, tried to push its capability in materials handling and test processes well ahead of the rest of its capabilities. The resulting strain has made it hard for the group to maintain a stable organization. By contrast, Hewlett-Packard's personal computer manufacturing group has tried to push ahead at a slower and steadier pace—but along a very broad front.

Third, although it is appealing in theory for companies to move as a single entity through these stages, the real work of development occurs at the business-unit level. Certainly, it is nice to have backing from a central corporate office so that several business units can evolve together and help each other, but it is at the business unit, not corporate, level that the critical nuts-and-bolts coordination among factors and across functions takes place.

With these three points in mind, we now turn to a consideration of the stages themselves. We will give special attention to the shift from Stage 3 to Stage 4 because this transition is the most difficult of all and because reaching Stage 4 has the largest payoff in terms of competitive success. In fact, Stage 4 operations characterize all companies that have achieved the status of world-class manufacturers.

STAGE 1

This lowest stage represents an "internally neutral" orientation toward manufacturing: top managers regard the function as neutral—incapable of influencing competitive success. Consequently, they seek only to minimize any negative impact it may have. They do not expect manufacturing (indeed, they tend to discourage it from trying) to make a positive contribution.

Stage 1 organizations typically view manufacturing capability as the direct result of a few structural decisions about capacity, facilities, technology, and vertical integration. Managers attach little or no strategic importance to such infrastructure issues as work force policies, planning and measurement systems, and incremental process improvements. When strategic issues involving manufacturing do arise, management usually calls in outside experts in the belief that its own production organization lacks the necessary expertise (a self-fulfilling prophecy).

When faced with the need to make a change in facilities, location, or process technology, its production managers run into top-level insistence to remain flexible and reactive so as not to get locked into the wrong decisions. Similarly, they are expected to source all manufacturing equipment from outside suppliers and to rely on these suppliers for most of their information about manufacturing technology and new technological developments.

On balance, Stage 1 organizations think of production as a low-tech operation that can be staffed with low-skilled workers and managers. They employ detailed measurements and controls of operating performance, oriented to near-term performance, to ensure that manufacturing does not get too far offtrack before corrective action can be taken. The aim is not to maximize the function's competitive value but to guard against competitively damaging problems.

Not surprisingly, the top managers of such companies try to minimize their involvement with, and thus their perceived dependence on, manufacturing. They concern themselves primarily with major investment decisions, as viewed through the prism of their capital budgeting process. As a result, they tend to regard their company's production facilities and processes as the embodiment of a series of once-and-for-all decisions. They are uneasy with the notion that manufacturing is a *learning* process that can create and expand its own capabilities—and may therefore not be totally controllable. Hence, they will agree to add capacity only when the need becomes obvious and, when they do, prefer to build large general-purpose facilities employing known—that is, "safe"—technologies purchased from outside vendors. Eager to keep the manufacturing function as simple as possible, they feel justified in thinking that "anybody ought to be able to manage manufacturing," an attitude reflected in their assignment of people to that department.

This Stage 1 view occurs both in companies whose managers see the manufacturing process as simple and straightforward and in those whose managers do not think it likely to have much impact on overall competitive position. Many consumer products and service companies fall into this category. So, too, do a number of sophisticated high-technology companies, which regard *product* technology as the key to competitive success and *process* technology as, at best, neutral.

Experience shows, however, that the competitive difficulties encountered by many U.S. consumer electronics and electrical equipment manufacturers have their roots in the attitude that manufacturing's role is simply to assemble and test products built from purchased components. Even in these high-tech companies, the manufacturing operation can appear clumsy and unprepared when confronted with such straightforward tasks as providing adequate production capacity, helping suppliers solve problems, and keeping equipment and systems up-to-date. With a self-limiting view of what manufacturing can do, managers find it difficult to upgrade their labor-intensive, low-technology processes when products involving a new generation of technology appear. Nor can their unfocused, general-purpose facilities compete effectively with the highly focused, specialized plants of world-class competitors.

STAGE 2

The second stage in our progression also represents a form of manufacturing "neutrality," but Stage 2 companies seek a competitive or "external" neutrality (parity with major competitors) on the manufacturing dimension rather than the internal ("don't upset the apple cart") neutrality of Stage 1. Typified by—but not restricted to—companies in traditional, manufacturing-intensive industries like steel, autos, and heavy equipment, Stage 2 organizations seek competitive neutrality by:

Following industry practice in matters regarding the work force (industrywide bargaining agreements with national unions, for example), equipment purchases, and the timing and scale of capacity additions.

Avoiding, where possible, the introduction of major, discontinuous changes in product or process. In fact, such changes tend to come—if at all—from competitors well outside the mainstream of an industry.

Treating capital investments in new equipment and facilities as the most effective means for gaining a temporary competitive advantage.

Viewing economies of scale related to the production rate as the most important source of manufacturing efficiency.

As noted, this approach to manufacturing is quite common in America's smokestack industries, most of which have an oligopolistic market structure and a well-defined set of competitors that share a vested interest in maintaining the status quo. It is also common in many companies engaged in electronic instrument assembly and pharmaceutical production, which consider manufacturing to be largely standardized and unsophisticated and which assume product development people can be entrusted with designing process changes whenever they are needed. Like those in Stage 1, Stage 2 companies—when they make an improvement in their process technology—rely on sources outside of manufacturing; unlike companies in Stage 1, however, they often turn to their own (largely product-oriented) R&D labs as well as to outside suppliers.

Top managers of Stage 2 companies regard resource allocation decisions as the most effective means of addressing the major strategic issues in manufacturing. Offensive investments to gain competitive advantage are usually linked to new products; manufacturing investments (other than those for additional capacity to match increases in the demand for existing products) are primarily defensive and cost-cutting in nature. They are usually undertaken only when manufacturing's shortcomings have become obvious.

STAGE 3

Stage 3 organizations expect manufacturing actively to support and strengthen the company's competitive position. As noted in Exhibit 1, these organizations view manufacturing as "internally supportive" in that its contribution derives from and is dictated by overall business strategy. That contribution includes:

Screening decisions to be sure that they are consistent with the organization's competitive strategy.

Translating that strategy into terms meaningful to manufacturing personnel.

Seeking consistency within manufacturing through a carefully thought-out sequence of investments and systems changes over time.

Being on the lookout for longer term developments and trends that may have a significant effect on manufacturing's ability to respond to the needs of other parts of the organization.

Formulating a manufacturing strategy, complete with plant charters and mission statements, to guide manufacturing activities over an extended period of time.

Companies often arrive at Stage 3 as a natural consequence of both their success in developing an effective business strategy, based on formal planning processes, and their wish to support that strategy in all functional areas. They want manufacturing to be creative and to take a long-term view in managing itself. When push comes to shove, however, the majority of them act as if such creativity is best expressed by making one or two bold moves—the introduction of robots, just-in-time, or CAD/CAM, for example—while they continue to run most of the function as a Stage 2 activity. The beer industry is a good case in point: after building a number of new, large-scale facilities in the 1970s and rationalizing their existing operations, it began to drift back into a "business as usual" attitude toward the manufacturing function.

While Stage 2 companies at times also pursue advances in manufacturing practice, they tend to regard these in strictly defensive terms: as a means of keeping up with their industry. Stage 3 companies, however, view technological progress as a natural response to changes in business strategy and competitive position.

Another characteristic of Stage 3 organizations is that their manufacturing managers take a broad view of their role by seeking to understand their company's business strategy and the kind of competitive advantage it is pursuing. Some of these managers even follow career paths that lead to general management. Notwithstanding the potential for advancement or the greater equality of titles and pay across all functions in Stage 3 companies, manufacturing managers are expected only to support the company's business strategy, not to become actively involved in helping to formulate it.

STAGE 4

The fourth and most progressive stage of manufacturing development arises when competitive strategy rests to a significant degree on a company's manufacturing capability. By this we do not mean that manufacturing dictates strategy to the rest of the company but only that strategy derives from a coordinated effort among functional peers—manufacturing very much among them.

As noted in Exhibit I, the role of manufacturing in Stage 4 companies is "externally supportive," in that it is expected to make an important contribution to the competitive success of the organization. The leading companies in process-intensive industries, for example, usually give manufacturing a Stage 4 role, for here the evolution of product and process technologies is so intertwined that a company virtually must be in Stage 4 to gain a sustainable product advantage.

What then is special about Stage 4 companies?

They anticipate the potential of new manufacturing practices and technologies and seek to acquire expertise in them long before their implications are fully apparent.

They give sufficient credibility and influence to manufacturing for it to extract the full potential from production-based opportunities.

They place equal emphasis on structural (buildings and equipment) and infrastructural (management policies) activities as potential sources of continual improvement and competitive advantage.

They develop long-range business plans in which manufacturing capabilities are expected to play a meaningful role in securing the company's strategic objectives. By treating the manufacturing function as a strategic resource—that is, as a source of strength by itself as well as a means for enhancing the contribution of other functions—they encourage the interactive development of business, manufacturing, and other functional strategies.

Stage 4 organizations are generally of two types. The first includes those companies like Emerson Electric, Texas Instruments, Mars (candy), and Blue Bell, whose business strategies place primary emphasis on a manufacturing-based competitive advantage such as low cost. In fact, these companies sometimes regard their manufacturing functions as so important a source of competitive advantage that they relegate other functions to a secondary or derivative role—an action which can be just as dysfunctional as relegating manufacturing to a reactive role. The other type of Stage 4 company seeks a balance of excellence in all its functions and pursues "externally supportive" Stage 4 roles for each of its integrated functions. We describe in detail two such organizations in a later section of this article.

In both types of organization, manufacturing complements its traditional involvement in the capital budgeting process with a considerable amount of qualitative analysis to compensate for the blind spots and biases inherent in financial data. In addition, there are extensive formal and informal horizontal interactions between manufacturing and other functions that greatly facilitate such activities as product design, field service, and sales training. Manufacturing's direct participation in formulating overall business strategy further enhances this functional interaction. Finally, equally with the other functions, manufacturing is a valued source of general management talent for the entire organization.

Managing the Transition

Because the four stages just outlined fall along a continuum, they suggest the path that a company might follow as it seeks to enhance the contribution of its manufacturing function. They suggest, too, the speed with which a company might follow that path. The inertia of most large organizations—their entrenched attitudes and practices—favors a gradual, systematic, and cumulative movement from one developmental stage to the next, not an effort to skip a stage by throwing more resources at problems. Getting from here to there is not simply a question of applying endless resources. Indeed, managing the transition between stages represents a significant and often dramatic challenge for most organizations.

At the least, successfully negotiating such a transition requires leadership from within the manufacturing function. Managing change in an established operation is always difficult, but here that difficulty is compounded by the need to bring all manufacturing personnel to a new view of things long familiar. Consider, for example, the kinds of production choices mentioned in Exhibit II.

As a company or business unit moves along the continuum, dealing with vendors or making facilities choices requires many changes: cost-minimization goals give way to a concern for enlisting vendors' critical capabilities, and planning for general-purpose facilities gives way to an appreciation of focused factories. Said another way, managing these transitions requires a special kind of leadership because the task at hand is to change how people think, not merely how they can be instructed to act.

Nowhere is this deep shift in viewpoint more important than in attitudes toward a company's human resources. As Exhibit III (courtesy of our colleague, Earl Sasser) suggests, Stages 1, 2, and 3 adhere fairly closely to the traditional "command-and-control" style of human

Exhibit III. Alternative views of work force management

Stages 1, 2, and 3 traditional, static	Stage 4 broad potential, dynamic
Command and control	Learning
Management of effort	Management of attention
Coordinating information	Problem-solving information
Direct (supervisory) control	Indirect (systems and values) control
Process stability/worker independence	Process evolution/worker dependence

resource management. Now, to be sure, moving from Stage 1 to Stage 2 and then on to Stage 3 requires an ever more polished execution of that style, with enhanced management development efforts and more thoughtful analysis of underlying commands. But there is no radical shift within these stages in the way managers think of the work force's contribution to overall competitive performance. In Stage 4, however, the dominant approach to the work force must be in terms of teamwork and problem solving, not command-and-control. In the earlier stages the key leadership task is the management of controlled effort, but getting to Stage 4—and prospering there—demands instead the management of creative experimentation and organizational learning.

WHY MOVE AT ALL?

Most young companies assign either Stage 1 or Stage 2 roles to manufacturing, to some extent because these roles require little attention and specific knowledge on the part of senior managers. In the United States, companies tend to start out with a unique product or with the identification of an unexploited niche in a market. As a result, they place primary emphasis on marketing, product design, or other non-manufacturing functions. Top management does not see the need to become smart about—or give close attention to—the work of production.

Companies are likely to remain at their initial stage until external pressures force a move. As long as no direct competitor successfully develops Stage 3 or Stage 4 manufacturing capabilities, they will find Stages 1 and 2 comfortable, secure, and apparently effective. The post-World War II experience of many U.S. industries convinced a generation of managers that a policy of stability can remain satisfactory for decades, a view reinforced by the stable economic growth associated with the 1960s. What they first saw as common practice they came to see as *good* practice.

In general, the transition from Stage 1 to Stage 2 comes when problems arise in the manufacturing function that can be solved by the "safe" application of an already proven practice. It can also occur if managers decide that the leading companies in their industry owe at least part of their success to their manufacturing process. The transition to Stage 3, however, usually begins when managers come to doubt the effectiveness of their traditional approaches or to wonder about the implications of new manufacturing technologies. A direct threat from a major competitor that has moved to a higher stage or a recognition of the competitive advantages of moving to Stage 3 (or the potential perils of not doing so) may also trigger action.

During the early 1980s all these factors came together to encourage literally hundreds of companies to shift toward Stage 3. In many industries, long dominated by a few large companies following stable competitive ground rules, the sudden appearance of foreign competition and globalized markets jolted laggards into action. With no end to such competitive pressures in sight, many more companies are likely to attempt transitions to Stage 3 over the next several years.

Unfortunately many, if not most, of these companies are unlikely to achieve a full, lasting move to Stage 3 before they revert to Stage 2. The reasons for such a retreat are subtle, yet powerful. Moving from Stage 2 to Stage 3 often occurs in a crisis atmosphere when—as with U.S. producers of steel, autos, and machine tools—managers and workers alike see their real objective as regaining competitive parity with their attackers. The changes that are required to adapt fully to Stage 3 require such sustained effort and broad-based support, however, that these companies may not be able to cement them in place before improved business conditions relieve some of the competitive pressure. The natural tendency, of course, is to return to a "business as usual" Stage 2 mentality as soon as the crisis appears to have passed.

The great irony here is that too quick success often spells doom for permanent change. If, as often happens, the managers responsible for building manufacturing to Stage 3 levels are quickly promoted into other responsibilities and other, lesser managers are left to be the caretakers of recent changes, the necessary follow-up activities may not occur.

THE BIG JUMP TO STAGE 4

However difficult it is to get from Stage 2 to Stage 3, our experience suggests that the shift from Stage 3 to Stage 4 demands an effort substantially greater both in kind and in degree. Earlier transitions, which take place largely within the manufacturing function, are a form of "manufacturing fixing itself." Moving to Stage 4, however, involves changing the way that the *rest* of the organization thinks about manufacturing and interacts with it. Because coordination among functions is crucial, manufacturing must first have its own house in order. Entering Stage 4 is not something an organization simply chooses to do. It must first pay its dues by having done all the appropriate groundwork.

The differences between Stages 3 and 4 should not be underestimated. In Stage 3, manufacturing considerations feed into business strategy, but the function itself is still seen as reactive (in that its role is a derived one), not as a source of potential competitive advantage. Stage 4 implies a deep shift in manufacturing's role, in its self-image, and in the view of it held by managers in other functions. It is, at last, regarded as an equal partner and is therefore expected to play a major role in strengthening a company's market position. Equally important, it helps the rest of the organization see the world in a new way. Stage 3 companies will, for example, treat automation as essentially a cost-cutting and labor-saving activity. A Stage 4 manufacturing operation will bring automation into focus as a means of boosting process precision and product quality.

There is an expectation in Stage 4 that all levels of management will possess a high degree of technical competence and will be aware of how their actions may affect manufacturing activities. Further, they are expected to have a general understanding of the way products, markets, and processes interact and to manage actively these interactions across functions. Traditional approaches to improving performance—providing flexibility through excess capacity, for example, or raising delivery dependability through holding finished-goods inventory, or reducing costs through improvements in labor productivity—no longer are considered as the only way to proceed. Tighter integration of product design and process capabilities can also lead to increased flexibility, as well as to faster deliveries (through shorter production cycle times) and to lower costs (through improved product quality and reliability).

Most American top managers, in our experience, regard the transition from Stage 1 to Stage 2, and then on to Stage 3, as a desirable course to pursue. Yet few view achieving Stage 4 capabilities as an obvious goal or strengthen their companies' manufacturing functions with the clear intent of moving there.

In fact, most companies that reach Stage 3 do not perceive a move to Stage 4 as either essential or natural. Their managers, believing that Stage 3 provides 90% of the benefits attainable, resist spending the extra effort to advance further. Many prefer to play it safe by remaining in Stage 3 for a sustained period before deciding how and whether to move on. A sizable number doubt the value of Stage 4—some because they think it extremely risky in organizational terms; others because they feel threatened by the kind of initiatives manufacturing might take when unleashed. One company, in fact, ruled out a move to Stage 4 as being potentially destabilizing to its R&D group, which historically had played the key role in establishing the company's competitive advantage.

Although the benefits of operating in Stage 4 will vary from company to company and will often be invisible to managers until they are just on the edge of Stage 4 operations, four variables can serve as a sort of litmus test for a company's real attitude toward the competitive role its manufacturing organization can—and should—play and thus indicate its placement in Stage 3 or Stage 4.

THE AMOUNT OF ONGOING IN-HOUSE INNOVATION.   Stage 4 organizations continually invest in process improvements, not only because they benefit existing products but also because they will benefit future products. This is not to say these companies are uninterested in big-step improvements, but that they place great importance on the cumulative value of continual enhancements in process technology.

THE EXTENT TO WHICH A COMPANY DEVELOPS ITS OWN MANUFAC-TURING EQUIPMENT.   The typical Stage 3 operation continues to rely on outside suppliers for equipment development. A Stage 4 company wants to know more than its suppliers about everything that is critical to its business. It may continue to buy much of its equipment, but it will also produce enough internally to ensure that it is close to the state-of-the-art in equipment technology.

Our experience with Stage 4 German and Japanese manufacturers is that they follow this practice much more than most of their American counterparts. Yet even in Germany, where leading companies develop their own equipment, suppliers such as those making machine tools remain strong and innovative. Reducing their market does not cripple their competitive viability. Instead, the increased competition and the greater technical sophistication among equipment users have made the interactions between manufacturers and suppliers more innovative for both.

THE ATTENTION PAID TO MANUFACTURING INFRASTRUCTURE.   Stage 4 managers take care to integrate measurement systems, manufacturing planning and control procedures, and work force policies in their structural decisions on capacity, vertical integration, and the like. They do not necessarily give infrastructure and structural elements equal weight, but they look on both as important, and complementary, sources of competitive strength.

THE LINK BETWEEN PRODUCT DESIGN AND MANUFACTURING PROCESS DESIGN.   Stage 3 companies focus on improving the hand-offs from product design to manufacturing; in Stage 4 the emphasis is on the parallel and interactive development of both products and processes.

If managers choose not to attempt the transition to Stage 4, that choice should be made intentionally, not by default or through a failure to understand the kind of benefits that new stage could offer. Rather, it should reflect a reasoned judgment that the risks were too great or the rewards insufficient.

Getting There from Here

Two examples of organizations that, in the early 1980s, chose to attempt the transition to Stage 4 are General Electric's dishwasher operation (at the business-unit level) and IBM (at the corporate level). Taking a closer look at these two experiences may help bring into focus the benefits of, and the obstacles to, a successfully managed transition.

GENERAL ELECTRIC DISHWASHER

Dishwashers are one of several major consumer appliances that GE has produced for decades. In the late 1970s GE's dishwasher strategic business unit (SBU) did a careful self-analysis and concluded that it had dated and aging resources: a 20-year-old product design, a 10- to 20-year-old manufacturing process, and an aging work force (average seniority of 15 to 16 years) represented by a strong, traditional union. Its manufacturing operations were primarily located, together with five other major appliance plants, at GE's Appliance Park in Louisville, Kentucky. A single labor relations group dealt with all of the site's 14,000 hourly workers, whose relations with management were neutral at best.

Nevertheless, it was a very successful business, holding the leading position in the U.S. dishwasher market and turning out about one-third of the units sold. In late 1977, as part of its normal planning for product redesign, the SBU proposed to corporate management that it invest $18 million in the incremental improvement of the product and its manufacturing process. With dishwasher manufacturing more or less at Stage 2 (it was essentially following "GE Appliance Park manufacturing practice"), those involved saw the request as a proposed foray into Stage 3, and expected the unit to return to Stage 2 once the improvements in products and processes began to age.

GE's senior managers normally would have approved such an investment and allowed the SBU to carry on with its traditional approach. In this case, however, they asked a number of tough questions about the long-term prospects for the business and encouraged SBU managers to think about pursuing a more innovative and aggressive course. The idea of making a fundamental change in the SBU's strategy gained rapid support from some key middle managers, who saw major opportunities if GE could break out of its traditional thinking. They began laying the groundwork for a solid move to Stage 3.

Over the next several months, as this reformulated proposal to upgrade product design and manufacturing processes began to take shape, the nature of the dishwasher business suggested possible benefits from moving on through Stage 3 to Stage 4:

> GE product designers had developed a top-of-the-line product with a plastic tub and plastic door liner. Although currently more expensive than the standard steel model, it offered significantly improved operating performance and used proprietary GE materials.

More disciplined product design could increase component standardization because little of the product was visible after installation.

Since only 55% of U.S. households owned dishwashers, there was considerable growth potential in the primary market as well as a sizable replacement market.

In combination with GE's strong competitive position, these factors led management to conclude that if the "right" product were introduced at the "right" price and with the "right" quality, GE could greatly expand both industry demand and its own market share, particularly in the private label business.

Accordingly, SBU managers decided not just to fix current problems but to do it right. They jettisoned their modest proposal for incremental product and process improvement and developed much bolder proposals requiring an investment of more than $38 million.

This revised plan rested on a major commitment to improve the factory's working environment through better communication with the work force as well as to encourage its involvement in redesigning the manufacturing process. Laying the groundwork for this new relationship took almost two years, but the time was well spent. Once established, this relationship markedly enhanced the contribution manufacturing could make to the overall business of the SBU.

The new plan also called for a complete redesign of the product around a central core consisting of a single-piece plastic tub and a single-piece plastic door. To ensure that the product would meet quality standards, management established stringent specifications for GE and for its vendors and demanded that both internal and external suppliers reduce their incidence of defects to one-twentieth of the levels formerly allowed. To meet the new specifications and the new cost targets, managers now had to carry out process and product development in tandem, not separate them as they had done in the past.

The revised proposal addressed, as well, the design of the production process. Automation was essential—not just to reduce costs but also to improve quality. Thus, modifications in product design had to reflect the capabilities and constraints of the new process. In addition, that process had to accommodate more worker control and shorter manufacturing cycle times, along with other nontraditional approaches to improve flexibility, quality, delivery dependability, and the integration of product testing with manufacturing.

By late 1980, there was general agreement on the major building blocks of this new strategy. Each of the functions—product design,

Exhibit IV. General Electric dishwasher SBU redesign

Performance measure	1980-1981	1983	1984 Goal
Service call rate (index)*	100	70	55
Unit cost (index)	100	90	88
Number of times tub or door is handled	27 + 27	1 + 3	1 + 3
Inventory turns	13	25	28
Reject rates (mechanical/ electrical test)	10 %	3 %	2.5 %
Output per employee (index)	100	133	142

*Lower is better.

marketing, and manufacturing—was to move aggressively toward defining its contribution in Stage 4 terms. To manufacturing management also fell the task of helping to develop performance measures that, if tracked over subsequent years, would indicate how well the function was carrying out its responsibilities.

As Exhibit IV shows, by the end of 1983 there was pronounced improvement in such important areas as service call rates, unit costs, materials handling, inventory turns, reject rates, and productivity—with a promise of still further improvements in 1984. Nor was this all. Other benefits included a 70% reduction in the number of parts, the elimination of 20 pounds of weight in the finished product (and thus reduced freight costs), and much more positive worker attitudes. Perhaps most important of all was the large jump in market share that GE won in the 12 months following the new product's introduction. Indeed, during the summer of 1983, *Consumer Reports* rated it as offering the best value among U.S. dishwashers.

Although these results were impressive, SBU managers also gained a much better understanding of the effort needed to secure fully a Stage 4 position for manufacturing. Their experience underlined the need to treat product and process design in a more iterative and interactive fashion and the importance of involving the work force in solving problems.

Of late, a rebounding economy with increased consumer demand has turned up pressure on the SBU to revert to its traditional view that output is paramount, no matter the compromises. Hence, even though the SBU's manufacturing function is now in Stage 4, it must doggedly fight to stay there and to help the rest of the organization complete the transition rather than allow itself to drift back toward Stage 3.

IBM CORPORATION

In the early 1980s, IBM viewed its worldwide activities as comprising 13 major businesses including, for example, typewriters and large computer systems. Like its competitors in each of these product markets, IBM faced rapidly changing environments and so had to be especially careful in designing and coordinating strategies. Hence, in each, the manufacturing organization was expected to play a role equal to that of the other major functions in developing and executing overall business strategy. Unlike its competitors, most of whom still assigned Stage 2 or Stage 3 roles to manufacturing, IBM recognized that production—responsible for 49% of IBM's assets, 110,000 of its employees, and 40% of its final product costs—had much to contribute to the competitive advantage of each business.

IBM's worldwide strategy for moving the manufacturing operations of each business into Stage 4 required those businesses to address seven areas of concern in a manner consistent with a Stage 4 approach to production. These areas were:

LOW COST.   IBM firmly believed that to be successful it must be the low-cost producer in each of its businesses, success being defined as having the best product quality, growing as fast or faster than the market, and being profitable. Reaching this low-cost position required stabilizing the manufacturing environment (reducing uncertainty wherever possible) and linking manufacturing more effectively to marketing and distribution. To this end, marketing had "ownership" of finished-goods inventory, and factory production rates were to be smoothed out by the adoption of a 90-day shipping horizon. In addition, IBM decided to design products around certain standard modules and, although it

produced different configurations of these standard modules to customer order, it would not manufacture customized modules.

INVENTORIES.   IBM's goal was to reduce inventories significantly, first
by measuring stock carefully and frequently and then by reducing
"order churn" (the fluctuation in mix and volume that occurs before
an order actually gets into the final production schedule). Lower in-
process inventories, derived in part from the adoption of a just-in-time
philosophy and from the standardization of components, helped IBM
cut its inventory costs by hundreds of millions of dollars within 18
months while supporting ever-increasing sales.

QUALITY.   IBM estimated that 30% of its products' manufacturing
cost—the total cost of quality prevention, detection, and appraisal—
arose directly from not doing it right the first time. Significant improvements in the quality and manufacturability of design, the pursuit
of zero defects, and the systematic stress testing of products during
design and manufacturing all contributed to the lowering of these costs.

AUTOMATION.   Automation in a Stage 4 orientation is of value in that
it leads to higher product quality, encourages interaction between
product design and process design, and cuts overhead. This, in turn,
means managing the evolution of the manufacturing process according to a long-term plan, just as with product evolution.

ORGANIZATION.   To provide the product design and marketing functions with a better linkage with manufacturing, IBM defined an additional level of line manufacturing management, a "production management center," which was responsible for all plants manufacturing
a product line. For example, the three large system plants (located in
France, Japan, and the United States) were all under a single production management center that served as the primary linkage with marketing for that product line, as well as with R&D's efforts to design
new products. Such centers were intended not only to create effective
functional interfaces but also to be responsible for planning manufacturing processes, defining plant charters, measuring plant performance, and ensuring that the processes and systems employed by different facilities were uniformly excellent.

MANUFACTURING SYSTEMS.   The purpose here was to develop integrated systems that provided information, linked directly to strategic
business variables, for both general and functional managers. Such

systems had to be compatible with each other yet flexible enough for each business to be able to select the modules it needed. As part of this systems effort, IBM re-thought its entire manufacturing measurement system with the intent of reducing its historical focus on direct labor and giving more emphasis to materials, overhead, energy, and indirect labor. IBM believed that its manufacturing systems, like its product lines, should be made up of standard modules based on a common architecture. Each business could then assemble its own customized configuration yet still communicate effectively with other IBM businesses.

AFFORDABILITY.   By making external competitiveness, not internal rules of thumb, the basis for evaluating manufacturing performance, IBM no longer evaluated manufacturing against its own history but rather against its competitors. As part of this concern with affordability, IBM also sought to reduce its overhead, which exceeded 25% of total manufacturing costs.

Out of these seven areas of concern emerged a set of three management principles fully in harmony with the move to a Stage 4 appreciation of the competitive contribution that manufacturing can make. The first—emphasizing activities that facilitate, encourage, and reward effective interaction between manufacturing and both marketing and engineering—requires people able to regard each other as equals and to make significant contributions to areas other than their own. Information, influence, and support should—and must—flow in both directions.

The second principle recognizes that product and process technologies must interact. Process evolution (including automation) and product evolution must proceed in tandem. Indeed, IBM uses the terms "process windows" and "product windows" to describe these parallel paths and the opportunities they offer to exploit state-of-the-art processes in meeting customer needs and competitive realities.

The third principle is a focus of attention and resources on only those factors—manufacturing, quality, and overhead reduction, for example—that are essential to the long-term success of the business.

Getting Things Moving in Your Company

Our experience suggests that building manufacturing excellence requires that managers do more than simply understand the nature of the current role that manufacturing plays in their organizations and develop a plan for enhancing its competitive contribution. They must also communicate their vision to their organizations and prepare the ground for the changes that have to be made.

In virtually all the Stage 4 companies we have seen, at least one senior manager has been a key catalyst for the transition. Such leaders spring from all functional backgrounds and are concerned not to elevate manufacturing at the expense of other functions but to see their companies "firing on all cylinders." Seeking ways to integrate all functions into an effective whole, they must be strong enough, persuasive enough, and tough enough to push beyond conventional management thinking and to force their organizations to grapple with the deeper challenges prevailing in the increasingly competitive world of industry.

Today, there is considerable pessimism in some quarters about the long-term prospects for U.S. manufacturing. We are neither pessimistic nor optimistic; the answer "lies not in our stars but in ourselves." We have seen many organizations focus their efforts on achieving Stage 4 and make incredible improvements in short periods of time. Unfortunately, we have also seen many of them subsequently lose that commitment. After making tremendous strides, they begin to get comfortable and fall behind again.

Manufacturing can contribute significantly to the competitive success of any business. But it takes managers with determination, vision, and the ability to sustain focused effort over a long period of time and often in the face of stiff organizational resistance. The industrial race is no longer decided (if it ever was) by a fast and furious last-minute cavalry charge. It is a long, patient, persistent process of working together to clear the land, cultivate the fields, and continually extend the frontiers of an organization's capabilities.

2
The Productivity Paradox

Wickham Skinner

American manufacturers' near-heroic efforts to regain a competitive edge through productivity improvements have been disappointing. Worse, the results of these efforts have been paradoxical. The harder these companies pursue productivity, the more elusive it becomes.

In the late 1970s, after facing a severe loss of market share in dozens of industries, U.S. producers aggressively mounted programs to revitalize their manufacturing functions. This effort to restore the productivity gains that had regularly been achieved for over 75 years has been extraordinary. (Productivity is defined by the Bureau of Labor Statistics as the value of goods manufactured divided by the amount of labor input. In this article "productivity" is used in the same sense, that is, as a measure of manufacturing employees' performance.) Few companies have failed to measure and analyze productivity or to set about to raise output/input ratios. But the results overall have been dismal.

From 1978 through 1982 U.S. manufacturing productivity was essentially flat. Although results during the past three years of business upturn have been better, they ran 25% lower than productivity improvements during earlier, postwar upturns.

Consider, for example, the XYZ Corporation, which I visited recently. The company operates a large manufacturing plant, where a well-organized productivity program, marshaling its best manufacturing talent, has been under way for three years. Its objective was to boost productivity so as to remove a 30% competitive cost disadvantage.

The program has included: appointing a corporate productivity manager; establishing departmental productivity committees; raising the number of industrial engineering professionals by 50%; carrying out operation-by-operation analyses to improve efficiency levels, avoid waste, and simplify jobs; retraining employees to work "smarter not harder"; streamlining work flow and materials movement; replacing out-of-date equipment; retooling operations to cut operator time; tightening standards; installing a computerized production control system; training foremen in work simplification; emphasizing good housekeeping and cleanliness; and installing a computer-based, measured-day work plan, which allows for daily performance reports on every operation, worker, and department.

For all this effort—and all the boost it gave to production managers' morale—little good has come of the program. Productivity has crept up by about 7% over three years, but profits remain negligible and market share continues to fall. As one executive said, "It's been great finally getting management support and the resources needed to get this plant cleaned up and efficient. But it is extremely discouraging to have worked so hard and, after three years, to be in worse competitive shape than when we started. I don't know how long we can keep trying harder when it doesn't seem to be getting us anywhere."

Unfortunately, XYZ's frustration with a full-out effort that achieves only insignificant competitive results is typical of what has been going on in much of American industry. Why so little competitive return—even a negative return—on so much effort? Is it the high value of the dollar, which cheapens imports? Is the cost gap just too great for us to overcome? Or are we going at the problems in the wrong way? What is going wrong? Why this apparent paradox?

The Wrong Approach

With these questions in mind, I have visited some 25 manufacturing companies during the last two years. Never have I seen so much energetic attention to productivity starting from the top and ricocheting all the way through organizations. This is American hustle and determination at its best. Productivity committees, productivity czars, productivity seminars, and productivity campaigns abound.

But the harder these companies work to improve productivity, the less they sharpen the competitive edge that *should* be improved by better productivity. Elusive gains and vanishing market share point not to a lack of effort but to a central flaw in how that effort is conceived. The very way managers define productivity improvement and the tools they use to achieve it push their goal further out of reach.

Resolutely chipping away at waste and inefficiency—the heart of most productivity programs—is not enough to restore competitive health. Indeed, a focus on cost reductions (that is, on raising labor output while holding the amount of labor constant or, better, reducing it) is proving harmful.

Let me repeat: not only is the productivity approach to manufacturing management not enough (companies cannot cut costs deeply enough to restore competitive vitality); it actually hurts as much as it helps. It is an instinctive response that absorbs managers' minds and diverts them from more effective manufacturing approaches.

Chipping away at productivity . . .

. . . IS MOSTLY CONCERNED WITH DIRECT LABOR EFFICIENCY, although direct labor costs exceed 10% of sales in only a few industries. Thus even an immense jump in productivity—say 20%—would not reverse the fortunes of import-damaged industries like autos, consumer electronics, textile machinery, shoes, or textiles.

. . . FOCUSES EXCESSIVELY ON THE EFFICIENCY OF FACTORY WORKERS. By trying to squeeze out better efficiency from improved attitudes and tighter discipline on a person-by-person and department-by-department basis, the approach detracts attention from the structure of the production system itself.

Production experience regularly observes a "40 40 20" rule. Roughly 40% of any manufacturing-based competitive advantage derives from long-term changes in manufacturing structure (decisions, for example, concerning the number, size, location, and capacity of facilities) and basic approaches in materials and work force management. Another 40% comes from major changes in equipment and process technology. The final 20%—no more—rests on conventional approaches to productivity improvement.

What this rule says is that the least powerful way to bolster competitive advantage is to focus on conventional productivity and cost-cutting approaches. Far more powerful are changes in manufacturing structure and technology. The rule does not, of course, say "Don't try to improve productivity." These well-known tools are easy to use and do help to remove unnecessary fat. But they quickly reach the limits of what they can contribute. Productivity is the wrong tree to bark up.

. . . IGNORES OTHER WAYS TO COMPETE THAT USE MANUFACTURING AS A STRATEGIC RESOURCE.   Quality, reliable delivery, short lead times, customer service, rapid product introduction, flexible capacity, and efficient capital deployment—these, not cost reduction, are the primary operational sources of advantage in today's competitive environment.

. . . FAILS TO PROVIDE OR SUPPORT A COHERENT MANUFACTURING STRATEGY.   By assuming that manufacturing's essential task is to make a company the low-cost producer in its industry, this approach rashly rules out other strategies.

Most of the productivity-focused programs I have seen blithely assume that competitive position lost on grounds of higher cost is best recovered by installing cost-reduction programs. This logic is tempting but wrong. These programs cannot succeed. They have the wrong targets and misconstrue the nature of the competitive challenge they are supposed to address. Worse, they incur huge opportunity costs. By tying managers at all levels to short-term considerations, they short-circuit the development of an aggressive manufacturing strategy.

But they also do harm. These programs can, for example, hinder innovation. As William Abernathy's study of auto manufacturers has shown, an industry can easily become the prisoner of its own massive investments in low-cost production and in the organizational systems that support it.[1] When process costs and constraints drive both product and corporate strategy, flexibility gets lost, as does the ability to rapidly introduce product changes or develop new products.

Even more is at stake than getting locked into the wrong equipment. Managers under relentless pressure to maximize productivity resist innovation. Preoccupied as they are with this week's cost performance, they know well that changes in processes or systems will wreak havoc with the results on which they are measured. Consequently, innovations that lead to, say, better service or shorter lead times for product changeovers are certain to suffer.

Innovation is not, however, all that suffers. A full-out concentration on productivity frequently creates an environment that alienates the work force. Pressure for output and efficiency are the staples of factory life as hourly workers experience it. Engineers and supervisors tell them what to do, how to do it, and how long they may take. Theirs is an often unhappy, quota-measured culture—and has been for more than 150 years. In such an environment, even the most reasonable requests are resented.

Recent admirers of the Japanese argue that low cost and high quality can go hand in hand. Indeed, in the right setting managers need not trade one for the other. But in an efficiency-driven operation, this logic can be a trap. When low cost is the goal, quality often gets lost. But when quality is the goal, lower costs do usually follow.

The will to make large investments in radically new process technology gets lost too. The slow adoption of such manufacturing technologies as CAD/CAM, robotics, and flexible machining centers reflects managers' wise assumptions that these investments would initially drive productivity down.

Fears that several years of debugging and learning to use the new gear would hurt productivity have already cost many companies valuable time in mastering these process technologies. Even more troubling, the companies have failed to acquire a strategic resource that could help them restore their competitive position. A productivity focus inevitably forces managers into a short-term, operational mindset. When productivity is driving, experimentation takes a backseat.

The emphasis on direct costs, which attends the productivity focus, leads a company to use management controls that focus on the wrong targets. Inevitably, these controls key on direct labor: overhead is allocated by direct labor; variances from standards are calculated from direct labor. Performance in customer service, delivery, lead times, quality, and asset turns are secondary. The reward system based on such controls drives behavior toward simplistic goals that represent only a small fraction of total costs while the real costs lie in overhead and purchased materials.

Why has this gone on year after year even as the cost mix has steadily moved away from direct labor? By now our accounting and control systems are pathetically old-fashioned and ineffective. But nothing changes. Our continuing obsession with productivity as the be-all measure of factory performance is to blame, not the stubbornness of accountants.

When managers grow up in this atmosphere, their skills and vision never fully develop. They instinctively seize on inefficiencies and waste while missing broad opportunities to compete through manufacturing. The harsh fact is that generations of production managers have been stunted by this efficiency-driven mentality. Theirs is the oldest management function, yet today it is often the most backward. Unable to join finance, marketing, and general management in thinking strategically about their businesses, they are cut off from corporate leadership. As my recent study of 66 "comers" in production management shows, 10 or 15 years' immersion in a productivity-directed organization creates severe limitations of vision.[2] These limitations, in time, form a long-term mind-set that only a few can shake. Today the production function is seldom the place to find managers who can design competitive manufacturing structures.

Indeed, ever since Fredrick Winslow Taylor, our obsession with productivity and efficiency has spoiled the atmosphere of the factory. "Factory" is a bad word. Production managers first came into existence not as architects of competitive systems but as custodians of large, capital-intensive assets. Their job was to control and coordinate all factors of production so as to minimize costs and maximize output. This single dimension of performance is deeply ingrained in the profession and until recently has sufficed as a basis of evaluation.

Not surprisingly, it created a negative, penny-pinching, mechanistic culture in most factories—a culture that has driven out and kept away creative people at all levels. Who among our young today wishes to work in an environment where one is told what to do, how to do it, when to do it, is measured in minutes and sometimes seconds, is supervised closely to prevent any inefficiencies, and is paced by assembly lines or machines to produce at a rapid and relentless pace?

Today's problems in making the factory into a more attractive place to work are not new. They are the direct outcome of the 150-year history of an institution based on productivity. As long as cost and efficiency are the primary measurements of factory success, the manufacturing plant will continue to repel many able, creative people.

Breaking Out

Faced with this paradox—efforts to improve productivity driving competitive success further out of reach—a number of companies have broken out of the bind with extraordinary success. Their experience suggests, however, that breaking loose from so long-established a mind-set is not easy. It requires a change in culture, habits, instincts, and ways of thinking and reasoning. And it means modifying a set of values that current reward systems and day-to-day operational demands reinforce. This is a tall order.

Every company I know that has freed itself from the paradox has done so, in part, by:

RECOGNIZING THAT ITS APPROACH TO PRODUCTIVITY WAS NOT WORK-ING WELL ENOUGH TO MAKE THE COMPANY COST COMPETITIVE.   This recognition allowed managers to seek strategic objectives for manufacturing other than those determined primarily by cost.

About 12 years ago, a key division of American Standard adopted a "become the low-cost producer" strategy. Its productivity-driven focus did little to reduce costs but had an immediate negative effect on quality, delivery, and market share. What Standard needed was a totally new manufacturing strategy—one that allowed different areas of the factory to specialize in different markets and quality levels. When this approach replaced the low-cost strategy, the division regained its strong competitive position within three years.

ACCEPTING THE FACT THAT ITS MANUFACTURING WAS IN TROUBLE AND NEEDED TO BE RUN DIFFERENTLY. In the mid-1970s officers of the Copeland Corporation, a large producer of refrigeration compressors, decided that their industry was fast becoming mature. An analysis of their nearly obsolete production facilities and equipment made it clear that manufacturing had become a corporate millstone. Without a major change in the number, size, location, and focus of these facilities, long-term survival would be impossible. Copeland made these changes. The results (described later) were remarkable.

DEVELOPING AND IMPLEMENTING A MANUFACTURING STRATEGY (see box). When production managers actively seek to understand (and, in some cases, to help develop) the competitive strategy of relevant business units, they are better able to work out the objectives for their own function that will turn it into a competitive weapon. The requirements of such a manufacturing strategy will then determine needed changes in the manufacturing system's structure and infrastructure.

At Copeland, this approach led to order-of-magnitude improvements in quality, shortened delivery cycles, lower inventory investments, and much greater flexibility in product and volume changes.

ADOPTING NEW PROCESS TECHNOLOGY. Changes in equipment and process technology are powerful engines of change. Bringing such technology on line helps force adjustments in work flow, key skills, and information systems as well as in systems for inventory control, materials management, and human resource management. There are few more effective means of loosening up old ways of organizing production.

General Electric and Deere & Company have made wholesale process changes at their dishwasher and locomotive (GE) and tractor (Deere) plants—changes that boosted product quality and reliability. Timken and Cooper Industries have each made large investments in radical

---

Manufacturing strategy

A manufacturing strategy describes the competitive leverage required of—and made possible by—the production function. It analyzes the entire manufacturing function relative to its ability to provide such leverage, on which task it then focuses each element of manufacturing structure. It also allows the *structure* to be managed, not just the short-term, operational details of cost, quality, and delivery. And it spells out an internally consistent set of structural decisions designed to forge manufacturing into a strategic weapon. These structural decisions include:

What to make and what to buy.

The capacity levels to be provided.

The number and sizes of plants.

The location of plants.

Choices of equipment and process technology.

The production and inventory control systems.

The quality control system.

The cost and other information systems.

Work force management policies.

Organizational structure.

---

new technologies that speeded up their ability to deliver new products and customer specials.

MAKING MAJOR CHANGES IN THE SELECTION, DEVELOPMENT, ASSIGN-MENTS, AND REWARD SYSTEMS FOR MANUFACTURING MANAGERS. The successful companies I looked at decided they needed a new breed of production leader—managers able to focus on a wider set of objectives than efficiency and cost. It was, however, no simple matter to find or train this new breed.

Some, in fact, turned up in unexpected places: marketing, sales, engineering, research, general management. As a group, they were good team builders and problem solvers and had broad enough experience to hold their own in top corporate councils. Their companies considered them among the most promising, high-potential "comers" for future leadership at the highest levels.

Only when manufacturers were willing to try such novel approaches to the competitive challenges facing them have they broken loose from the productivity paradox and transformed their production function into a strategic weapon. There is hope for manufacturing in America, but it rests on a different way of managing in this oldest of managerial professions.

As we have seen, our pursuit of productivity is paradoxical: the more we pursue it, the more elusive it becomes. An obsession with cost reduction produces a narrowness of vision and an organizational backlash that work against its underlying purpose. To boost productivity in its fullest sense—that is to unleash a powerful team of people supported by the right technology—we must first let go of old-fashioned productivity as a primary goal. In its place we must set a new, simple but powerful objective for manufacturing: to be competitive.

Notes

1. William J. Abernathy and Kenneth Wayne, "Limits of the Learning Curve," *Harvard Business Review*, September–October 1974, p. 109.
2. Wickham Skinner, "The Taming of Lions: How Manufacturing Leadership Evolved, 1780–1984," in *The Uneasy Alliance*, ed. Kim B. Clark, Robert H. Hayes, and Christopher Lorenz (Boston: Harvard Business School Press, 1985), p. 63.

3
The Service Factory

Richard B. Chase and David A. Garvin

The factory of the future is *not* a place where computers, robots, and flexible machines do the drudge work. That is the factory of the present, which, with money and brains, any manufacturing business can build. Of course, any competitor can build one too—which is why it is becoming harder and harder to compete on manufacturing excellence alone. Lower costs, higher quality, and greater product variety are like table stakes in poker—the price that companies pay to enter the game. Most products can be quickly and easily imitated; and the most automated design and production processes cannot decisively beat the second most automated. Who wins and who loses will be determined by how companies play, not simply by the product or process technologies that qualify them to compete.

The manufacturers that thrive into the next generation, then, will compete by bundling services with products, anticipating and responding to a truly comprehensive range of customer needs. Moreover, they will make the factory itself the hub of their efforts to get and hold customers—activities that now are located in separate, often distant, parts of the organization. Production workers and factory managers will be able to forge and sustain new relationships with customers because they will be in direct and continuing contact with them. Manufacturing, in short, will become the cortex of the business. Today's flexible factories will become tomorrow's service factories.

About 200 years ago, when horse-drawn carriages were made largely by craftsmen, the most successful carriage maker was invariably the most accommodating. Though he prided himself on being a technician—a manufacturer—his success depended heavily on his willingness and ability to talk with customers at key points: before the sale, so he could get a clear idea of what the client needed and what features would satisfy him; during the manufacturing process, so he could incorporate any necessary changes in the product; and after delivery, so he could learn what features had worked (and what hadn't) and what the client needed for maintenance, repair, and replacement.

Mass production overtook customized craftsmanship because customers came to value standardized goods over higher priced, personalized goods. As a result, work grew increasingly compartmentalized through the division of labor. Craftsmanship (that is, manufacturing) became separated from downstream activities, like sales and postpurchase service, as well as from upstream activities, like new-product development and design. Gradually, manufacturing received more and more of its information and instructions through filters—divisions and departments that were separated, functionally and physically, from the production site. Not surprisingly, manufacturing managers complained that those who defined their work rarely understood it or cared enough about its details, problems, or technical possibilities.

For decades, companies muddled through. In recent years, as Japanese competition put pressure on manufacturing businesses everywhere, manufacturers have worked mightily and successfully to educate workers and break down some of the barriers between their upstream activities and the work of the factory. They have encouraged interfunctional communication between product designers and manufacturing engineers and between R&D and quality managers on the factory floor.

These imaginative efforts to accelerate product innovation and improve manufacturing performance were necessary and important. But they are no longer adequate. Today downstream activities have to be joined to the tasks of the factory too. Increasingly, factory personnel have the means to support the sales force, service technicians, and consumers. This support should, and will, be used. Competition is shifting away from how companies build their products to how well they serve customers before and after they build them.

Some of America's best-run companies—Hewlett-Packard, Allen-Bradley, Caterpillar, Frito-Lay—already operate factories whose activities reflect the new role of service in manufacturing competition. None of their facilities is a complete service factory. We are still many years from that. But in the range of upstream and downstream activities these factories perform, and in the degree of interaction between production workers and customers, they point the way to the future.

Service for a manufacturing company inescapably revolves around its products—their design, features, durability, repairability, distribution, and ease of installation and use. Even the most traditional factories of yesterday proffered service of a kind, but their conception of service was narrow. To old-guard factory managers, service was little more than a commitment to meeting due dates. Logistics and distribution urged the factory to complete orders in a timely fashion, to give advance notice of delivery problems, and to package materials for ease of shipment and damage control. Customers were simply numbers on a production schedule.

Managers in flexible factories have broadened the concept of service to include both a commitment to product variety and a capacity to see the customer in specialized terms. The key to flexibility has been the ability to produce small lot sizes efficiently and to change over quickly from one product to another. Yet even the most flexible factories are not capitalizing on the full range of services they could provide. As a result, they are bypassing competitive opportunities.

Factories generate information and skills that are critical for product design. Among them are accurate and timely feedback on the manufacturability of new designs, the ability to construct prototypes quickly, and the capability of introducing engineering change orders smoothly. But factories are also a resource for helping customers with installation, maintenance, and troubleshooting. The people who make products are often more knowledgeable about their performance, variability, and repair than the people in field service.

Such product experts can also contribute decisively to sales and marketing efforts. Not only do factories generate quality information that helps sales, but producers of very sophisticated products—chip makers, for instance—prove the quality of their products by showing customers that their procedures are virtually infallible. Factories can serve as real-time demonstrators of the technology and systems the company sells. They can also help make salespeople more responsive by supplying detailed cost and production data for competitive bidding and cross-selling and by making an ever-increasing range of products. Once the products have been sold, the factory can also participate in after-sales support by providing accurate and easily accessible information about the status of orders and by replenishing critical parts and products without delay.

Building a full-fledged service factory—one that offers all these services—in one fell swoop would be difficult. The way to reach that goal is to start by identifying a focused set of customer needs and then try to fill them with all deliberate speed, beginning with those services the factory is particularly good at. This means coalescing around a single service model that is so explicit and transparent that the whole organization can easily understand what needs to be done and why.

Here we propose four alternatives; there are undoubtedly more.

The Laboratory

The factory's competence in testing new products and processes and in ensuring manufacturability and quality equips it also to serve as a lab. The archetype is the pilot plant. Factory managers make crucial information available to the rest of the business: data on product performance and architecture to R&D; process parameters to designers; capacity restrictions to sales and marketing. To do so, they need processes that are heavily instrumented, equipment that is capable of fine adjustments, operators who are technically skilled, and documentation that is careful and precise.

Allegheny Ludlum, a large manufacturer of specialty steel, has developed a formal system of process experiments, often high-risk experiments governed by special procedures to encourage innovation. High-risk experiments are those that push the frontiers of steel making; more traditional experiments aim to modify or improve existing operations that remain imperfectly understood.

For example, in the mid-1980s, Allegheny Ludlum began a series of experiments to develop a metallic replacement for the ceramic substrate in automotive catalytic converters. The experiments involved a new family of alloys, which are difficult and time-consuming to manufacture. To begin the experiments, R&D or manufacturing people first obtained sign-offs from the senior vice president of the technical division and the vice presidents of technical services, production, and sales; then, operating managers ran the experiments freely, knowing that the results would not appear in their budgets or detract from their margins.

The company supports such experimentation with an extremely detailed cost accounting system—100,000 standards, tracking costs for every department, machine, process, grade, width, and gauge of steel. As a result, every experiment yields useful cost and productivity information. The system also tracks defect rates and other quality data. Experimentation has produced impressive results: between 1984 and 1988, the productivity of Allegheny's melt shop and continuous caster improved 7% to 8% per year.

The CEO of Chaparral Steel, a highly successful mini-mill, is explicit about this approach. He is trying, he says, to get his company's research and development done right on the factory floor. First-line supervisors enjoy regular sabbaticals, during which they visit other steel mills, explore new technologies, and visit customers. They bring fresh, often experimental ideas back to the factory and take the lead in introducing them to the shop floor.

Laboratories do more, however, than perform experiments. They also supply supporting data based on rigorous tests—like the clinical labs that support physicians. Such information can also alleviate customers' concerns about product failures and flawed performance. Because customers are less patient and more insistent than ever, the factory that's close to them and does its own product experimentation can respond to their concerns quickly and directly by providing hard data with which they can make judgments about product quality, flexibility, and the like.

At Hewlett-Packard's Fort Collins Systems Division, which makes computers and technical workstations, the quality department has played a lead role in generating information crucial to customers. At first, quality managers developed customer surveys and collected field data on competitors' products for their own use. Then they discovered that marketing viewed the initiative as an encroachment. So they suggested forming a new partnership drawing on the factory's special expertise. The quality department embraced the role of a service department for marketing, working with members of the technical marketing staff to support field sales and service personnel. According to Henry Kohoutek, the quality manager: "The focus for selecting opportunities to contribute was shifted to the marketing staff, who knew well where help was needed and would be appreciated."

Over time, new kinds of information were generated, packaged, and presented in novel formats: product-quality data sheets; test conditions and test-result data summarized in easily understandable ways that impressed customers; videotapes documenting actual product tests and field performance. The quality department also cultivated direct contacts with sales and service personnel through training sessions, presentations, and guided tours through its facilities. Marketing now covers nearly all the associated costs from its own budget.

The Consultant

Hewlett-Packard's experience is closely related to another factory service—problem solving out in the field. Many companies sell technical expertise along with the product. Most use so-called "systems engineers" or technical service people. Yet factory workers can constitute a pool of talent that can perform some of these tasks. The more factory people work with design, marketing, and quality, and the greater the sophistication of the machines they run, the more they come to think like product and process engineers. In the words of one product designer we know, they become "experts on what the product is trying to be." Factory people can teach customers quality control techniques. They could also be made a part of a customer's design team, consulting on manufacturability, or could help customers solve production difficulties.

Raritan River Steel Company, a metal-rod fabricator, sends factory workers out with salespeople to troubleshoot customers' quality problems; after returning to the factory, they develop solutions with co-workers on the shop floor. In one case, a customer's problem was traceable to a subtle manufacturing flaw—minute scratches on the surface of a rod—that only a worker's trained eye could identify.

Tektronix, a manufacturer of electronic equipment, has pioneered direct communication between customers and shop-floor employees. Into the shipping carton of every oscilloscope it sells, the company inserts a postcard listing the names of the workers who built the scope along with an "800" number to a phone on the shop floor. Every day the factory gets several calls from customers; the six people working in the repair area who answer them have all received telephone training.

Customers call for various reasons: questions about the use of their oscilloscopes, complaints about quality performance, requests for information about other Tektronix products, and so on. Workers and managers meet daily to discuss these calls; if necessary, further conversations with the customer follow up the meetings. In some cases, workers will call customers six months after delivery to find out how well their products are performing.

Of course, to be useful consultants, factory workers must know more about their products and markets than they can absorb by daily osmosis. They should get training in basic quality assurance techniques and education in key technical concepts and terminology. They must also be at ease dealing with customers and even perhaps in making formal presentations.

The Showroom

Another, somewhat unexpected way a factory can be used to advantage, especially in high-tech businesses, is as a showroom. The factory can serve as a working demonstration of the systems, processes, and products it manufactures. It can also dramatize the company's manufacturing superiority and, by implication, its superior quality or reliability.

Allen-Bradley, a manufacturer of industrial automation controls, uses its computer-integrated manufacturing operation in Milwaukee in just these ways. The facility is a 150 feet by 300 feet "factory within a factory." Within 24 hours of order placement, it can produce 1,025 different electronic contactors and relays in lot sizes down to one and with zero defects.

Even before this facility was constructed, the company's sales group had developed a "productivity pyramid" to show the linkages among the various levels of factory control (computer controls at higher and lower levels—plan level, center level, and so forth) and had seized on the idea of using the company's own operations to prove the system's plausibility. The Milwaukee plant also shows off Allen-Bradley's software products, and it models what would otherwise be an abstract and elusive systems architecture.

The factory can also reinforce customer perceptions of product quality. Copeland Corporation, a manufacturer of air-conditioning compressors, introduced a new model in the 1970s and built a state-of-the-art facility equipped with programmable controllers and other advanced automation. The corporation then arranged customer tours to demonstrate the plant's precision manufacturing and exhaustive test procedures and to underline the product's reliability. Copeland seized 25% of the market in two years.

For the factory to be a successful showroom, three things are needed. Marketing and manufacturing personnel have to work closely together to both understand customers' expectations and fulfill them. Manufacturing managers and shop-floor employees have to be well trained in communication and presentation. And the factory's layout must allow for stopping points and audiovisual aids to highlight processes with the greatest sales potential.

At Frito-Lay's Vancouver, Washington plant, for example, entrances and exits have been enlarged to accommodate large groups of visitors, and microphones and loudspeakers have been located at key observation points. Floors have been reconditioned for safety, and public affairs people have developed three different tours, one tailored to wholesalers, one to retailers, and, of course, one to snackers. One of these tours was critical to landing a $2 million account.

The Dispatcher

Finally, the factory can be the linchpin of after-sales support. Service backup is of obvious importance in emerging industries, where the technology is new and products lack a track record. But factories can also be organized to help companies differentiate products in mature businesses. They can provide customers with quick replacements for defective or worn parts and ensure speedy replenishment of stocks to help customers avoid downtime and stock-outs. An unavailable part can idle an expensive machine—indeed, an entire factory.

Effectiveness as a dispatcher requires an unprecedented level of flexibility. The factory must be able to anticipate demand surges and respond immediately to customers' crises.

For decades, Caterpillar has been extraordinarily skilled at parts control, warehousing, and logistics; it promises to have repair parts for its tractors and earth-moving equipment available anywhere in the world within 48 hours. This responsiveness is emphasized more than ever by Caterpillar's sales force. Today Caterpillar often advises customers in the area of logistical support and related services and has an active consulting practice.

In clothing, personal care, and small appliance businesses, which are often subject to fads and shifts in fashion, quick responsiveness to the retail trade is crucial. The Limited, a clothing retailer, electronically links its hundreds of stores to a single, centralized computer at its Columbus, Ohio headquarters and then to its Hong Kong textile mills through a real-time system that allows the mills to begin reproducing hot-selling items at the end of the first week of sales.

Such responsiveness depends on ever-tighter customer linkages, which can be achieved in several ways. In the most innovative approach, sometimes called interorganizational systems, factories supply customers with computer terminals that are linked directly to the factory's order-entry and production-control system. Inland Steel uses interorganizational systems, as does Levi Strauss. Several leading food companies are exploring the possibility of linking their order-entry systems to the computers that compile data from supermarket scanners so that they can bypass the purchasing departments entirely.

Companies can also tighten customer linkages more conventionally, without sophisticated information systems. Usually, this requires interfunctional teams consisting of representatives from sales, logistics, and manufacturing. At Frito-Lay's Vancouver plant, for instance, logistics and sales managers and plant personnel schedule regular (weekly, monthly, quarterly) contacts, in person and by telephone. Joint training events are common. Teams work together to reduce late deliveries, eliminate stale product, resolve breakage problems, and meet special promotion needs. The result has been rapid sales growth and, in 1988, the highest combined service and quality rating of any of Frito-Lay's full-mix plants.

Each of these models—laboratory, consultant, showroom, and dispatcher—shows a distinctive approach to factory service. They also show how services overlap. A factory cannot become a good dispatcher without excellent customer information; it cannot become a good consultant without detailed product and process knowledge. Factories become service factories when their managers and workers understand customers' needs as deeply and directly as they know their own products.

Not all factory managers welcome the changes a service factory requires. Most companies used to seal off their core production technology and discouraged interaction with groups outside the factory. Manufacturing managers sought to maximize efficiency and protect the line from outside disturbances; they buffered themselves by storing inventories in locations that were set off from the rest of the organization and from customers.

The managers of service factories, in contrast, have to work in an open system. They need direct and accessible connections to design, to marketing, and to strategic planning, as well as to customers. Computers and telecommunications can help here, to be sure. Computerized ordering systems, expert systems to manage complex sales, computerized logs for after-sales support, computerized catalogs for replacement parts, 24-hour answering machines to take customer complaints, inexpensive fax machines—all of these speed up communication and break down functional barriers.

But what drives the open systems approach is strategy, not technology—the fact that management sees the competitive advantages of working more collaboratively. At Frito-Lay's Vancouver plant, the best example of an open system we've come across, the technology is nothing more than a telephone.

Tomorrow's leading manufacturing companies will be the ones whose managers unleash the service potential of their factories. Competition demands it. Technology makes it possible. Indeed, the competitive forces driving companies to differentiate products with new and imaginative services are simultaneously empowering factory organizations to deliver them.

Think again about the division of labor, how the factory organization has evolved—and why. Victorian capitalists (and, later, the "scientific management" movement led by Frederick Winslow Taylor) divided human labor into ever more simplified and automatic tasks. The goal was improved productivity: if every worker did a small part of the job, unskilled workers could build products more quickly and efficiently (if less pleasurably) than craftsmen. The point was to compete on price.

The Japanese raised this principle to a higher, more sophisticated standard. Taking their cues from Taylor and his disciples, Japanese managers have analyzed production processes with astonishing precision—movements in microseconds, tolerances in fractions of microns. Originally, the idea was simply to make people work more efficiently. But this attention to detail also laid the groundwork for just-in-time and computerized manufacturing. Japanese factories were organized to deliver low-cost products fast without sacrificing superior quality or flexibility. (You could always buy a luxurious, indestructible car in just the right color. But not off the lot, and not for three months' wages.)

To stay in the game, U.S. manufacturers have had to reform their processes and practices. Many have succeeded. Today Harley-Davidson stands up to Honda because of its embrace of quality improvements and just-in-time production methods, when a few years ago the company was on the brink of financial disaster. Every business now has to master the science of manufacturing—the analysis, subdivision, and control of tightly defined conversion tasks. Otherwise, its factories will remain hopelessly unfit for world competition and for the computer programs that might run and monitor the line.

Moreover, U.S. industry now has to select, train, and retrain workers who use and compete with smart (and not so smart) machines. Today direct labor averages less than 15% of the cost of most manufactured goods; in five years that number is likely to seem as extravagant as 3% defect rates recently did.

As factories employ fewer and fewer people, those who remain need to know how to deal with complex machines, software interfaces, and design problems, and how to track quality and appreciate customers.

Increasingly, as Peter Drucker and others have argued, the factory requires knowledge workers who will add value by thinking more like general managers, by contributing, as no computer can, by seeing the production system whole and suggesting fresh ways to enhance products. The result is that factory workers and managers will know more about selected aspects of their products' performance and potential than anyone else in the organization.

Drucker has noted that the imperatives of information-based competition are breaking down barriers within businesses and making functional divisions obsolete. He might have added that divisions among upstream and downstream activities are evaporating too. Marketing, research and development, design, manufacturing, sales, after-sales service—all are folding into one another. The service tasks of business can no longer be separated neatly and sequentially from the work of the factory. If factory personnel are indispensible to the interfunctional teams that generate excellent designs—as they are—how much more essential they must be to a business that competes on service.

4
The Emerging Theory of Manufacturing

Peter F. Drucker

We cannot build it yet. But already we can specify the "postmodern" factory of 1999. Its essence will not be mechanical, though there will be plenty of machines. Its essence will be conceptual—the product of four principles and practices that together constitute a new approach to manufacturing.

Each of these concepts is being developed separately, by different people with different starting points and different agendas. Each concept has its own objectives and its own kinds of impact. Statistical Quality Control is changing the social organization of the factory. The new manufacturing accounting lets us make production decisions as business decisions. The "flotilla," or module, organization of the manufacturing process promises to combine the advantages of standardization and flexibility. Finally, the systems approach embeds the physical process of making things, that is, manufacturing, in the economic process of business, that is, the business of creating value.

As these four concepts develop, they are transforming how we think about manufacturing and how we manage it. Most manufacturing people in the United States now know we need a new theory of manufacturing. We know that patching up old theories has not worked and that further patching will only push us further behind. Together these concepts give us the foundation for the new theory we so badly need.

Author's note: I wish to acknowledge gratefully the advice and criticism I received on this piece from Bela Gold and Joseph Maciariello, friends and colleagues at the Claremont Graduate School.

The most widely publicized of these concepts, Statistical Quality Control (SQC), is actually not new at all. It rests on statistical theory formulated 70 years ago by Sir Ronald Fisher. Walter Shewhart, a Bell Laboratories physicist, designed the original version of SQC in the 1930s for the zero-defects mass production of complex telephone exchanges and telephone sets. During World War II, W. Edwards Deming and Joseph Juran, both former members of Shewhart's circle, separately developed the versions used today.

The Japanese owe their leadership in manufacturing quality largely to their embrace of Deming's precepts in the 1950s and 1960s. Juran too had great impact in Japan. But U.S. industry ignored their contributions for 40 years and is only now converting to SQC, with companies such as Ford, General Motors, and Xerox among the new disciples. Western Europe also has largely ignored the concept. More important, even SQC's most successful practitioners do not thoroughly understand what it really does. Generally, it is considered a production tool. Actually, its greatest impact is on the factory's social organization.

By now, everyone with an interest in manufacturing knows that SQC is a rigorous, scientific method of identifying the quality and productivity that can be expected from a given production process in its current form so that control of both attributes can be built into the process itself. In addition, SQC can instantly spot malfunctions and show where they occur—a worn tool, a dirty spray gun, an overheating furnace. And because it can do this with a small sample, malfunctions are reported almost immediately, allowing machine operators to correct problems in real time. Further, SQC quickly identifies the impact of any change on the performance of the entire process. (Indeed, in some applications developed by Deming's Japanese disciples, computers can simulate the effects of a proposed change in advance.) Finally, SQC identifies where, and often how, the quality and productivity of the entire process can be continuously improved. This used to be called the "Shewhart Cycle" and then the "Deming Cycle"; now it is *kaizen*, the Japanese term for continuous improvement.

But these engineering characteristics explain only a fraction of SQC's results. Above all, they do not explain the productivity gap between Japanese and U.S. factories. Even after adjusting for their far greater reliance on outside suppliers, Toyota, Honda, and Nissan turn out two or three times more cars per worker than comparable U.S. or European plants do. Building quality into the process accounts for no more than one-third of this difference. Japan's major productivity gains are the result of social changes brought about by SQC.

The Japanese employ proportionately more machine operators in direct production work than Ford or GM. In fact, the introduction of SQC almost always increases the number of machine operators. But this increase is offset many times over by the sharp drop in the number of nonoperators: inspectors, above all, but also the people who do not *do* but *fix*, like repair crews and "fire fighters" of all kinds.

In U.S. factories, especially mass-production plants, such nonoperating, blue-collar employees substantially outnumber operators. In some plants, the ratio is two to one. Few of these workers are needed under SQC. Moreover, first-line supervisors also are gradually eliminated, with only a handful of trainers taking their place. In other words, not only does SQC make it possible for machine operators to be in control of their work, it makes such control almost mandatory. No one else has the hands-on knowledge needed to act effectively on the information that SQC constantly feeds back.

By aligning information with accountability, SQC resolves a heretofore irresolvable conflict. For more than a century, two basic approaches to manufacturing have prevailed, especially in the United States. One is the engineering approach pioneered by Frederick Winslow Taylor's "scientific management." The other is the "human relations" (or "human resources") approach developed before World War I by Andrew Carnegie, Julius Rosenwald of Sears Roebuck, and Hugo Münsterberg, a Harvard psychologist. The two approaches have always been considered antitheses, indeed, mutually exclusive. In SQC, they come together.

Taylor and his disciples were just as determined as Deming to build quality and productivity into the manufacturing process. Taylor asserted that his "one right way" guaranteed zero-defects quality; he was as vehemently opposed to inspectors as Deming is today. So was Henry Ford, who claimed that his assembly line built quality and productivity into the process (though he was otherwise untouched by Taylor's scientific management and probably did not even know about it). But without SQC's rigorous methodology, neither scientific management nor the assembly line could actually deliver built-in process control. With all their successes, both scientific management and the assembly line had to fall back on massive inspection, to fix problems rather than eliminate them.

The human-relations approach sees the knowledge and pride of line workers as the greatest resource for controlling and improving quality and productivity. It too has had important successes. But without the kind of information SQC provides, you cannot readily distinguish productive activity from busyness. It is also hard to tell whether a proposed modification will truly improve the process or simply make things look better in one corner, only to make them worse overall.

Quality circles, which were actually invented and widely used in U.S. industry during World War II, have been successful in Japan because they came in after SQC had been established. As a result, both the quality circle and management have objective information about the effects of workers' suggestions. In contrast, most U.S. quality circles of the last 20 years have failed despite great enthusiasm, especially on the part of workers. The reason? They were established without SQC, that is, without rigorous and reliable feedback.

A good many U.S. manufacturers have built quality and productivity into their manufacturing processes without SQC and yet with a minimum of inspection and fixing. Johnson & Johnson is one such example. Other companies have successfully put machine operators in control of the manufacturing process without instituting SQC. IBM long ago replaced all first-line supervisors with a handful of "managers" whose main task is to train, while Herman Miller achieves zero-defects quality and high productivity through continuous training and productivity-sharing incentives.

But these are exceptions. In the main, the United States has lacked the methodology to build quality and productivity into the manufacturing process. Similarly, we have lacked the methodology to move responsibility for the process and control of it to the machine operator, to put into practice what the mathematician Norbert Wiener called the "human use of human beings."

SQC makes it possible to attain both traditional aspirations: high quality and productivity on the one hand, work worthy of human beings on the other. By fulfilling the aims of the traditional factory, it provides the capstone for the edifice of twentieth century manufacturing that Frederick Taylor and Henry Ford designed.

Bean counters do not enjoy a good press these days. They are blamed for all the ills that afflict U.S. manufacturing. But the bean counters will have the last laugh. In the factory of 1999, manufacturing accounting will play as big a role as it ever did and probably even a bigger one. But the beans will be counted differently. The new manufacturing accounting, which might more accurately be called "manufacturing economics," differs radically from traditional cost accounting in its basic concepts. Its aim is to integrate manufacturing with business strategy.

Manufacturing cost accounting (cost accounting's rarely used full name) is the third leg of the stool—the other legs being scientific management and the assembly line—on which modern manufacturing industry rests. Without cost accounting, these two could never have become fully effective. It too is American in origin. Developed in the 1920s by General Motors, General Electric, and Western Electric (AT&T's manufacturing arm), the new cost accounting, not technology, gave GM and GE the competitive edge that made them worldwide industry leaders. Following World War II, cost accounting became a major U.S. export.

But by that time, cost accounting's limitations also were becoming apparent. Four are particularly important. First, cost accounting is based on the realities of the 1920s, when direct, blue-collar labor accounted for 80% of all manufacturing costs other than raw materials. Consequently, cost accounting equates "cost" with direct labor costs. Everything else is "miscellaneous," lumped together as overhead.

These days, however, a plant in which direct labor costs run as high as 25% is a rare exception. Even in automobiles, the most labor intensive of the major industries, direct labor costs in up-to-date plants (such as those the Japanese are building in the United States and some of the new Ford plants) are down to 18%. And 8% to 12% is fast becoming the industrial norm. One large manufacturing company with a labor-intensive process, Beckman Instruments, now considers labor costs "miscellaneous." But typically, cost accounting systems are still based on direct labor costs that are carefully, indeed minutely, accounted for. The remaining costs—and that can mean 80% to 90%— are allocated by ratios that everyone knows are purely arbitrary and totally misleading: in direct proportion to a product's labor costs, for example, or to its dollar volume.

Second, the benefits of a change in process or in method are primarily defined in terms of labor cost savings. If other savings are considered at all, it is usually on the basis of the same arbitrary allocation by which costs other than direct labor are accounted for.

Even more serious is the third limitation, one built into the traditional cost accounting system. Like a sundial, which shows the hours when the sun shines but gives no information on a cloudy day or at night, traditional cost accounting measures only the costs of producing. It ignores the costs of nonproducing, whether they result from machine downtime or from quality defects that require scrapping or reworking a product or part.

Standard cost accounting assumes that the manufacturing process turns out good products 80% of the time. But we now know that even with the best SQC, nonproducing time consumes far more than 20% of total production time. In some plants, it accounts for 50%. And nonproducing time costs as much as producing time does—in wages, heat, lighting, interest, salaries, even raw materials. Yet the traditional system measures none of this.

Finally, manufacturing cost accounting assumes the factory is an isolated entity. Cost savings in the factory are "real." The rest is "speculation"—for example, the impact of a manufacturing process change on a product's acceptance in the market or on service quality. GM's plight since the 1970s illustrates the problem with this assumption. Marketing people were unhappy with top management's decision to build all car models, from Chevrolet to Cadillac, from the same small number of bodies, frames, and engines. But the cost accounting model showed that such commonality would produce substantial labor cost savings. And so marketing's argument that GM cars would lose customer appeal as they looked more and more alike was brushed aside as speculation. In effect, traditional cost accounting can hardly justify a product *improvement*, let alone a product or process *innovation*. Automation, for instance, shows up as a cost but almost never as a benefit.

All this we have known for close to 40 years. And for 30 years, accounting scholars, government accountants, industry accountants, and accounting firms have worked hard to reform the system. They have made substantial improvements. But since the reform attempts tried to build on the traditional system, the original limitations remain.

What triggered the change to the new manufacturing accounting was the frustration of factory-automation equipment makers. The potential users, the people in the plants, badly wanted the new equipment. But top management could not be persuaded to spend the money on numerically controlled machine tools or robots that could rapidly change tools, fixtures, and molds. The benefits of automated equipment, we now know, lie primarily in the reduction of nonproducing time by improving quality (that is, getting it right the first time) and by sharply curtailing machine downtime in changing over from one model or product to another. But these gains cost accounting does not document.

Out of this frustration came Computer-Aided Manufacturing-International, or CAM-I, a cooperative effort by automation producers, multinational manufacturers, and accountants to develop a new cost accounting system. Started in 1986, CAM-I is just beginning to influence manufacturing practice. But already it has unleashed an intellectual revolution. The most exciting and innovative work in management today is found in accounting theory, with new concepts, new approaches, new methodology—even what might be called new economic philosophy—rapidly taking shape. And while there is enormous controversy over specifics, the lineaments of the new manufacturing accounting are becoming clearer every day.

As soon as CAM-I began its work, it became apparent that the traditional accounting system could not be reformed. It had to be replaced. Labor costs are clearly the wrong unit of measurement in manufacturing. But—and this is a new insight—so are all the other elements of production. The new measurement unit has to be time. The costs for a given period of time must be assumed to be fixed; there are no "variable" costs. Even material costs are more fixed than variable, since defective output uses as much material as good output does. The only thing that is both variable and controllable is how much time a given process takes. And "benefit" is whatever reduces that time. In one fell swoop, this insight eliminates the first three of cost accounting's four traditional limitations.

But the new cost concepts go even further by redefining what costs and benefits really are. For example, in the traditional cost accounting system, finished-goods inventory costs nothing because it does not absorb any direct labor. It is treated as an "asset." In the new manufacturing accounting, however, inventory of finished goods is a "sunk cost" (an economist's, not an accountant's, term). Stuff that sits in inventory does not earn anything. In fact, it ties down expensive money and absorbs time. As a result, its time costs are high. The new accounting measures these time costs against the benefits of finished-goods inventory (quicker customer service, for instance).

Yet manufacturing accounting still faces the challenge of eliminating the fourth limitation of traditional cost accounting: its inability to bring into the measurement of factory performance the impact of manufacturing changes on the total business—the return in the marketplace of an investment in automation, for instance, or the risk in not making an investment that would speed up production changeovers. The in-plant costs and benefits of such decisions can now be worked out with considerable accuracy. But the business consequences are indeed speculative. One can only say, "Surely, this should help us get more sales," or "If we don't do this, we risk falling behind in customer service." But how do you quantify such opinions?

Cost accounting's strength has always been that it confines itself to the measurable and thus gives objective answers. But if intangibles are brought into its equations, cost accounting will only raise more questions. How to proceed is thus hotly debated, and with good reason. Still, everyone agrees that these business impacts have to be integrated into the measurement of factory performance, that is, into manufacturing accounting. One way or another, the new accounting will force managers, both inside and outside the plant, to make manufacturing decisions as *business* decisions.

Henry Ford's epigram, "The customer can have any color as long as it's black," has entered American folklore. But few people realize what Ford meant: flexibility costs time and money, and the customer won't pay for it. Even fewer people realize that in the mid-1920s, the "new" cost accounting made it possible for GM to beat Ford by giving customers both colors and annual model changes at no additional cost.

By now, most manufacturers can do what GM learned to do roughly 70 years ago. Indeed, many go quite a bit further in combining standardization with flexibility. They can, for example, build a variety of end products from a fairly small number of standardized parts. Still, manufacturing people tend to think like Henry Ford: you can have either standardization at low cost or flexibility at high cost, but not both.

The factory of 1999, however, will be based on the premise that you not only *can* have both but also *must* have both—and at low cost. But to achieve this, the factory will have to be structured quite differently.

Today's factory is a battleship. The plant of 1999 will be a "flotilla," consisting of modules centered either around a stage in the production process or around a number of closely related operations. Though overall command and control will still exist, each module will have its own command and control. And each, like the ships in a flotilla, will be maneuverable, both in terms of its position in the entire process and its relationship to other modules. This organization will give each module the benefits of standardization and, at the same time, give the whole process greater flexibility. Thus it will allow rapid changes in design and product, rapid response to market demands, and low-cost production of "options" or "specials" in fairly small batches.

No such plant exists today. No one can yet build it. But many manufacturers, large and small, are moving toward the flotilla structure: among them are some of Westinghouse's U.S. plants, Asea Brown Boveri's robotics plant in Sweden, and several large printing plants, especially in Japan.

The biggest impetus for this development probably came from GM's failure to get a return on its massive (at least $30 billion and perhaps

$40 billion) investment in automation. GM, it seems, used the new machines to improve its existing process, that is, to make the assembly line more efficient. But the process instead became less flexible and less able to accomplish rapid change.

Meanwhile, Japanese automakers and Ford were spending less and attaining more flexibility. In these plants, the line still exists, but it is discontinuous rather than tightly tied together. The new equipment is being used to speed changes, for example, automating changeovers of jigs, tools, and fixtures. So the line has acquired a good bit of the flexibility of traditional batch production without losing its standardization. Standardization and flexibility are thus no longer an either-or proposition. They are—as indeed they must be—melded together.

This means a different balance between standardization and flexibility, however, for different parts of the manufacturing process. An "average" balance across the plant will do nothing very well. If imposed throughout the line, it will simply result in high rigidity and big costs for the entire process, which is apparently what happened at GM. What is required is a reorganization of the process into modules, each with its own optimal balance.

Moreover, the relationships between these modules may have to change whenever the product, process, or distribution changes. Switching from selling heavy equipment to leasing it, for instance, may drastically change the ratio between finished-product output and spare-parts output. Or a fairly minor model change may alter the sequence in which major parts are assembled into the finished product. There is nothing very new in this, of course. But under the traditional line structure, such changes are ignored, or they take forever to accomplish. With competition intensifying and product life cycles shortening all the time, such changes cannot be ignored, and they have to be done fast. Hence the flotilla's modular organization.

But this organization requires more than a fairly drastic change in the factory's physical structure. It requires, above all, different communication and information. In the traditional plant, each sector and department reports separately upstairs. And it reports what upstairs has asked for. In the factory of 1999, sectors and departments will have to think through what information they owe to whom and what information they need from whom. A good deal of this information will flow sideways and across department lines, not upstairs. The factory of 1999 will be an information network.

Consequently, all the managers in a plant will have to know and understand the entire process, just as the destroyer commander has to know and understand the tactical plan of the entire flotilla. In the factory of 1999, managers will have to think and act as team members, mindful of the performance of the whole. Above all, they will have to ask: What do the people running the other modules need to know about the characteristics, the capacity, the plans, and the performance of *my* unit? And what, in turn, do we in my module need to know about theirs?

The last of the new concepts transforming manufacturing is systems design, in which the whole of manufacturing is seen as an integrated process that converts materials into goods, that is, into economic satisfactions.

Marks & Spencer, the British retail chain, designed the first such system in the 1930s. Marks & Spencer designs and tests the goods (whether textiles or foods) it has decided to sell. It designates one manufacturer to make each product under contract. It works with the manufacturer to produce the right merchandise with the right quality at the right price. Finally, it organizes just-in-time delivery of the finished products to its stores. The entire process is governed by a meticulous forecast as to when the goods will move off store shelves and into customers' shopping bags. In the last ten years or so, such systems management has become common in retailing.

Though systems organization is still rare in manufacturing, it was actually first attempted there. In the early 1920s, when the Model T was in its full glory, Henry Ford decided to control the entire process of making and moving all the supplies and parts needed by his new plant, the gigantic River Rouge. He built his own steel mill and glass plant. He founded plantations in Brazil to grow rubber for tires. He bought the railroad that brought supplies to River Rouge and carried away the finished cars. He even toyed with the idea of building his own service centers nationwide and staffing them with mechanics trained in Ford-owned schools. But Ford conceived of all this as a financial edifice held together by ownership. Instead of building a system, he built a conglomerate, an unwieldy monster that was expensive, unmanageable, and horrendously unprofitable.

In contrast, the new manufacturing system is not "controlled" at all. Most of its parts are independent—independent suppliers at one end, customers at the other. Nor is it plant centered, as Ford's organization was. The new system sees the plant as little more than a wide place in the manufacturing stream. Planning and scheduling start with shipment to the final customer, just as they do at Marks & Spencer. Delays, halts, and redundancies have to be designed into the system—a warehouse here, an extra supply of parts and tools there, a stock of old products that are no longer being made but are still occasionally demanded by the market. These are necessary imperfections in a continuous flow that is governed and directed by information.

What has pushed American manufacturers into such systems design is the trouble they encountered when they copied Japan's just-in-time methods for supplying plants with materials and parts. The trouble could have been predicted, for the Japanese scheme is founded in social and logistic conditions unique to that country and unknown in the United States. Yet the shift seemed to American manufacturers a matter of procedure, indeed, almost trivial. Company after company found, however, that just-in-time delivery of supplies and parts created turbulence throughout their plants. And while no one could figure out what the problem was, the one thing that became clear was that with just-in-time deliveries, the plant no longer functions as a step-by-step process that begins at the receiving dock and ends when finished goods move into the shipping room. Instead, the plant must be redesigned from the end backwards and managed as an integrated flow.

Manufacturing experts, executives, and professors have urged such an approach for two or three decades now. And some industries, such as petroleum refining and large-scale construction, do practice it. But by and large, American and European manufacturing plants are neither systems designed nor systems managed. In fact, few companies have enough knowledge about what goes on in their plants to run them as systems. Just-in-time delivery, however, forces managers to ask systems questions: Where in the plant do we need redundancy? Where should we place the burden of adjustments? What costs should we incur in one place to minimize delay, risk, and vulnerability in another?

A few companies are even beginning to extend the systems concept of manufacturing beyond the plant and into the marketplace. Caterpillar, for instance, organizes its manufacturing to supply any replacement part anywhere in the world within 48 hours. But companies like this are still exceptions; they must become the rule. As soon as we define manufacturing as the process that converts things into economic satisfactions, it becomes clear that producing does not stop when the product leaves the factory. Physical distribution and product service are still part of the production process and should be integrated with it, coordinated with it, managed together with it. It is already widely recognized that servicing the product must be a major consideration during its design and production. By 1999, systems manufacturing will have an increasing influence on how we design and remodel plants and on how we manage manufacturing businesses.

Traditionally, manufacturing businesses have been organized "in series," with functions such as engineering, manufacturing, and marketing as successive steps. These days, that system is often complemented by a parallel team organization (Procter & Gamble's product management teams are a well-known example), which brings various functions together from the inception of a new product or process project. If manufacturing is a system, however, every decision in a manufacturing business becomes a manufacturing decision. Every decision should meet manufacturing's requirements and needs and in turn should exploit the strengths and capabilities of a company's particular manufacturing system.

When Honda decided six or seven years ago to make a new, upscale car for the U.S. market, the most heated strategic debate was not about design, performance, or price. It was about whether to distribute the Acura through Honda's well-established dealer network or to create a new market segment by building separate Acura dealerships at high cost and risk. This was a marketing issue, of course. But the decision was made by a team of design, engineering, manufacturing, and marketing people. And what tilted the balance toward the separate dealer network was a manufacturing consideration: the design for which independent distribution and service made most sense was the design that best utilized Honda's manufacturing capabilities.

Full realization of the systems concept in manufacturing is years away. It may not require a new Henry Ford. But it will certainly require very different management and very different managers. Every manager in tomorrow's manufacturing business will have to know and understand the manufacturing system. We might well adopt the Japanese custom of starting all new management people in the plant and in manufacturing jobs for the first few years of their careers. Indeed, we might go even further and require managers throughout the company to rotate into factory assignments throughout their careers—just as army officers return regularly to troop duty.

In the new manufacturing business, manufacturing is the integrator that ties everything together. It creates the economic value that pays for everything and everybody. Thus the greatest impact of the manufacturing systems concept will not be on the production process. As with SQC, its greatest impact will be on social and human concerns—on career ladders, for instance, or more important, on the transformation of *functional* managers into *business* managers, each with a specific role, but all members of the same production and the same cast. And surely, the manufacturing businesses of tomorrow will not be run by financial executives, marketers, or lawyers inexperienced in manufacturing, as so many U.S. companies are today.

There are important differences among these four concepts. Consider, for instance, what each means by "the factory." In SQC, the factory is a place where people work. In management accounting and the flotilla concept of flexible manufacturing, it is a place where work is being done—it makes no difference whether by people, by white mice, or by robots. In the systems concept, the factory is not a place at all; it is a stage in a process that adds economic value to materials. In theory, at least, the factory cannot and certainly should not be designed, let alone built, until the entire process of "making"—all the way to the final customer—is understood. Thus defining the factory is much more than a theoretical or semantic exercise. It has immediate practical consequences on plant design, location, and size; on what activities are to be brought together in one manufacturing complex; even on how much and in what to invest.

Similarly, each of these concepts reflects a particular mind-set. To apply SQC, you don't have to think, you have to do. Management accounting concentrates on technical analysis, while the flotilla concept focuses on organization design and work flow. In the systems concept, there is great temptation to keep on thinking and never get to the doing. Each concept has its own tools, its own language, and addresses different people.

Nevertheless, what these four concepts have in common is far more important than their differences. Nowhere is this more apparent than in their assumption that the manufacturing process is a configuration, a whole that is greater than the sum of its parts. Traditional approaches all see the factory as a collection of individual machines and individual operations. The nineteenth century factory was an assemblage of machines. Taylor's scientific management broke up each job into individual operations and then put those operations together into new and different jobs. "Modern" twentieth century concepts—the assembly line and cost accounting—define performance as the sum of lowest cost operations. But none of the new concepts is much concerned with performance of the parts. Indeed, the parts as such can only underperform. The process produces results.

Management also will reflect this new perspective. SQC is the most nearly conventional in its implications for managers, since it does not so much change their job as shift much of it to the work force. But even managers with no business responsibility (and under SQC, plant people have none) will have to manage with an awareness of business considerations well beyond the plant. And every manufacturing manager will be responsible for integrating people, materials, machines, and time. Thus every manufacturing manager ten years hence will have to learn and practice a discipline that integrates engineering, management of people, and business economics into the manufacturing process. Quite a few manufacturing people are doing this already, of course—though usually unaware that they are doing something new and different. Yet such a discipline has not been systematized and is still not taught in engineering schools or business schools.

These four concepts are synergistic in the best sense of this much-abused term. Together—but only together—they tackle the conflicts that have most troubled traditional, twentieth century mass-production plants: the conflicts between people and machines, time and money, standardization and flexibility, and functions and systems. The key is that every one of these concepts defines performance as productivity and conceives of manufacturing as the physical process that adds economic value to materials. Each tries to provide economic value in a different way. But they share the same theory of manufacturing.

5

Making Mass Customization Work

B. Joseph Pine II, Bart Victor, and Andrew C. Boynton

Continuous improvement at Toyota Motor Company is now a business legend. For three decades, Toyota enlisted its employees in a relentless drive to find faster, more efficient methods to develop and make low-cost, defect-free cars. The results were stupendous. Toyota became the benchmark in the automobile industry for quality and low cost.

The same, however, cannot be said for mass customization, Toyota's latest pioneering effort. With U.S. companies finally catching up, Toyota's top managers set out in the late 1980s to use their highly skilled, flexible work force to make varied and often individually customized products at the low cost of standardized, mass-produced goods. They saw this approach as a more advanced stage of continuous improvement.

As recently as early 1992, Toyota seemed to be well on its way to achieving its goals of lowering its new-product-development time to 18 months, offering customers a wide range of options for each model, and manufacturing and delivering a made-to-order car within three days.

In the last 18 months, however, Toyota has run into trouble and has had to retreat, at least temporarily, from its goal of becoming a mass customizer. As production costs soared, top managers widened product-development and model life cycles and asked dealers to carry more inventory. After Toyota's investigations revealed that 20% of the product varieties accounted for 80% of the sales, it reduced its range of offerings by one-fifth.

Author's note: IBM Consulting Group partners and consultants contributed significantly to the development of the ideas in this article. The research was sponsored in part by the IBM Consulting Group and the IBM Advanced Business Institute.

What happened? Was Toyota's new goal off-base in the first place, or was the mass-customization program a victim of troublesome economic times? Many analysts believe that Japan's recession and the devaluation of the dollar against the yen were the culprits that forced Toyota's pullback. These factors had undermined the company's competitive position and were causing its profits to slide. But, according to Toyota top managers, these weren't the only reasons for the company's retrenchment. They acknowledged that they had learned the hard way that mass customization is not simply continuous improvement plus.

All too often, executives at manufacturing as well as service companies that have been pursuing continuous improvement do not realize that mass customization is a distinct and, generally, a very unfamiliar way of doing business. This mistake is understandable. The frequent process enhancements generated by continuous improvement can increase the inherent flexibility of those processes. And, as a work force gets better and better, expanding its range of skills, it can handle an increasingly complex set of tasks, such as assembling a variety of products or delivering tailored services.

While executives are correct in thinking that continuous improvement is a prerequisite for mass customization, one thing is becoming clear from the experiences of companies such as Toyota, Amdahl, and Dow Jones. Continuous improvement and mass customization require very different organizational structures, values, management roles and systems, learning methods, and ways of relating to customers. (See box.)

In continuous-improvement systems, tightly linked teams bridge disparate functions that typically interact with each other in a predictable, sequential manner. A hallmark is the conviction that every process must contribute to satisfying the customer by constantly and incrementally achieving higher quality. But a big difference from mass-customizing systems is that workers do not question the basic design of the product that they are assigned to build; they assume it to be what customers want.

Continuous-improvement organizations school workers in tools and techniques to help them improve the tasks they must perform. The fundamental precept is to learn by doing a task and then do it better. Managers of such organizations lead everyone on a relentless mission to eliminate waste and enhance quality through a vision of "being the best," while still ensuring reliable outcomes from routine tasks. These managers are eternally striving to tighten the links between processes so that every team and individual worker knows how its function

---

Understanding the Differences

Mass Production

The traditional mass-production company is bureaucratic and hierarchical. Under close supervision, workers repeat narrowly defined, repetitious tasks. Result: low-cost, standard goods and services.

Continuous Improvement

In continuous-improvement settings, empowered, cross-functional teams strive constantly to improve processes. Managers are coaches, cheering on communications and unceasing efforts to improve. Result: low-cost, high-quality, standard goods and services.

Mass Customization

Mass customization calls for flexibility and quick responsiveness. In an ever-changing environment, people, processes, units, and technology reconfigure to give customers exactly what they want. Managers coordinate independent, capable individuals, and an efficient linkage system is crucial. Result: low-cost, high-quality, customized goods and services.

---

affects others and ultimately the quality of the product or service. They must be coaches who constantly urge employees to interact, converse, improve, and do what is right for the team. They try to foster values that create a sense of community because the interests of the individual are subsumed within the interests of the team, the company, and the customer.

Mass customization, on the other hand, requires a *dynamic network* of relatively autonomous operating units. Each *module* is typically a specific process or task, like making a given component, a distinctive welding method, or performing a credit check. The modules, which may include outside suppliers and vendors, typically do not interact or come together in the same sequence every time. Rather, the combination of how and when they interact to make a product or provide a service is constantly changing in response to what each customer wants and needs. From continually trying to meet these demands, the mass-customization organization learns what new capabilities it requires. Its employees are on a quest to increase their own skills, as well as those of the unit and the network, in a never-ending campaign to expand the number of ways the company can satisfy customers.

Managers in these ever-changing settings are coordinators whose success depends on how well they perfect the links that make up the dynamic network. They strive to make it ever easier and less costly for the process modules to come together to satisfy unique customer requests. And they lead the effort to increase the range of things that the organization can do. They must create a culture that places a high value on the diversity of employees' capabilities because the greater the diversity of the modules, the greater the range of customization the organization can offer.

What all this boils down to is that mass customization is a totally different world from continuous improvement. It is a world in which the unpredictable nature of each customer's demands is considered an opportunity. To exploit that opportunity, the organization must perpetually generate new product teams. The key to success is designing a linkage system that can bring together whatever modules are necessary—instantly, costlessly, seamlessly, and frictionlessly.

When Mass Customization Cannot Work

Continuous improvement can certainly be a subset of mass customization. The autonomous operating units within a mass customizer can and should strive to continuously improve their processes. But as Toyota, for one, seems to have finally realized, mass customization generally cannot be a subset of continuous improvement.

One of the main causes of Toyota's recent problems was that it had been pursuing mass customization but had retained the structures and systems of continuous-improvement organizations. By doing this, Toyota ended up not succeeding at mass customization and, at the same time, undermining its continuous-improvement efforts.

For example, Toyota assumed that its work force had attained the skills needed to handle production of its rapidly growing range of product offerings. But when the frequently changing tasks butted up against the limit of workers' capabilities, managers did not realize that the problems stemmed from a failure to transform the organization. Rather than developing the loose network necessary to make a mass-customization organization work, Toyota managers turned to machines. Over time, this ended up weakening the skills of the workers and thus violated an essential tenet of continuous improvement. It also caused internal friction.

One action Toyota took was to invest heavily in robots. But as one Toyota manager later commented, "Robots don't make suggestions."

Toyota also installed monitors at some stations along the assembly line that told workers how to put together a particular car. And the company installed computer-controlled spotlights illuminating the bins containing the right components. These measures deprived employees of opportunities to learn and think about the processes and, therefore, reduced their ability to improve them.

Another big problem at Toyota was that product proliferation took on a life of its own. Like mindless continuous improvers, engineers created technically elegant features regardless of whether customers wanted the additional choices. In mass customization, customer demand drives model varieties.

A third problem arose when Toyota's management, in its pursuit of low-cost customization, pushed product-development teams to use more common components across its models. At Toyota, project leaders have overall responsibility for the development of a given model, but separate teams develop individual components, such as brake systems or transmissions, which ideally will be used in several models. Project leaders felt that the intensifying pressure to share components was forcing them to compromise their models, and they began to resist. Eventually, the company couldn't achieve targeted levels for sharing design expertise, components, and production processes, and overall product development costs rose.

Other companies have also been attempting to achieve mass customization with less than optimal results. Some of their experiences highlight the potential pitfalls companies can encounter in trying to make this leap.

Nissan, Mitsubishi, and Mazda have run into many of the same problems that hurt Toyota. Nissan, for example, reportedly had 87 different varieties of steering wheels, most of which were great engineering feats. But customers did not want many of them and disliked having to choose from so many options.

Amdahl, which built its business on a low-cost strategy but never made the move to continuous improvement, adopted a goal similar to Toyota's: deliver a custom-built mainframe in a week. However, Amdahl did not achieve its objective through flexible process capabilities, a dynamic network, or anything else resembling mass customization. It stocked inventory for every possible combination that customers could order, an approach that ended up saddling it with hundreds of millions of dollars in excess inventory.

Dow Jones, through *The Wall Street Journal* and its other news-gathering resources, has a storehouse of information that it can customize and then deliver in a number of ways, including newswires, faxes, and on-line computer systems. Dow Jones, however, has not yet found the right formula for packaging services at a low price that would allow it to increase its share of the market. We suspect that two factors are responsible. Dow Jones seems to be trying to push a somewhat customized product out the door rather than first determining what customers truly need and how they want it delivered. The company also doesn't appear to have developed the organizational capabilities that would enable it to lower its costs enough to expand the still emerging market for customized information.

Despite the fact so many companies are struggling, scores of others are joining the quest. The appeal is understandable. Mass customization offers a solution to a basic dilemma that has plagued generations of executives.

Breaking New Ground

Until the widespread adoption of continuous improvement began about 15 years ago, either/or dichotomies dictated most managerial choices. A company could pursue a strategy of providing large volumes of standardized goods or services at a low cost, or it could decide to make customized or highly differentiated products in smaller volumes at a high cost. In other words, companies had to choose between being efficient mass producers and being innovative specialty businesses. Quality and low cost and customization and low cost were assumed to be trade-offs.

This old competitive dictum was grounded in the seemingly well-substantiated notion that the two strategies required very different ways of managing, and, therefore, two distinct organizational forms.

The *mechanistic* organization, so named because of the management emphasis on automating tasks and treating workers like machines, consists of a bureaucratic structure of functionally defined, highly compartmentalized jobs. Managers and industrial engineers study and define tasks, and workers execute them. Employees learn their jobs by following rigid rules under tight supervision.

In contrast, the *organic* organization, so named because of its fluid and ever-changing nature, is characterized by an adaptable structure of loosely defined jobs. These are typically held by highly skilled craftsmen. They learn through apprenticeships and experience, are governed by personal or professional standards, and are motivated by a desire to create a unique or breakthrough product.

The mechanistic organization, whether in a manufacturing or a service setting, gives managers the control and predictability required to achieve high levels of efficiency. The organic organization yields the craftsmanship needed to pursue a differentiation or niche strategy. Each of these organizational forms has innate limitations, however, which in the past have forced managers to choose one or the other. Almost all change is anathema to the mechanistic organization. And the artistry and informality at the heart of the organic organization defy efforts to regulate and control.

The development of the continuous-improvement and the mass-customization models show that companies *can* overcome the traditional trade-offs. In other words, companies can have it all.

Continuous improvement has enabled thousands of companies to realize lower costs than traditional mass producers and still achieve the distinctive quality of craft producers. But mass customization has enabled its adherents, which are as varied as Motorola, Bell Atlantic, the diversified insurer United Services Automobile Association (USAA), TWA Getaway Vacations, and Hallmark, to go a step further. These companies are achieving low costs, high quality, and the ability to make highly varied, often individually customized products.

Is Your Company Ready for Mass Customization?

Since achieving mass customization requires nothing less than a transformation of the business, managers must assess whether their companies must and whether in fact they can make the transformation.

Not all markets are appropriate for mass customization. Customers of commodity products like oil, gas, and wheat, for example, do not demand differentiation. In other markets, like public utilities and government services, regulation often bars customization. In some markets, the possible variations in services or products simply are of little value to customers. Also, variety in and of itself is not necessarily customization, and it can be dangerously expensive. Some consumer electronics retailers and supermarkets today are experiencing a backlash from customers confused by too broad a range of choices.

Continuous improvement will continue to be a very viable strategy for companies whose markets are relatively stable and predictable. But those companies whose markets are highly turbulent because of factors like changing customer needs, technological advances, and diminishing product life cycles are ripe for mass customization.

To have even a chance of successfully becoming a mass customizer, though, companies must first achieve high levels of quality and skills and low cost. For this reason, it seems impossible for mass producers to make the leap without first going through continuous improvement.

Westpac, the Australian financial services giant, is a case in point. It spent huge sums attempting to become a mass customizer by automating both the creation and delivery of its products. It wanted to install software building blocks that would allow it to create new financial products like mortgages and securities more quickly. Strategically, the move made sense. Deregulation had spawned a dizzying array of new products and services, and intensifying competition had caused significant downward pressure on prices.

Westpac tried to leapfrog continuous improvement by going from mass production directly to mass customization. The challenges of automating inflexible processes, building on ossified products, and trying to create a fluid network within a hierarchical organization—particularly at a time when the company was in poor financial condition due to intensifying competition in depressed markets—proved too difficult. Westpac has had to scale back significantly its ambitious dreams of becoming a tailored-product factory.

As we have stressed, even a company that has mastered continuous improvement must change radically the way it is run to become a successful mass customizer. A company must break apart the long-lasting, cross-functional teams and strong relationships built up for continuous improvement to form dynamic networks. It must change the focus of employee learning from incremental process improvement to generating ever-increasing capabilities. And leaders must replace a vision of "being the best" in an industry with an ideology of satisfying whatever customers want, when they want it.

The traditional mechanistic organization, aimed at achieving low-cost mass production, is segmented into very narrow compartments, often called functional or vertical silos, each of which performs an isolated task. Information is passed up, and decisions are handed down. Compensation of employees, who are viewed as mere cogs in the wheel, is generally based on standardized, narrowly defined job levels or categories.

In continuous-improvement organizations, the control system is much more, although never completely, horizontal. Increasingly, teams have not only responsibility for but also authority over a problem or task area. Such organizations are moving to much more generalized and overlapping job descriptions as well as to team-based compensation.

When mass customization is the objective, organizations structured around cross-functional teams can create horizontal silos just as isolated and ultimately damaging to the long-term health of the organization as vertical silos have been. When Toyota expanded dramatically its variety, for example, it found that tightly linked teams did not share easily across their boundaries to improve the general capabilities of the company. As a result, the costs of increasing variety rapidly outstripped any value it was creating for customers.

To achieve successful mass customization, managers need first to turn their processes into modules. Second, they need to create an architecture for linking them that will permit them to integrate rapidly in the best combination or sequence required to tailor products or services. The coordination of the overall dynamic network is often centralized, while each module retains operational authority for its particular process. Job descriptions become increasingly broad and may even disappear. And compensation for each module, whether it's a team or an individual, is based on the uniqueness and value of the contributions it makes toward producing the product.

Making Mass Customization Work

The key to coordinating the process modules is a linkage system with four key attributes.

1. *Instantaneous.* Processes must be able to be linked together as quickly as possible. First, the product or service each customer wants must be defined rapidly, preferably in collaboration with the customer. Mass customizers like Dell Computer, Hewlett-Packard, AT&T, and LSI Logic use special software that records customer desires and translates them into a design of the needed components. Then the design is quickly translated into a set of processes, which are integrated rapidly to create the product or service.

2. *Costless.* Beyond the initial investment required to create it, the linkage system must add as little as possible to the cost of making the product or service. Many service businesses have databases that make available all the information they know about their customers and their requirements to all the modules, so nothing new needs to be regenerated. USAA, for example, uses image technology that can scan

and electronically store paperwork and a companywide database, so every representative who comes into contact with a customer knows everything about him or her.

3. *Seamless.* An IBM executive once commented, correctly, "You always ship your organization." What he meant was, if you have seams in your organization, you are going to have seams in your product, such as programs that do not work well together in a computer system. Since a dynamic network is essentially constructing a new, *instant team* to deal with every customer interaction, the occasions for "showing the seams" are many indeed. The recent adoption of case workers or case managers is one way service companies like USAA and IBM Credit Corporation avoid this. These people are responsible for the company's relationship with the customer and for coordinating the creation of the customized product or service. They ensure that no seams appear.

4. *Frictionless.* Companies that are still predominantly continuous improvers may have the most trouble attaining this attribute. The need to create instant teams for every customer in a dynamic network leaves no time for the kind of extensive team building that goes on in continuous-improvement organizations. The instant teams must be frictionless from the moment of their creation, so information and communications technologies are mandatory for achieving this attribute. These technologies are necessary to find the right people, to define and create boundaries for their collective task, and to allow them to work together immediately without the benefit of ever having met.

USING TECHNOLOGY

In mechanistic organizations, the primary use of technology is to automate tasks, replacing human labor with mechanical or digital machines. People are sources of variation and are relatively costly, so mass producers often try to automate their companies as much as possible. This has the natural effect of reducing the numbers and skills of the work force.

In continuous-improvement companies, where workers are not only allowed but also encouraged to think about their jobs and how processes can be improved, technology is primarily used to augment workers' knowledge and skills. Measurement and analysis programs, computerized decision-support systems, videoconferencing, and even machine tools are aids, not people replacements.

In the dynamic networks of mass customizers, technology still automates tasks where that makes sense. Certainly, technology must augment people's knowledge and skills, but the elements of mass customization require that technology must also automate the links between modules and ensure that the people and the tools necessary to perform them are brought together instantly. Communication networks, shared databases that let everyone view the customer information simultaneously, computer-integrated manufacturing, workflow software, and tools like groupware (such as Lotus Notes) can automate the links so that a company can summon exactly the right resources to service a customer's unique desires and needs.

Many managers still view the promises of advanced technologies through the lens of mass production. But for mass customizers, the promise of technology is not the lights-out factory or the fully automated back office. It is used as a tool to tap more effectively all the diverse capabilities of employees to service customers.

While automating the links between modules is crucial, often some modules themselves can be automated by adopting, for example, a flexible manufacturing system that can choose instantly any product component within its wide envelope of variety. Motorola's Bravo pager factory in Boynton Beach, Florida, for example, can produce pagers—thanks to hardware and software modularity—in lot sizes as small as one within hours of an order arriving from a customer. The pager business is also a good example of how a mass customizer can automate links between modules. At Motorola, a sales rep and a customer design together, on a rep's laptop computer, the set of pagers (out of 29 million possible combinations) that exactly meets that customer's needs. Then the almost fully automated dynamic network takes over. The rep plugs the laptop into a phone and transmits one or more designs to the factory. Within minutes, a bar code is created with all the steps that a flexible manufacturing system needs to produce the pager.

As wonderful as these technological miracles sound, it is important to realize that technology is also potentially harmful. Mass customizers must periodically overhaul the linkages that they have adopted because as the market, the nature of their businesses, and the competition change, and as technology advances, any linkage system inevitably will become obsolete.

Another caveat: in this age when automated systems are handling daily millions of customer orders and inquiries placed via phones or computer systems, mass customizers must constantly be on their guard against eliminating their opportunities to learn what their customers like or dislike. Companies must always make it possible for their customers to "drop out" of the automated system so they can talk to a real person who is committed to helping them.

LEARNING FROM FAILURE

In the mechanistic organization, learning how to do something better is the prerogative of management and its collection of industrial engineers and supervisors. Workers only need to learn to do what is assigned to them; they don't have to think about it as well. The breakthrough of continuous improvement was the acknowledgment that workers' experience and know-how can help managers solve production problems and contribute toward tightening variances and reducing errors.

The differences between organizational learning in continuous-improvement and in mass-customization companies are most visible when you see how the two treat defects. Continuous-improvement organizations look at them as *process failures*, which the Japanese consider "treasures" because they provide the knowledge to fix problems and to ensure that failure never recurs.

In the dynamic networks of mass-customization organizations, defects are considered *capability failures:* the inability to satisfy the needs of some specific customer or market. They are still valuable treasures; but rather than sparking a spate of process-improvement activities, these defects call on the organization to renew itself by enhancing the flexibility within its processes, joining with another organization that has the needed capability, or even creating completely new process capabilities—whatever it takes to ensure that the customer is satisfied and, therefore, that capability failure doesn't happen again.

Capturing customer feedback on capability failures is crucial to sustaining any advantage that mass customization yields. A company that does this well is USAA, which targets its financial services and consumer goods to events in a customer's life, such as buying a house or car, getting married, or having a baby. Its information system allows sales reps to get customer feedback quickly on the phone and route it instantly to the appropriate department for analysis and action.

At Computer Products, Inc., a manufacturer of power supplies, marketing managers and engineers cold-call customers every day not to make a sale but to understand their problems and needs and to discuss product ideas. They then enter the information into a database that serves as an invaluable reference throughout the product-development cycle. Applied Digital Data Systems, a unit of AT&T's NCR subsidiary, uses a database system to store all its production information, including workers' comments and suggestions, and then regularly analyzes it to improve both its processes and products.

The capability to codesign and even coproduce products with customers provides mass customizers with the ability to capture valuable new knowledge. Motorola's and USAA's systems are good examples of this, as is Bally Engineered Structures Inc.'s (see "Overcoming the Hurdles at Bally"). This is very different from what goes on in both mass-production and continuous-improvement organizations. Typically, in those settings, there are almost no individual customer interactions that generate new knowledge.

Overcoming the Hurdles at Bally

In 1990, Tom Pietrocini, president of Bally Engineered Structures Inc. of Bally, Pennsylvania, decided that his company had to become a mass customizer to survive. He concluded that Bally had to change from a company that made specific products, like refrigerated rooms and walk-in coolers, to one that could make a growing range of products tailored to individual customers' needs but at the cost of standard mass-produced goods. Ideally, just what those products might be would be determined largely by how customers wanted Bally to use its hopefully ever-expanding set of capabilities to satisfy them.

It is too early to claim victory. With its markets still severely depressed, Bally is struggling. But its product range has widened to include even cleanrooms for the pharmaceutical industry, and today every product is tailored for each customer. Much more significant are the sweeping changes within the company that made the move to mass customization possible, such as the restructuring of process capabilities into modules that can be summoned in the numbers and combinations needed to create anything a particular customer seeks.

When Pietrocini joined Bally in 1983, it was a staid, high-cost mass producer that had been struggling to compete in a mature, cyclical industry soon to be wracked by price wars. It had positioned itself as a "quality" manufacturer, a strategy that had consigned it to the unenviable position of having to persuade customers to pay increasingly high premiums for its marginally better products.

Realizing this was untenable, Pietrocini started turning Bally into a lean, cost-efficient manufacturer that could grow by gaining market share. He hoped to achieve this by using the continuous-improvement approach to reduce significantly the number of defects and the time required to fill orders. Over several years, he broke down barriers between functions, created quality teams that were given wide latitude to make changes, and instilled within employees the belief that it was each person's responsibility not just to do a job but to figure out ways to do it better.

He developed an organization in which people talked to each other about production problems and enjoyed solving them together. They were driven by the vision of being the number one walk-in refrigerator company.

Bally was making considerable progress in enhancing its quality and bringing its costs in line with the rest of the industry when the last recession hit. That brought the already staggering industry to its knees. Before joining Bally, Pietrocini had worked in the auto-parts business, where he had twice expanded operations only to have to shrink them drastically during the OPEC-induced oil crises. After those painful experiences, he was loath to assume that Bally's market would fully rebound after the recession. He judged that continuous improvement alone would not be able to save the company and decided instead to remake it into an organization that thrives on the fickleness of customers and the turbulence of the markets.

Unlike many CEOs who have embarked on the road to mass customization only to stumble badly, Pietrocini committed his company with his eyes wide open. He understood that becoming a mass customizer would entail radical changes in organizational structure, systems, and culture. And during the last three years, he has succeeded at methodically transforming the $50 million company.

This transformation would not have been possible if Bally were still a mass producer. In those days, no one in manufacturing thought much about customers, let alone about their needs and wants. Aside from quality and cost levels that were out of kilter with the industry's, innovation—in terms of both products and processes—had stagnated at Bally. Although the continuous-improvement efforts gave Bally a fighting chance of making the leap to mass customization, the pillars of that approach were also obstacles that had to be removed. Even employee's perceptions of what Bally's business was got in the way of transformation.

As part of the continuous-improvement drive, Pietrocini had worked to convince employees that they were integral members of what was going to be "the best walk-in refrigerator company." That was fine when a good goal was continuing to do today what was done yesterday, only better. But this perception was an impediment to becoming a mass customizer.

Workers had questioned, for instance, whether Bally should be making under-the-counter blast chillers, which process food instead of just storing it.

Now Pietrocini is trying to get employees to view the company in terms of its capabilities and values rather than as a maker of a concrete set of products. He preaches that things like efficiency, flexibility, and quality are the end rather than the means to achieving a rather limited purpose. He points out that customer demands and Bally's widening array of process capabilities will determine what it will create.

Pietrocini also had to find ways to ensure that Bally's capabilities kept expanding. He encouraged employees to listen to and learn from every customer, and not just to depend on customer-reported defects or periodic customer satisfaction surveys for feedback, as had been the tradition.

Bally's experience with one customer is a case in point. This customer decided to abandon Bally because his walk-in-freezers' floors kept wearing out in as little as 18 months. Bally engineers discovered that the customer was cleaning the freezers with hot steam, something they were not designed to endure.

Bally would never had been able to advance the existing technology for making its products to the point where they could withstand the kind of punishment, but the company didn't simply write off the customer as unreasonable as it might have done in the past. Instead, a project team made up of people from various areas of the company worked on a solution part-time for two years. Ultimately, the team developed a completely new, patented technology that prevented moisture from entering crevices and destroying the floor. Bally not only won back this customer but also has used the technology for others.

Bally's structure also had to change radically to make the leap to mass customization. Before Pietrocini joined the company, Bally was producing modular panels that theoretically should have enabled it to customize individual orders. But the organization's structure was so rigid, it made doing so very difficult. Customers had to choose from a set number of standard product offerings in a catalog. Then, because of the bureaucratic way that the company processed orders, it took weeks just to get them to the shop floor. In addition, manufacturing processes were organized in a sequential order that left no room for modifications.

Bally has now not only broken up its tightly integrated set of processes but also has greatly expanded it. In the old days, when every order reached the factory floor, the foam panels, metal skins, corners, floors, ceilings, doors, and refrigeration units needed to cool the structure were built in largely that sequence. Since then, the number of customer options has soared from 12 to 10,000. And to create these options, Bally has greatly increased its number of process modules, so it can offer such features as welded construction and a much wider range of finishes and air- and electrical-control systems. Different modules are now called on to make each specific order, whether it is for a blast chiller, a clean room, or a freezer that can withstand steam cleaning.

The nervous system of Bally's new dynamic network is a sophisticated information-management system that Bally calls the computer-driven intelligence network (CDIN). A sales rep can custom-design each order in the customer's office on a laptop computer connected to the CDIN via a modem. Once the design is completed, manufacturing software in the CDIN defines the precise combination of process modules required to make the product.

The network electronically connects everyone in the company, was well as independent sales reps, suppliers, and customers. The CDIN's databases contain nearly all the information Bally uses, including such things as leads, quotes, designs, purchase orders, and the skills and experiences of all Bally employees. This allows everyone to access the information they need to know without having to contend with functional boundaries. It also enables everyone to find quickly the people who have the skills they need for whatevery issue that arises.

"We're a company of 400 people that behaves as if it were a company of 4 people, who talk to each other every day to decide how to best satisfy the customer of the moment," Pietrocini says.

CREATING A VISION

In addition to different attitudes about customer interactions, leaders of continuous-improvement companies and mass customizers foster very different approaches to the future. The former think they know what the organization needs to do to succeed in the future, whereas the latter believe that it's impossible to know and heresy to try because the future should be shaped by each successive customer order.

Leaders of continuous-improvement organizations provide a vision of not just what is to be done today but also what needs to be realized tomorrow, and this can work, provided that the market is relatively stable. Their vision is often expressed in terms of some competitive ideal of customer satisfaction. Allstate's "To be the best," Federal Express's "Never let the best get in the way of better," and Steelcase's "To provide the world's best office environment products, services, systems, and intelligence" are good examples. The common vision provides everyone in the company with the motivation, direction, and control necessary to continue improving all the time. Without a sustained vision, a company's attempts at process improvement can become lost in "program-of-the-month" fads or lip service to quality.

The highly turbulent marketplace of the mass customizer, with its ever-changing demand for innovation and tailored products and services, doesn't result in a clear, shared vision of that market. A standard product or market vision isn't just insufficient; it simply doesn't make sense. In a true mass-customization environment, no one knows exactly what the next customer will want, and, therefore, no one knows exactly what product the company will be creating next. No one knows what market-opportunity windows will open, and, therefore, no one can create a long-term vision of certain products to service those markets. But everyone does know that the next customer will want something and the next market opportunity is out there somewhere.

Many companies are articulating this scenario by using words like "anything," "anywhere," and "anytime." Peter Kann, chief executive of Dow Jones, describes his organization's strategic goal as providing "business and financial news and information however, wherever, and whenever customers want to receive it." Nissan's vision for the year 2000 is the "Five A's": any volume, anytime, anybody, anywhere, and anything. Motorola's pager group has a TV ad that asks, "How do you use your Motorola pager?" Various people answer with phrases like, "Anytime," "For anything," and "Anywhere I want."

No matter what they are called, such ideologies say two things about an organization: one, we don't know exactly what we'll have to provide to whom, and two, within our growing envelope of capabilities, we do know that we have or can acquire the capabilities to give customers what they want.

Leaders who can articulate such an ideology and create the dynamic network that can make it happen will succeed in moving their organizations far beyond continuous improvement to the new competitive arena of mass customization.

PART

II

Improving Competitiveness through Investments in Technology and Facilities

1
The Focused Factory

Wickham Skinner

The threat posed by foreign competition, the problem of industries suffering from "blue-collar blues," and the increasing complexity and frustration of life in the factory have forced public attention back to the industrial sector of the economy. Many years of taking our industrial health and leadership for granted abruptly ended in the 1970s when our declining position in world markets weakened the dollar and became a national issue.

In the popular press and at the policy level in government, the issue has been seen as a "productivity crisis." The National Commission on Productivity was established in 1971. The concern with productivity has appealed to many managers who have firsthand experience with our problems of high costs and low efficiency.

So pessimism now pervades the outlook of many managers and analysts of the U.S. manufacturing scene. The recurring theme of this gloomy view is that (a) U.S. labor is the most expensive in the world, (b) its productivity has been growing at a slower rate than that of most of its competitors, and therefore (c) our industries sicken one by one as imports mushroom and unemployment becomes chronic in our industrial population centers.

Author's note: This article is an analysis based on my cases written in the electronics, plastics, textile, steel, and industrial equipment industries, supplemented by recent project research in the furniture industry. Financial support for this work provided by the Harvard Business School Division of Research and course development funds is gratefully acknowledged.

In this article, I shall offer a more optimistic view of the productivity dilemma, suggesting that we need not feel powerless in competing against cheaper foreign labor. Rather, we have the opportunity to effect basic changes in the management of manufacturing, which could shift the competitive balance in our favor in many industries. What are these basic changes? I can identify four:

1. Seeing the problem not as "How can we increase productivity?" but as "How can we compete?"
2. Seeing the problem as encompassing the efficiency of the *entire* manufacturing organization, not only the efficiency of the direct labor and the work force. (In most plants, direct labor and the work force represent only a small percentage of total costs.)
3. Learning to focus each plant on a limited, concise, manageable set of products, technologies, volumes, and markets.
4. Learning to structure basic manufacturing policies and supporting services so that they focus on one explicit manufacturing task instead of on many inconsistent, conflicting, implicit tasks.

A factory that focuses on a narrow product mix for a particular market niche will outperform the conventional plant, which attempts a broader mission. Because its equipment, supporting systems, and procedures can concentrate on a limited task for one set of customers, its costs and especially its overhead are likely to be lower than those of the conventional plant. But, more important, such a plant can become a competitive weapon because its entire apparatus is focused to accomplish the particular manufacturing task demanded by the company's overall strategy and marketing objective.

In spite of their advantages, my research indicates that focused manufacturing plants are surprisingly rare. Instead, the conventional factory produces many products for numerous customers in a variety of markets, thereby demanding the performance of a multiplicity of manufacturing tasks all at once from one set of assets and people. Its rationale is "economy of scale" and lower capital investment.

However, the result more often than not is a hodgepodge of compromises, a high overhead, and a manufacturing organization that is constantly in hot water with top management, marketing management, the controller, and customers.

A simple but telling example of a failure of focus is uncovered in this case study of a manufacturer, the American Printed Circuit Company (APC).

APC was a small company which had been growing rapidly and successfully. Its printed circuits were custom-built in lots of 1 to 100 for about 20 principal customers and were used for engineering tests and development work. APC's process consisted of about 15 operations using simple equipment, such as hand-dipping tanks, drill presses, and manual touch-ups. There was considerable variation in the sequence and processes for different products. Delivery was a major element for success, and price was not a key factor.

APC's president accepted an order from a large computer company to manufacture 20,000 printed circuit boards—a new product for the company—at a price equivalent to about one-third of its average mix of products. APC made the decision to produce these circuit boards in order to build volume, broaden the company's range of markets, and diversify the line. The new product was produced in the existing plant.

The result was disastrous. The old products were no longer delivered on time. The costs of the new printed circuit boards was substantially in excess of the bid price. The quality on all items suffered as the organization frenetically attempted to meet deliveries. Old customers grew bitter over missed deliveries, and the new customer returned one-third of the merchandise for below-spec quality. Such heavy losses ensued that the APC company had to recapitalize. Subsequently, the ownership of the company changed hands.

The purpose of this article is to set forth the advantages of focused manufacturing. I shall begin with the basic concepts of the focused factory, then follow with an analysis of the productivity phenomenon, which tends to prevent the adoption of the focused plant concept. Finally, I shall offer some specific steps for managing manufacturing to accomplish and take advantage of focus.

Basic Concepts

From my study of approximately 50 plants in six industries, I can pinpoint three basic concepts underlying focused manufacturing. Consider:

1. There are many ways to compete besides by producing at low cost. This statement may be self-evident to the reader (particularly, to one in an industry which has been badly hit by low-priced foreign imports and has been attempting to compete with better products, quality, or customer service and delivery). Nevertheless, it still needs saying for two reasons.

One is simply the persistent attitude that ways of competing other than on the basis of price are second best. The other is that a company which starts out with higher manufacturing costs than its competitors is in trouble regardless of whatever else it does.

While these assumptions may be true of industries with mature products and technologies, they are not at all true of products in earlier stages of their life cycles. In fact, in many U.S. industries, companies are being forced to shift to products in which technological innovation in the form of advanced features is a more critical element of competitive advantage than cost.

2. A factory cannot perform well on every yardstick. There are a number of common standards for measuring manufacturing performance. Among these are short delivery cycles, superior product quality and reliability, dependable delivery promises, ability to produce new products quickly, flexibility in adjusting to volume changes, low investment and hence higher return on investment, and low costs.

These measures of manufacturing performance necessitate trade-offs—certain tasks must be compromised to meet others. They cannot all be accomplished equally well because of the inevitable limitations of equipment and process technology. Such trade-offs as costs versus quality or short delivery cycles versus low inventory investment are fairly obvious. Other trade-offs, while less obvious, are equally real. They involve implicit choices in establishing manufacturing policies.

Within the factory, managers can make the manufacturing function a competitive weapon by outstanding accomplishment of one or more of the measures of manufacturing performance. But managers need to know: "What must we be especially good at? Cost, quality, lead times, reliability, changing schedules, new product introduction, or low investment?"

Focused manufacturing must be derived from an explicitly defined corporate strategy which has its roots in a corporate marketing plan. Therefore, the choice of focus cannot be made independently by production people. Instead, it has to be a result of a comprehensive analysis of the company's resources, strengths and weaknesses, position in the industry, assessment of competitors' moves, and forecast of future customer motives and behavior.

Conversely, the choice of focus cannot be made without considering the existing factory because a given set of facilities, systems, and people skills can do only certain things well within a given time period.

3. Simplicity and repetition breed competence. Focused manufacturing is based on the concept that simplicity, repetition, experience, and homogeneity of tasks breed competence. Furthermore, each key functional area in manufacturing must have the same objective, derived from corporate strategy. Such congruence of tasks can produce a manufacturing system that does limited things very well, thus creating a formidable competitive weapon.

MAJOR CHARACTERISTICS

Five key characteristics of the focused factory are:

1. Process technologies: Typically, unproven and uncertain technologies are limited to one per factory. Proven, mature technologies are limited to what their managers can easily handle, typically two or three (e.g., a foundry, metal working, and metal finishing).

2. Market demands: These consist of a set of demands including quality, price, lead times, and reliability specifications. A given plant can usually only do a superb job on one or two demands at any time.

3. Product volumes: Generally, these are of comparable levels, such that tooling, order quantities, materials handling techniques, and job contents can be approached with a consistent philosophy. But what about the inevitable short runs, customer specials, and one-of-a-kind orders that every factory must handle? The answer is usually to segregate them. This is discussed later.

4. Quality levels: These employ a common attitude and set of approaches so as to neither overspecify nor overcontrol quality and specifications. One frame of mind and set of mental assumptions suffice for equipment, tooling, inspection, training, supervision, job content, materials handling.

5. Manufacturing tools: These are limited to only one (or two at the most) at any given time. The task at which the plant must excel in order to be competitive focuses on one set of internally consistent, doable, noncompromised criteria for success.

My research evidence makes it clear that the focused factory will outproduce, undersell, and quickly gain competitive advantage over the complex factory. The focused factory does a better job because repetition and concentration in one area allow its work force and managers to become effective and experienced in the task required for success. The focused factory is manageable and controllable. Its problems are demanding, but limited in scope.

Productivity Phenomenon

The conventional wisdom of manufacturing management has been and continues to be that the measure of success is productivity. Now that U.S. companies in many industries are getting beaten hands down by overseas competitors with lower unit costs, we mistakenly cling to the old notion that "a good plant is a low-cost plant." This is simply not so. A low-cost plant may be a disaster if the company has sacrificed too much in the way of quality, delivery, flexibility, and so forth, in order to get its costs down.

Too many companies attempt to do too many things with one plant and one organization. In the name of low investment in facilities and spreading their overheads, they add products, markets, technologies, processes, quality levels, and supporting services which conflict and compete with each other and compound expense. They then hire more staff to regulate and control the unmanageable mixture of problems.

In desperation, many companies are now "banging away" at anything to reduce the resulting high costs. But we can only regain competitive strength by stopping this process of increasing complexity and overstaffing.

This behavior is so illogical that the phenomenon needs further explanation. Our plants are generally managed by extremely able people; yet the failure to focus manufacturing on a limited objective is a common managerial blind spot. What happens to produce this defect in competent managers? Engineers know what can and cannot be designed into planes, boats, and building structures. Engineers accept design objectives that will accomplish a specific set of tasks which are possible, although difficult.

In contrast, most of the manufacturing plants in my study attempted a complex, heterogeneous mixture of general and special-purpose equipment, long- and short-run operations, high and low tolerances, new and old products, off-the-shelf items and customer specials, stable and changing designs, markets with reliable forecasts and unpredictable ones, seasonal and nonseasonal sales, short and long lead times, and high and low skills.

LACK OF CONSISTENT POLICIES

It is not understood, I think, that each of the contrasting features just noted generally demands conflicting manufacturing tasks and hence different manufacturing policies. The particular mix of these features should determine the elements of manufacturing policy. Some of these elements are the following:

Size of plant and its capacity.

Location of plant.

Choice of equipment.

Plant layout.

Selection of production process.

Production scheduling system.

Use of inventories.

Wage system.

Training and supervisory approaches.

Control systems.

Organizational structure.

Instead of designing elements of manufacturing policy around one manufacturing task, what usually happens? Consider, for example, that the wage system may be set up to emphasize high productivity, production control to maximize short lead times, inventory to minimize stock levels, order quantities to minimize setup times, plant layout to minimize materials handling costs, and process design to maximize quality.

While each of these decisions probably looks sensible to the professional specialist in his field, the conventional factory consists of six or more inconsistent elements of manufacturing structure, each of which is designed to achieve a different implicit objective.

Such inconsistency usually results in high costs. One or another element may be excessively staffed or operated inefficiently because its task is being exaggerated or misdirected. Or several functions may require excess staff in order to control or manage a plant which is unduly complex.

But often the result is even more serious. My study shows that the chief negative effect is not on productivity but on ability to compete. The plant's manufacturing policies are not designed, tuned, and focused as a whole on that one key strategic manufacturing task essential to the company's success in its industry.

REASONS FOR INCONSISTENCY

Noncongruent manufacturing structures appear to be common in U.S. industry. In fact, my research revealed that a fully consistent set of manufacturing policies resulting in a congruent system is highly rare. Why does this situation occur so often? In the cases I studied, it seemed to come about essentially for one or more of these reasons:

> Professionals in each field attempted to achieve goals which, although valid and traditional in their fields, were not congruent with goals of other areas.
>
> The manufacturing task for the plant subtly changed while most operating and service departments kept on the same course as before.
>
> The manufacturing task was never made explicit.
>
> The inconsistencies were never recognized.
>
> More and more products were piled into existing plants, resulting in an often futile attempt to meet the manufacturing tasks of a variety of markets, technologies, and competitive strategies.

Let me elaborate on the first and last set of causes we have just noted.

"PROFESSIONALISM" IN THE PLANT.   Production system elements are now set up or managed by professionals in their respective fields, such as quality control, personnel, labor relations, engineering, inventory management, materials handling, systems design, and so forth.

These professionals, quite naturally, seek to maximize their contributions and justify their positions. They have conventional views of success in each of their particular fields. Of course, these objectives are generally in conflict.

I say "of course" not to be cynical. These fields of specialty have come into existence for many different reasons—some to reduce costs, others to save time, others to minimize capital investments, still others to promote human cooperation and happiness, and so on. So it is perfectly normal for them to pull in different directions, which is exactly what happens in many plants.

This problem is not totally new. But it is changing because professionalism is increasing; we have more and more experts at work in different parts of the factory. So it is a growing problem.

PRODUCT PROLIFERATION. The combination of increasing foreign and domestic competition plus an accelerating rate of technological innovation has resulted in product proliferation in many factories. Shorter product life, more new products, shorter runs, lower unit volumes, and more customer specials are becoming increasingly common. The same factory which five years ago produced 25 products may today be producing 50 to 100.

The inconsistent production system grows up, not simply because there are more products to make—which is of course likely to increase direct and indirect costs and add complexity and confusion—but also because new products often call for different manufacturing tasks. To succeed in some tasks may require superb technological competence and focus; others may demand extremely short delivery; and still others, extremely low costs.

Yet, almost always, new products are added into the existing mix in the same plant, even though some new equipment may be necessary. The rationale for this decision is usually that the plant is operating at less than full capacity. Thus the logic is, "If we put the new products into the present plant, we can save capital investment and avoid duplicating overheads."

The result is complexity, confusion, and worst of all a production organization which, because it is spun out in all directions by a kind of centrifugal force, lacks focus and a doable manufacturing task. The factory is asked to perform a mission for Product A which conflicts with that of Product B. Thus the result is a hodgepodge of compromises.

When we may have, in fact, four tasks and four markets, we make the mistake of trying to force them into one plant, one set of equipment, one factory organization, one set of manufacturing policies, and so on. We try to cram into one operating system the ability to compete in an impossible mix of demands. Each element of the system attempts to adjust to these demands with variation, special sections, complex procedures, more people, and added paperwork.

In my opinion this syndrome, starting with added market demands and ending with incongruent internal structures, to a large extent accounts for the human frustrations, high costs, and low competitive abilities we see so much of in U.S. industry today.

Who gets the blame? The manufacturing executive, of course, gets it from corporate headquarters for high costs, poor productivity, low quality and reliability, and missed deliveries. In turn he tends to blame the situation on anything which makes sense, such as poor market forecasts, subpar labor, unconcern over quality, inept engineering designs, faulty equipment, and so forth.

Probably all such factors contribute and, undoubtedly, they all add to the pressure on production people. But what is not perceived is that a given production organization, as we noted earlier, can only do certain things well; trade-offs are inevitable.

Experience accomplishes wonders, but a diffused organization with conflicting structural elements and competing manufacturing tasks accumulates experience and specialized competence very slowly.

Toward Manufacturing Focus

A new management approach is needed in industries where diverse products and markets require companies to manufacture a broad mix of items, volumes, specifications, and customer demand patterns. Its emphasis must be on building competitive strength. One way to compete is to focus the entire manufacturing system on a limited task precisely defined by the company's competitive strategy and the realities of its technology and economics. A common objective produces synergistic effects rather than internal power struggles between professionalized departments. This approach can be assisted by these guiding rules:

Centralize the factory's focus on relative competitive ability.

Avoid the common tendency to add staff and overhead in order to save on direct labor and capital investment.

Let each manufacturing unit work on a limited task instead of the usual complex mix of conflicting objectives, products, and technologies.

This management approach can be thought of as focused manufacturing, for it is the opposite of the under-one-roof diffusion process of the conventional factory. Instead of permitting the whirling diversity of tasks and ingredients, top management applies a centripetal force, which constantly pulls inward toward one central focus—the one key manufacturing task. The result is greater simplicity, lower costs, and a manufacturing and support organization that is directed toward successful competition.

ACHIEVING THE FOCUSED PLANT

In my experience, manufacturing managers are generally astounded at the internal inconsistencies and compromises they discover once they put the concept of focused manufacturing to work in analyzing their own plants.

Then, when they begin to discern what the company strategy and market situation are implicitly demanding and to compare these implicit demands with what they have been trying to achieve, many submerged conflicts surface.

Finally, when they ask themselves what a certain element of the structure or of the manufacturing policy was designed to maximize, the built-in cross-purposes become apparent.

At the risk of seeming to take a cookbook approach to an inevitably complex set of issues, let me offer a recipe for the focused factory based on an actual but disguised example of an industrial manufacturing company which attempted to adapt its operations to this concept.

Consider this four-step approach of, say, the WXY Company, a producer of mechanical equipment:

1. Develop an explicit, brief statement of corporate objectives and strategy. The statement should cover the next three to five years, and it should have the substantial involvement of top management, including marketing, finance, and control executives.

In its statement, the top management of the WXY Company agreed to the following:

> Our corporate objective is directed toward increasing market share during the next five years via a strategy of (1) tailoring our product to individual customer needs, (2) offering advanced and special product features at a modest price increment, and (3) gaining competitive advantage via rapid product development and service orientation to customers of all sizes.

2. Translate the objectives-and-strategy statement into "what this means to manufacturing." What must the factory do especially well in order to carry out and support this corporate strategy? What is going to be the most difficult task it will face? If the manufacturing function is not sharp and capable, where is the company most likely to fail? It may fail in any one of the elements of the production structure, but it will probably do so in a combination of some of them.

To carry on with the WXY Company example, such a manufacturing task might be defined explicitly as follows:

> Our manufacturing task for the next three years will be to introduce specialized, customer-tailored new products into production, with lead times which are substantially less than those of our competitors.

> Since the technology in our industry is changing rapidly, and since product reliability can be extremely serious for customers, our most difficult problems will be to control the new-product introduction process, so as to solve technical problems promptly and to maintain reliability amid rapid changes in the product itself.

3. Make a careful examination of each element of the production system. How is it now set up, organized, focused, and manned? What is it now especially good at? How must it be changed to implement the key manufacturing task?

4. Reorganize the elements of structure to produce a congruent focus. This reorganization focuses on the ability to do those limited things well which are of utmost importance to the accomplishment of the manufacturing task.

To complete the example of the WXY Company, Exhibit I lists each major element of the manufacturing system of the company, describes its present focus in terms of that task for which it was implicitly or inadvertently aimed, and lists a new approach designed to bring consistency, focus, and power to its manufacturing arm.

What stands out most in this exhibit is the number of substantial changes in manufacturing policies required to bring the production system into a total consistency. The exhibit also features the implicit conflicts between many manufacturing tasks in the present approach, which are the result of the failure to define one task for the whole plant.

The reader may perceive a disturbing implication of the focused plant concept—namely, that it seems to call for major investments in new plants, new equipment, and new tooling, in order to break down the present complexity.

For example, if the company is currently involved in five different products, technologies, markets, or volumes, does it need five plants, five sets of equipment, five processes, five technologies, and five organizational structures? The answer is probably *yes*. But the practical

Exhibit I. Conflicting manufacturing tasks implied by incongruent elements of the present production system

Production system elements	Present approach (conventional factory)	Implicit manufacturing tasks of present approach	Changed approach (focused factory)
Equipment and process policies	One large plant; special purpose equipment; high-volume tooling; balanced capacity with functional layout.	Low manufacturing costs on steady runs of a few large products with minimal investment.	Separate old, standardized products and new customized products into two plants within a plant (PWP). For new PWP, provide general purpose equipment, temporary tooling, and modest excess capacity with product-oriented layout.
Work-force management policies	Specialized jobs with narrow job content; incentive wages; few supervisors; focus on volume of production per hour.	Low costs and efficiency.	Create fewer jobs with more versatility. Pay for breadth of skills and ability to perform a variety of jobs. Provide more foremen for solving technical problems at workplace.
Production scheduling and control	Detailed, frequent sales forecasts; produce for inventory economic or sizes of finished goods; small, decentralized production scheduling group.	Short delivery lead times.	Procure to order special parts and stock of common parts based on semi-annual forecast. Staff production control to closely schedule and centralize parts movements.
Quality control	Control engineers and large inspection groups in each department.	Extremely reliable quality.	No change.
Organizational structure	Functional; production control under superintendents of each area; inspection reports to top.	Top performance of the objectives of each functional department, i.e., many tasks.	Organize each PWP by program and project in order to focus organizational effort on bringing new products into production smoothly and on time.

solution need not involve selling the big multipurpose facility and decentralizing into five small facilities.

In fact, the few companies that have adopted the focused plant concept have approached the solution quite differently. There is no need to build five plants, which would involve unnecessary investment and overhead expenses.

The more practical approach is the "plant within a plant" (PWP) notion in which the existing facility is divided both organizationally and physically into, in this case, five PWPs. Each PWP has its own facilities in which it can concentrate on its particular manufacturing task, using its own work-force management approaches, production control, organization structure, and so forth. Quality and volume levels are not mixed; worker training and incentives have a clear focus; and engineering of processes, equipment, and materials handling are specialized as needed.

Each PWP gains experience readily by focusing and concentrating every element of its work on those limited essential objectives which constitute its manufacturing task. Since a manufacturing task is an offspring of a corporate strategy and marketing program, it is susceptible to either gradual or sweeping change. The PWP approach makes it easier to perform realignment of essential operations and system elements over time as the task changes.

Conclusion

The prevalent use of "cost" and "efficiency" as the conventional yardsticks for planning, controlling, and evaluating U.S. plants played a large part in the increasing inability of many of the approximately 50 companies included in my research to compete successfully. However, such goals are no longer adequate because competition is getting rougher and, in particular, because a strictly low-cost, high-efficiency strategy is apparently becoming less viable in many industries.

While the economy has moved toward an era of more advanced technologies and shorter product lives, we have not readjusted our concepts of production to keep up with these changes. Instead, we have continued to use "productivity" and "economies of scale" as guiding objectives. Both feature only one element of competition (i.e., costs), and both are now obsolete as general, all-purpose guides in manufacturing management.

But I have concluded that the focused plant is a rarity. With the mistaken rationale that the keys to success are limited investment, economies of scale, and full utilization of existing plant resources to achieve low costs, we keep adding new products to plants which were once focused, manageable, and competitive.

Reversing the process, however, is not impossible. In most cases I have studied, capital investment in facilities is not difficult to justify when payoffs that will result from organizational simplicity are taken into account. Resources for simplifying the focus of a manufacturing complex are not hard to acquire when the expected payoff is the ability to compete successfully, using manufacturing as a competitive weapon.

Moreover, better customer service and competitive position typically support higher margins to cover capital investments. And when studied carefully, the economies of scale and the effects of less than full utilization of plant equipment are seldom found to be as critical to productivity and efficiency as classical economic approaches often predict.

The U.S. problem of "productivity" is real indeed. But seeing the problem as one of "how to compete" can broaden management's horizon. The focused factory approach offers the opportunity to stop compromising each element of the production system in the typical general-purpose, do-all plant which satisfies no strategy, no market, and no task.

Not only does focus provide punch and power, but it also provides clear goals which can be readily understood and assimilated by members of an organization. It provides, too, a mechanism for reappraising what is needed for success, and for readjusting and shaking up old, tired manufacturing organizations with welcome change and a clear sense of direction.

In many sectors of U.S. industry, such change and such a new sense of direction are needed to shift the competitive balance in our favor.

2
Postindustrial Manufacturing

Ramchandran Jaikumar

As global competition grows ever fiercer in manufacturing indus-tries, American managers are adopting a new battle cry: "Beat 'em with technology or move—over there." Indeed, since 1975, the boom in information-intensive processing technologies has been explosive. A close look at how U.S. managers are actually using these technolo-gies, however, silences their battle cry in a hurry. Yes, they are buy-ing the hardware of flexible automation—but they are using it very poorly. Rather than narrowing the competitive gap with Japan, the technology of automation is widening it further.

With few exceptions, the flexible manufacturing systems installed in the United States show an astonishing lack of flexibility. In many cases, they perform worse than the conventional technology they replace. The technology itself is not to blame; it is management that makes the difference. Compared with Japanese systems, those in U.S. plants produce an order-of-magnitude less variety of parts. Further-more, they cannot run untended for a whole shift, are not integrated with the rest of their factories, and are less reliable. Even the good ones form, at best, a small oasis in a desert of mediocrity.

Lest this sound unduly harsh, consider the facts summarized in Exhibit I. In 1984 I conducted a focused study of 35 flexible manufac-turing systems (FMSs) in the United States and 60 in Japan, a sample that represented more than half the installed systems in both coun-tries. The kinds of products they made—large housings, crankcases, and the like—were comparable in size and complexity, and required simi-lar metal-cutting times, numbers of tools, and precision of parts. The U.S. systems had an average of seven machines and the Japanese, six.

Exhibit I.   *Comparison of FMSs studied in the United States and Japan*

	United States	Japan
System development time years	2.5 to 3	1.25 to 1.75
Number of machines per system	7	6
Types of parts produced per system	10	93
Annual volume per part	1,727	258
Number of parts produced per day	88	120
Number of new parts introduced per year	1	22
Number of systems with untended operations	0	18
Utilization rate* two shifts	52 %	84 %
Average metal-cutting time per day hours	8.3	20.2

*Ratio of actual metal-cutting time to time available for metal cutting.

Here the similarities end. The average number of parts made by an FMS in the United States was 10; in Japan the average was 93, almost ten times greater. Seven of the U.S. systems made just 3 parts. The U.S. companies used FMSs the wrong way—for high-volume production of a few parts rather than for high-variety production of many parts at low cost per unit. Thus the annual volume per part in the United States was 1,727; in Japan, only 258. Nor have U.S. installations exploited opportunities to introduce new products. For every new part introduced into a U.S. system, 22 parts were introduced in Japan. In the critical metal-working industries, from which these numbers come, the United States is not using manufacturing technology effectively. Japan is.

I have spent several years examining the experiences of companies that have installed FMSs. (See appendix "Primary Research" for details of the study.) The object has been to observe the most sophisticated form of information-intensive technology in manufacturing. Flexible systems resemble miniature factories in operation. They are natural laboratories in which to study computer-integrated manufacturing, which is rapidly becoming the battleground for manufacturing supremacy around the globe.

The battle is on, and the United States is losing badly. It may even lose the war if it doesn't soon figure out how better to use the new technology of automation for competitive advantage. This does not mean investing in more equipment; in today's manufacturing environment, it is how the equipment is used that is important. Success comes from achieving continuous process improvement through organizational learning and experimentation.

Technology Leadership

The FMS installations surveyed in Exhibit I were, as noted, technically alike. They had similar machines and did similar types of work. The difference in results was mainly due to the extent of the installed base of machinery, the work force's technical literacy, and management's competence. In each of these areas, Japan was far ahead of the United States.

In the last five years, Japan has outspent the United States two to one in automation. During that time, 55% of the machine tools introduced in Japan were computer numerically controlled (CNC) machines, key parts of FMSs. In the United States, the figure was only 18%. Of all these machines installed worldwide since 1975, more than 40% are in Japan. What's more, over two-thirds of the CNC machines in Japan went to small and medium-sized companies.

Just counting how much of this technology companies use is not enough. Because software development lies at the heart of this increasingly information-intensive manufacturing process, the technological literacy of a company's workers is critical. In the Japanese companies I studied, more than 40% of the work force was made up of college-educated engineers, and all had been trained in the use of CNC machines. In the U.S. companies studied, only 8% of the workers were engineers, and less than 25% had been trained on CNC machines. Training to upgrade skills was 3 times longer in Japan than in the United States. Compared with U.S. plants, Japanese factories had an average of $2\frac{1}{2}$ times as many CNC machines, 4 times as many engineers, and 4 times as many people trained to use the machines.

MANAGEMENT'S ROLE

A skilled work force and a large installed base of equipment build the foundation for technological leadership. It is the competence of managers, however, that makes such leadership happen. To understand why, we should look more closely at recent experience with FMS technology.

A flexible manufacturing system is a computer-controlled grouping of semi-independent work stations linked by automated material-handling systems. The purpose of an FMS is to manufacture efficiently several kinds of parts at low to medium volumes. All activities in the system—metal cutting, monitoring tool wear, moving parts from one machine to another, setup, inspection, tool adjustment, material handling, scheduling, and dispatching—are under precise computer control. In operation, an FMS is a miniature automated factory.

The system at one prominent Midwestern heavy-equipment producer consisted of 12 machines that made just 8 different parts for a total volume of 5,000 units a year. Once the FMS went on line, management prevented workers from making process improvements by encouraging them not to make any changes. "If it ain't broke, don't fix it" became the watchword.

The FMS boosted machine uptime and productivity, but it did not come close to realizing its full—and distinctive—strategic promise. The technology was applied in a way that ignored its huge potential for flexibility and for generating organizational learning.

Management treated the FMS as if it were just another set of machines for high-volume, standardized production—which is precisely what it is not. Captive to old-fashioned Taylorism and its principles of scientific management, these executives separated the establishment of procedures from their execution, replaced skilled blue-collar machinists with trained operators, and emphasized machine uptime and productivity. In short, they mastered narrow-purpose production on expensive FMS technology designed for high-powered, flexible usage.

This is no way to run a railroad. Certainly, Frederick W. Taylor's work still applies—but not to this environment. Managing an FMS as if it were the old Ford plant at River Rouge is worse than wrong; it is paralyzing. In this case there was little, if any, attention given to process or program flexibility and almost no support for software improvement. Management failed to utilize the FMS's improved capabilities, from which even greater improvements might have flowed over time.

Not surprisingly, the flexibility achieved by this FMS was much less than that of a stand-alone CNC machining center. And that's the *good* news. The system had four operators per shift, each of whom was responsible for checking gauges, changing hydraulic fluid and parts like drill bits, and making simple diagnoses when something went wrong. These tasks, as specified by management, were very procedural, and no operator had the discretion to change procedures. If anything, the complexity of the FMS forced operators to stick more rigidly to procedure than they did at the stand-alone CNC machining centers.

GOALS FOR MANAGEMENT

How, then, should managers look at FMSs? About what should they ask? For one thing, development time. The systems in the United States take $2\frac{1}{2}$ to 3 years and about 25,000 man-hours to conceive, develop, install, and get running. Japanese systems take $1\frac{1}{4}$ to $1\frac{3}{4}$ years and 6,000 man-hours. Here, again, the difference is management. U.S. project teams are usually large groups made up of specialists who design systems for a much greater level of flexibility than their companies are prepared to use. This greater complexity means that projects not only take longer but have plenty of bugs when finished. Delays create enormous pressure on software engineers to take shortcuts and seek hard-wired fixes.

At the end of a project, as a rule, the team is disbanded. The engineers assigned to maintain a system, who are usually not its developers, are reluctant to make any changes. They know about all the bugs but are unwilling to tinker with things because "you never know what may happen." The result: inflexibility.

By contrast, the FMS installations in Japan are remarkably flexible.

This would not be so troublesome for the United States if the old-fashioned productivity of its systems, for which flexibility gets sacrificed, were better than that of Japanese systems. But it is not. The average utilization rate (metal-cutting time as a percentage of total time) of U.S. flexible manufacturing systems over two shifts was 52%, as opposed to 84% in Japan. Over three shifts, because of reliable untended operations, the figure in Japan was even higher.

Where does so huge a difference come from? In a word, the *reliability* designed into the system. In Japan, system designers strive to create operations that can run untended. Of the 60 FMSs I studied, 18 ran untended during the night shift. Such systems take more time and resources to develop than those that require even a single attendant, because designers have to anticipate all possible contingencies. But the additional costs are well worth it. So demanding a design objective leads in practice to a great deal of advance problem solving and process improvement. The entire project team remains with the system long after installation, continually making changes. Learning occurs throughout—and learning gets translated into ongoing process mastery and productivity enhancement. This learning is what gives rise to, and sustains, competitive advantage.

Most of the systems built in Japan after 1982 have achieved untended operations and system uptime of an astonishing 90% to 99%. Operators on the shop floor make continual programming changes and are responsible for writing new programs for both parts and systems as a whole. They are highly skilled engineers with multifunctional responsibilities. Like the designers, they work best in small teams. Most important, managers see FMS technology for what it is—flexible—and create operating objectives and protocols that capitalize on this special capability. Not bound by outdated mass-production assumptions, they view the challenge of flexible manufacturing as automating a job shop, not simply making a transfer line flexible. The difference in results is enormous, but the the vision that leads to it is in human scale. No magic here—just an intelligent process of thinking through what new technology means for how work should be organized.

FMS on Line

To find out more about this "job shop" approach, I examined more closely 22 FMS installations at Hitachi-Seiki, Yamazaki Mazak, Okuma, Murata, Mori-Seiki, Makino, and Fanuc. As Exhibit II shows,

Exhibit II. Comparison of Japanese FMSs with the systems they replaced

	FMSs	Conventional systems
Number of parts produced per system*	182	182
Number of systems with untended operations	18	0
Number of machine tools	133	253
Number of operators three shifts	129	601
Utilization rate two shifts	84 %†	61 %

*To make the comparison useful, I have held the number of parts made by each system constant.

†For three shifts, the figure is 92%

these systems far outperformed the conventional CNC equipment they replaced.

Both systems produced the same variety of parts. But the FMSs did it with five times fewer workers than the conventional systems. Moreover, it took only half as many flexible machines to produce the same volume of parts as conventional machines. The CNC machines used in both systems were identical; the FMSs, however, also employed robots, special material-handling equipment, automated storage systems, and tool-handling equipment. These support devices added another 30% to hardware costs, but they helped boost average uptime from 61% to 92% and made untended operations possible. These benefits alone more than justified the extra cost; better quality and reduced inventories were a bonus.

Potential FMS users often worry that the systems are difficult to justify strictly in economic terms. Based on the experiences of Japanese companies, these fears are groundless. All 22 systems I studied in Japan met their companies' ROI criterion of a three-year payback.

Even so, the impact of flexible manufacturing on the performance of a company reaches far beyond simple productivity rates and investment calculations. FMSs take on strategic importance when the installed base of flexible systems in a factory reaches a critical mass. Only when separate "islands of automation" in a plant start to link does management realize the possibilities for new kinds of competitive advantage via manufacturing.

Of the six Japanese companies that used flexible automation extensively, three had fully automated fabrication plants. At the time I visited them, they were the only flexible manufacturing factories in the world. Their productivity was stupendous.

Exhibit III compares the performance of one such factory before and after the introduction of total flexible automation, and Exhibit IV shows the effect of such performance on cost structure and competition in an industry. Specifically, the exhibit compares the manpower requirements of various manufacturing systems for metal-cutting operations: if it took 100 people in a conventional Japanese factory to make a certain number of machine parts, it would take 194 people in a conventional U.S. factory—but only 43 in a Japanese FMS-equipped factory. If U.S. companies mastered flexible automation as the Japanese have, they would have more than a fourfold increase in labor productivity. This efficiency in labor is part of the reason that smaller companies in Japan have been able to use FMS technology so effectively.

Perhaps even more interesting than such aggregate improvements are their components. The largest manpower reduction in the exhibit is in manufacturing overhead, where an FMS cuts the number of workers from 64 to 5. In engineering, an FMS cuts the number of workers from 34 to 16. One consequence of these reductions (92% in manufacturing overhead, but only 53% in engineering) is to change the composition of the work force: engineers now outnumber production workers three to one. This may not sound like much at first, but it signals a fundamental change in the environment of manufacturing.

Flexible automation shifts the arena of competition from manufacturing to engineering, from running the plant to planning it. In the FMS environment, engineering innovation and engineering productivity hold the keys to success. Engineering now performs the critical line function. Manufacturing has become, by comparison, a staff or support function.

Managing Above the Line

Picture a "lights out" factory operating untended, with general-purpose CNC machines that make a wide variety of parts and are capable of adapting easily to new demands. If two such factories compete with similar products, competition will focus on price. This is so because all

Exhibit III.   Performance of one factory before and after automation

		Before	After
	Types of parts produced per month*	543	543
	Number of pieces pro- duced per month*	11,120	11,120
	Floor space required	16,500 m²	6,600 m²
Equipment per system	CNC machine tools	66	38
	General- purpose machine tools	24	5
	Total	90	43
Personnel per system three shifts	Operators	170	36
	Distribution and production control workers	25	3
	Total	195	39
Average processing time per part† days	Machining time	35	3
	Unit assembly	14	7
	Final assembly	42	20
	Total	91	30

*To make the comparison useful, I have held these figures constant.

†This includes time spent in queue.

Exhibit IV.   *Manpower requirements for metal-cutting operations to make the same number of identical parts*

	Conventional systems		FMSs
	United States	Japan	Japan
Engineering	34	18	16
Manufacturing overhead	64	22	5
Fabrication	52	28	6
Assembly	44	32	16
Total number of workers	194	100	43

Note:
There is no column here for FMSs in the
United States because, at the time of this
study, no domestic machine tool producer
had an FMS on line.

costs in the development of tools, fixtures, and programs are sunk before the first unit is produced. The only variable costs are those of materials and energy, which usually amount to less than 10% of total costs.

Each factory's profits will erode over time as other companies acquire the same operating capabilities. How, then, would a company stay ahead? One way is by creating new physical assets in the form of better programmed and better managed equipment. Each plant's competitive fate would rest heavily on its ability to create facilities that generate performance advantages—and to do it faster than the competition. When the lion's share of costs are sunk before production starts, the creation and management of intellectual assets becomes the prime task of management.

This is manufacturing's new competitive environment. It may sound like something from the distant future, but the Japanese are doing it now. The crucial variable in this kind of environment is automation—the ability of an FMS to run untended. And Japanese manufacturing companies are becoming increasingly expert in that field.

Exhibit V summarizes my findings from 20 of the 22 Japanese FMSs on the extraordinary degree of automation reflected in different pro-

Exhibit V. Degree of automation in production activities of 20 Japanese FMSs in numbers of systems

	Metal-cutting operations	Material handling		Setup		Process control*	Production control		Inventory management	
		Parts	Tools	Parts	Tools		Planning	Dispatching	Parts	Tools
Manual	—	—	—	16	13	—	4	—	—	—
Manual with computer assistance	—	—	—	2	—	—	5	—	—	—
Automated with manual override	2	—	—	—	2	—	10	—	—	15
Untended†	18	20	20	2	5	20	1	20	20	5

*Tool monitoring, inspection, and feedback.

†To quality as untended, a system had to run without manual assistance for one shift a day and have a 98% utilization rate.

duction activities. Exhibit VI presents data from these 20 systems on the amount of manual labor time spent on the factory floor to support such levels of automation. Average system losses took 16.6% of total operating time, about a third the figure in U.S. systems. Each 144 hours of metal-cutting time took only 26 hours of manual effort, which included direct labor as well as required activities usually associated with manufacturing overhead. In the United States, manufacturing overhead activities are separated from direct labor and take about ten times longer.

In most plants, 26 hours of manual effort translate into two workers per system for each of two shifts. In all 22 of these FMSs, however, there was a third person on each shift, whose work accounted for part of the 26 hours of manual effort. By dividing the work among three people, the companies that had these systems purposely created extra time for such process-improvement activities as additional test cutting of new parts, observing machine behavior, and examining statistics on performance. In all 22 systems, each of the workers did these nonrequired—but immensely valuable—tasks. The number of people required to do all this in conventional systems making the same parts in the same companies was four times greater.

The distribution of the 26 hours of manual effort is also instructive. More than half were spent loading and unloading pallets. The other major activity, which took 7 hours, was mounting tools and qualifying them on machines. Together, these efforts accounted for 80% of the time spent on manual labor. Workers loaded pallets and mounted tools during the day shift, and the machines ran untended at night. Production planning, a weekly activity, took only one hour of a person's time. Systems making a large variety of parts also had automated methods for production planning. Those with a low variety of parts did it manually.

The FMS installations performed exceptionally well. Delivery performance in each system, tracked during a three-month period, was 100%. The high reliability of individual machines and of the system itself kept the variance in unscheduled downtime to only 2%. The scheduled slack for software testing and process experiments ranged from 4% to 9% of capacity and was more than enough to accommodate any variation in machine reliability. Each system met its production schedule, as long as the schedule observed the constraints of capacity. In addition, only six pieces in a thousand had a quality problem. Of these, three were reworked, usually by the operators themselves. The other three were scrapped. Tool breakage caused most

Exhibit VI. Production activities in an average FMS in Japan*

	Metal-cutting operations	Material handling		Setup		Process control	Production control		Inventory management		Total
		Parts	Tools	Parts	Tools		Planning	Dispatching	Parts	Tools	
Average system losses as a percentage of total time	1.6 %	5%	—	—	5%	2%	—	3%	—	—	16.6 %†
Manual labor time per system hours	2	—	—	11	7	3	2.5	.5	—	—	26

*An average FMS in Japan has six machines, creating a total of 144 hours of available metal-cutting time per day.

†This figure seems to imply that the system's utilization rate over three shifts would be 83.4%, not 92% as asserted in Exhibit II. There is no discrepancy; the figures don't match because problems in some areas, such as material handling, cause system losses that do not result in machine downtime.

of these quality problems, and the machine operators could make the necessary adjustments.

With such impressive levels of performance, few contingencies demanded management's attention. In fact, executives were largely absent from day-to-day operations. Instead of concerning themselves with internal operations, they focused their attention on how to meet competitive pressures on product performance. In the United States, on the other hand, managers spend so much time on routine problems with quality and production delivery schedules that they have virtually no time left over to plan for long-term process improvement.

As noted before, the prime task of management once the system has been made reliable is not to categorize tasks or regiment workers but to create the fixed assets—the systems and software—needed to make products. This calls for intellectual assets, not just pieces of hardware. Thus the new role of management in manufacturing is to create and nurture the project teams whose intellectual capabilities produce competitive advantage. What gets managed is intellectual capital, not equipment.

The technology of flexible manufacturing has led managers into a drastically altered competitive landscape. This new landscape has a number of important features:

A sharp focus on intellectual assets as the basis for a company's distinctive competence.

A heightened emphasis on the selection of the portfolio of projects a company chooses to manage.

A close attention to the market and to the special competence of process engineers.

A steady adjustment of product mix and price in order to maintain full capacity utilization.

A pointed emphasis on reducing fixed manufacturing costs and the time required to generate new products, processes, and programs.

An intensification of cost-based competition for manufactured products.

I am convinced that the heart of this new manufacturing landscape is the management of manufacturing projects: selecting them, creating teams to work on them, and managing workers' intellectual development. In company after company in Japan, systems engineers with a thorough knowledge of several disciplines have proved the key to the success of flexible manufacturing systems. One rigidly organized Japanese company, recognizing the importance of such versatile teams, now rotates experienced engineers through all manufacturing departments. Another, which already had job rotation, has begun to keep its engineers longer in each area so they can learn more from their FMS experience.

In contrast with the traditional Japanese approach of involving a large number of people in decision making, small teams of highly competent, engineering-oriented people have been most successful with flexible manufacturing. These groups have succeeded because they are given responsibility for both design and operations. They remain on a project until the FMS achieves 90% uptime and untended operations. Perhaps most important, in all the Japanese companies I studied, the teams came entirely from engineering and were given line responsibility for day-to-day operations.

New Mission Statement

The management of FMS technology is taking place in a different manufacturing environment, and thus consists of new imperatives:

Build small, cohesive teams. Very small groups of highly skilled generalists show a remarkable propensity to succeed.

Manage process improvement, not just output. FMS technology fundamentally alters the economics of production by drastically reducing variable labor costs. When these costs are low, little can be gained by reducing them further. The challenge is to develop and manage physical and intellectual assets, not the production of goods. Choosing projects that develop intellectual and physical assets is more important than monitoring the costs of day-to-day operations. Old-fashioned, sweat-of-the-brow manufacturing effort is now less important than system design and team organization.

Broaden the role of engineering management to include manufacturing. The use of small, technologically proficient teams to design, run, and improve FMS operations signals a shift in focus from managing people to managing knowledge, from controlling variable costs to managing fixed costs, and from production planning to project selection. This shift gives engineering the line responsibilities that have long been the province of manufacturing.

Treat manufacturing as a service. In an untended FMS environment, all of the tools and software programs required to make a part have to be created before the first unit is produced. While the same is true of typical parts and assembly operations, the difference in an FMS is that there are no allowances for in-the-line, people-intensive adjustments. As a result, competitive success increasingly depends on management's ability to anticipate and respond quickly to changing market needs. With FMS technology, even a small, specialized operation can accommodate shifts in demand. Manufacturing now responds much like a professional service industry, customizing its offerings to the preferences of special market segments.

Making flexibility and responsiveness the mission of manufacturing flies in the face of Taylor's view of the world, which for 75 years has shaped thinking about manufacturing. FMS technology points inevitably toward a new managerial ethos—an ethos dedicated to the building of knowledge in the flexible service of markets, not merely to the building of things. Scale is no longer the central concern. Size no longer provides barriers to entry. The minimum efficient scale for FMS operations is a cell of roughly six machines and fewer than a half a dozen people. That's the new reality.

Going to FMS-based operations does not require lots of money or people. It can be done—at its best, it is done—on a small scale. The critical ingredient here is nothing other than the competence of a small group of people. There is no Eastern mystery in this, no secrets known only to the Japanese. We can do it too—if we will.

What, after all, is a manufacturing company? Today, no artist would represent a factory as a huge, austere building with bellowing smokestacks. The behemoth is gone. The efficient factory is now an aggregation of small cells of electronically linked and controlled FMSs. New technology enables these operating cells to be combined in nonlinear ways. No shared base of infrastructure mandates large-scale production integration. The days of Taylor's immense, linear production systems are largely gone.

Unless U.S. managers understand the implications of Japan's mastery of FMS technology, their companies will fall further behind. Flexible manufacturing systems are no longer a theory, a pipe dream. They exist. And the leverage they provide on continuous process improvement is immense. Making automation work means a whole new level of process mastery. A large number of Japanese factories demonstrate its reality every day. They lead the way; we linger behind at our own peril.

Appendix: Primary Research

The research on which this article is based took three years and included the detailed study of 95 flexible manufacturing systems in the United States and Japan—more than half the installed FMSs at the time. I examined published and company records of all these installations, held long interviews with managers and system designers, and observed the systems in operation. I had two goals: first, to obtain an overview of the use of the systems, their capabilities, and where they succeed and fail; and, second, to understand why and how the successful ones work.

My choice of sites for the second part of this study reflected stringent conditions: all had to be in the same industry, the companies had to have a history of success with two or more systems, and the systems had to influence more than one FMS cell.

Only the machine tool industry in Japan met all these conditions. My choice was especially fortunate in that it is the mother industry for creating capital goods. Machine tool producers use their own products, and their process innovations quickly lead to product development in other areas. Further, the industry is fragmented; most companies are small and family owned. Because the U.S. metal-working industry is structurally similar to the machine tool industry in Japan (more than three-quarters of manufacturing output in the United States comes from operations with fewer than 50 people), my findings bear directly on how these technologies would affect most U.S. manufacturers.

Between 1972 and 1984, 23 companies in Japan built flexible manufacturing systems. Of these, 6 were nonmachine tool companies that wanted them for in-house use. The remaining 17 were machine tool companies; 16 built systems for their own use, 9 built systems for other companies, and 8 sold more than 2 systems. I visited 7 of these companies, including the only 3 that had fully automated factories, and examined in detail the operations of 22 systems.

3
Manufacturing Offshore Is Bad Business

Constantinos C. Markides and Norman Berg

July 1985: AT&T decides to transfer production of residential telephones from its only U.S. telephone manufacturing plant, in Shreveport, Louisiana, to Singapore.

February 1986: United Technologies announces it will close its diesel-engine parts plant in Springfield, Massachusetts and transfer operations to a nonunion plant in South Carolina and two plants in Europe.

February 1987: General Motors plans to phase out the production of A-body cars in the United States and move it to its Ramos Arizpe, Coahuila plant in Mexico.

For decades, foreign direct investment has been a common practice among American companies, so investments like these don't seem particularly noteworthy. But they are. In the past, U.S. companies went abroad primarily to secure a foreign market or to obtain raw materials. Now they go overseas to buy or make products and components to ship back to the United States. The new investments are not complementing domestic production; they are replacing it. (See Appendix.)

Manufacturers defend sourcing from overseas as the only way to compete with inexpensive, high-quality imports. They say that moving to cheap-labor countries like Mexico, Taiwan, and Malaysia for export back to the United States is allowing U.S. industry to regain its world standing. Economists generally approve. They consider the migration to low-wage areas an adjustment caused by changes in international comparative advantage.

Others are less enchanted by the trend. Labor unions claim that it deindustrializes the country and destroys American jobs. Some observers have argued that it "hollows" the nation's industrial base and threatens the standard of living.

In the debate over whether offshore manufacturing is good for the nation, it is always assumed that it is good for an individual company. But we challenge that notion. The mere fact that a lot of companies are doing it doesn't make it smart. Going overseas is hardly the panacea many people think it is. At best, it is just another quick fix. In their rush to save money, managers often lose sight of the high penalties of moving abroad. And by continually shifting manufacturing to the areas with the lowest labor costs, they are merely postponing the inevitable day of reckoning when they must confront the parts of the business that really need reform.

It's Not the Only Option

American manufacturers claim that going offshore is their only alternative if they are to stay competitive against foreign rivals. It's either offshore manufacturing or no manufacturing at all. As powerful as this argument may seem, it doesn't hold up well in light of several facts.

First, an increasing number of U.S. companies are responding to the import threat by improving their competitive position at home. They are convinced that creating long-term competitive advantage requires a commitment to a new way of doing business—not just a shortsighted attack on labor costs.

Take Eastman Kodak. After a disappointing 1985, in which earnings dropped 31% from the year before (excluding the $563 million Kodak lost when it withdrew from instant photography), the company decided to drastically change its strategy. While still relying on some offshore manufacturing, Kodak also embarked on an aggressive and multifaceted program to restore its competitive position at home. It made an all-out attempt to create long-term competitive advantage by addressing the business as a whole, not just isolated parts of it.

Consider some of the steps Kodak has taken or plans to take: reduce overhead by trimming employment, especially in middle management; revise the wage dividend plan; cut operating and expense budgets; eliminate inefficient operations and marginal product lines; reorganize internally; increase R&D expenditures; move into new technologies; introduce new products; and improve quality and cost efficiency. The effect of these changes was immediate: in 1986, sales grew by 9% to

$11.5 billion, while earnings from operations climbed 24% to $724 million. Earnings per share were $3.52 in 1987, versus only $1.10 in 1986.

Black & Decker is another case in point. It reduced its work force by 40%, consolidated operations to achieve economies of scale, eliminated hundreds of administrative positions at corporate headquarters, modernized plants, introduced new manufacturing methods, standardized models, expanded and upgraded marketing and engineering capabilities, and moved aggressively into the low end of the professional power-tool market. The results: for fiscal year 1986 the company reported net earnings of $6.3 million—that compares with a net loss of $158.4 million the previous year. EPS went from 49¢ to 95¢ between 1986 and 1987.

Litton Industries is making similar changes in its operations to fight foreign competition in microwave ovens. The company has redesigned its product line, improved the quality of its products, cut down on labor costs, and introduced new models.

Some companies have embraced automation to stay competitive. In 1985, GM had more than 4,000 programmable robots in operation; it expects to have 10,000 in place by the end of 1988. Xerox has spent more than $100 million to automate manufacturing and materials handling, and Fairchild Semiconductor moved its assembly operations back to the United States after automating the welding of semiconductor chips and the inventory tracking system.

Second, more Japanese companies are building manufacturing plants in the United States at precisely the time when many American companies are claiming it is impossible for them to stay home and be competitive. Every major Japanese automaker has an assembly plant in the States. By one count, there are more than 600 Japanese plants operating on American soil. Honda's plant in Marysville, Ohio, Nissan's plant in Smyrna, Tennessee, and Mazda's plant in Flat Rock, Michigan are but a few. Japanese electronics companies are also operating in the United States. Fujitsu, Hitachi, Mitsubishi, NEC, Toshiba—all have assembly or manufacturing facilities in America.

The Japanese are investing in the United States for four reasons: to increase their political clout and prevent further trade restrictions by creating jobs for Americans; to ensure access to the American market in case exports to the United States are restricted further; to get a better feel for their most important export market so they can be more responsive to it; and to hedge against fluctuations in the value of the dollar.

To be sure, the Japanese in the United States enjoy some advantages over existing U.S. plants. Because of a younger work force, they have low pension expenses and low insurance costs. They also have newer facilities. But these benefits are not the chief reason Japanese factories are competitive. The plants are successful because of their manufacturing techniques. Studies have shown that the main reason the Japanese were able to dominate the market for small cars over the last decade was not because of higher capital investment rates or more advanced technology but because of management philosophy and excellence in manufacturing.[1] By emphasizing superior product designs, high quality, minimum inventories, waste elimination, and worker participation, the Japanese emerged as the cost and quality leaders in the industry. Now, using the same techniques, the Japanese are outperforming domestic rivals on their home turf.

The ability of the Japanese to manufacture in the United States raises serious questions about the rationale American companies use for going offshore. In particular, if the Japanese can manufacture in the United States and still be competitive, why do U.S. companies have to go offshore to stay alive? More important, if U.S. companies have the option of becoming more competitive by improving manufacturing at home, why do they choose the quick fix of manufacturing offshore?

Third and last, Japanese companies have managed to stay competitive over the years without resorting to offshore manufacturing. Overseas production of the Japanese semiconductor industry, for instance, has amounted to less than 4% of total production.[2] Even when the yen got strong, the Japanese found it unnecessary to search for low-cost labor. They stayed world-class competitors by investing in automatic wire-bonding machines and by using flexible manufacturing.

In consumer electronics, the Japanese didn't go offshore but instead used intelligent product design and simple automation to stay competitive. In the early 1970s, while U.S. color TV manufacturers like RCA, GE, and Zenith were rushing to the Far East, Japanese manufacturers switched to 100% solid-state chassis, automated insertion and testing, and reduced component counts through extensive use of integrated circuits, early use of in-line tubes, and single-circuit board designs.

The few Japanese companies that chose to go offshore did so either to supply their export markets or, more commonly, to get around trade restrictions. Japanese textile companies went to Asia in the 1970s, for example, to avoid OMAs (orderly marketing agreements) imposed on exports of apparel to the United States and Europe. Similarly, Sanyo, Sony, and Hitachi have been moving manufacturing and assembly operations to Mexico to circumvent U.S. trade laws and to preempt American protectionism.

In the period 1985 to 1987, when the yen gained by more than 60% against the dollar, 53% of the 214 Japanese manufacturers responding to a Keidanren survey stated that they would cope with the strong yen by shifting their emphasis to domestic markets. They planned to do so by upgrading their products, incorporating greater value added, and minimizing costs. More important, 73% of the companies surveyed reported that they will not resort to more outside contracting, and 77% reported that they do not plan to cut wages. The 29% that planned to shift some production overseas were doing so to supply export markets, not the Japanese market. Nearly three-fourths of the companies expected to replace or had already replaced outside subcontracting with internal production. This behavior is in sharp contrast to that of American companies in the early 1980s when the dollar was strong.

The Bush Is Full of Thorns

Offshore manufacturing is not, then, the only option available to companies under competitive siege. It is, in fact, a poor option for many organizations. Managers should know that offshore manufacturing is not all roses and labor savings. Before they make the move, they should have a fuller picture of where they're headed. They should know that there are some powerful reasons *not* to go offshore.

The savings can cost a lot. Granted, companies can often save money on labor and materials by purchasing or manufacturing overseas, but other costs—some not so obvious—may well offset the gains. Offshore sourcing usually involves larger inventories, for example, and higher administrative costs. Parts made overseas are less likely to meet specifications, so quality costs may be higher. Factor in higher transportation expenses and tariffs, and don't forget the cost of training foreign workers.

It takes longer to get supplies from an offshore location, so companies operating abroad are slower to respond to changing market demands. That too has its price. In 1984, some big U.S. retailers were stuck with huge inventories of imported goods they had ordered the year before—when a slowdown in consumer spending was nowhere in sight!

These costs may seem obvious, but companies rarely take them into account when making the offshore manufacturing decision. According to a survey commissioned by the National Tooling and Machining Association, American tool and die makers routinely ignore these "hidden" costs of offshore manufacturing. Yet according to the survey, these costs typically add 5% to 15% to the foreign vendors' bid price for shipping, 3% for additional paperwork and communications, 5% to 10% for added inventory, and up to 35% for unanticipated design changes.

Other costs are less direct. Shifting some production operations overseas may prevent the company from exploiting economies of scale at home as well as abroad. The implications can be especially grave during a recession. Going offshore can also cause underutilization of existing manufacturing capacity and, ultimately, plant closings and layoffs.

Finally, companies that move outside the United States may lose valuable customers, who may switch to other U.S.-based suppliers. Italian chip maker Dynamit Nobel Silicon is among the foreign companies that opened a factory in the United States to be closer to its American customers. The managing director explained the decision by saying that "the distance between Italy and California is such that [customers] do not want to get any more than 10% of their needs from us."

You don't really save much on labor. On the surface, looking for low-wage sites for manufacturing is a logical way to reduce total production costs. But workers in less developed countries tend to be less productive than Americans, so a straight comparison of wages gives an inaccurate reading of the potential savings. Worse, in most businesses, direct labor is no longer a significant portion of total costs.

A survey of manufacturers by the National Association of Accountants found that on average labor represents only 15% of the cost of making a product. For most electronic items, labor is only 5% to 10% of the total cost. The wage savings are therefore unlikely to have a big impact overall. In some cases, they are offset by higher transportation costs alone. According to one expert, the typical cost of transporting a color TV set from Southeast Asia to the West Coast is 13% of its value at the time of shipping; making the set in Asia saves just 10%.[3]

Managers' preoccupation with labor costs deflects attention from the other 85% of the cost structure. Opportunities to save money in administration, inventory control, marketing, R&D, and distribution far exceed those relating to labor alone, but they are often overlooked.

You'll hollow the corporation. The semiconductor industry has split into two market segments: commodity and semicustom. Advocates of offshore manufacturing claim it doesn't matter if the commodity side of the business goes offshore in search of lower wages. As long as the design and R&D talent remains in the United States, so will the value added. Other industries have adopted this argument as well: as long as the company focuses on innovation, advanced technology, and excellent service, it doesn't really matter if it manufactures products abroad.

But a business cannot design in a vacuum. It cannot exploit new technologies if it has no chance to apply them. And it needs the profits from commodity production to fund R&D. The fact is, design and manufacturing are linked. A company that subcontracts its manufacturing to foreigners will soon lose the expertise to design and the ability to innovate, because it won't get the feedback it needs. Moving engineering offshore along with manufacturing is not a solution; it just accelerates the process. When companies do that, they give potential competitors not only finances and managerial expertise but also engineering skills.

The TV industry's inability to design and develop the new generation of TV products—the videocassette recorders and camcorders—is the perfect example. The U.S. television industry began assembling black and white sets overseas in the late 1960s. Assembly of color TVs soon followed black and white, and manufacturing followed assembly. By 1987, not one U.S. company was producing black and white TVs domestically, and only two—Zenith and Curtis Mathes—were making color TVs. Many people contend that the move offshore dispossessed U.S. manufacturers of manufacturing and design technologies needed to innovate or even compete with the innovators.

The semiconductor industry has fallen into the same trap. Americans have all but given up on the production of high-volume semiconductors such as 64K RAM chips. But memory chips are the cornerstone of semiconductor technology. Because they are a high-volume product, they serve as a testing ground for engineers trying to produce new technologies for other applications and for manufacturers trying to perfect delicate processes. In addition, they generate earnings for further research. By abandoning the commodity memory products, electronics companies put their design capabilities and technological leadership at risk.

Even normal product development suffers. As a senior executive of a large corporation explained: "I don't think people realize when they make the offshore decision that it is really a commitment to freeze the product. There is no way to make rapid design changes and product updates at a remote location."

Meanwhile, collaborators become competitors. The same senior executive continued: "To survive, the offshore manufacturer must build his own design or technology capability, and very quickly the game is over. He has the capability and the market." Consider Taiwan's Sunrise Plywood and Furniture. For years the company acted as an export platform for California's Mission Furniture. It relied on Mission's designs and blueprints to manufacture furniture suitable to American tastes. Now the Taiwanese company is one of Mission's competitors, exporting directly to the United States through its own marketing subsidiary.

The pattern is widespread. Hitachi, which has made microprocessors under license from Motorola, is now introducing its own 32-bit microprocessor. Toshiba, which acted as a supplier of copying machines to 3M, is now promoting its own brand name. Singatronics, which for years produced electronic games and pocket calculators for multinationals, is now pushing its own proprietary line of electronic medical instruments. And Daewoo, while still a subcontractor to U.S. companies, now sells its own personal computer.

The danger that collaboration will give way to competition is immediate and real. As the newly industrializing countries of Asia lose their advantage as low-wage producers to places like China and Thailand, they are increasingly anxious to develop their own technology-intensive industries and marketing capabilities. One executive of a large multinational told us, "Many Americans are naive about how insistent other nations have become on developing a full capability. Even in aerospace, it is hard to satisfy a coproduction requirement anymore by just letting the foreign plant rivet an aluminum assembly. The host country wants the whole technology, and it is not long before a competitor has been developed."

Many offer U.S. manufacturers incentives to bring their technology with them. Taiwan offers R&D facilities plus attractive loan packages. Malaysia has stepped up its efforts to get companies to invest in research, and Ireland has been encouraging foreign businesses to boost their product development efforts there.

U.S. companies that transfer technology across national borders don't have the same protection against piracy they enjoy at home. Indonesia, for example, has no patent protection at all. Korea denies copyright protection to software, semiconductors, or foreign works. Other countries require an importer of technology to license local companies to use that same technology for modest fees.

The advantage doesn't last. Offshore manufacturing is most promising when three conditions hold: the dollar is strong, foreign wages are low, and trade barriers are absent. None of these factors is within a company's control. Most of the offshore investments between 1982 and 1985 were motivated by the strong dollar. Now that the dollar is considerably weaker, running those operations is more expensive. U.S. companies that purchase or produce abroad are not as price competitive as they were three years ago; the price of their products has gone up, along with those of all the other imports. There is no simple solution to their dilemma. Deere & Company, for example, makes its small tractors for the U.S. market in Japan and its midsize models in Germany. As the dollar declines, Deere will have to either raise prices or lower profit margins. Indeed, the aggregate figures for Deere's return on sales show a marked drop between 1984 and 1986: from 2.3% to −6.3%.

Reducing offshore activities when the dollar weakens is not a realistic option. Most of the offshore investments are irreversible capital expenditures, and they are hard to liquidate. But even purchasing arrangements are hard to change overnight. And it's unwise to sever a sound relationship with a foreign supplier when you know that the dollar may strengthen in a year or two.

Moreover, foreign wages inevitably rise. As workers learn and become more productive, they command higher pay. And as foreign countries grow economically, workers want a bigger piece of the pie. In Mexico, the minimum wage was increased three times in 1986—in January, June, and October. In Taiwan, average monthly earnings in manufacturing quadrupled in a ten-year period, from 2,929 Taiwanese dollars in 1974 to 12,844 Taiwanese dollars in 1984. In Korea, employee compensation doubled from 1979 to 1984. U.S. companies could run themselves ragged chasing low wages from one country to another.

Remember too that the threat of protectionism always looms. Importers are always risking a toughening of import restrictions. When a country's trade surplus with the United States swells, protectionism pressures intensify. Taiwan's $15.7 billion surplus in 1986, for instance, heightened pressures in the United States to impose trade restrictions on Taiwanese products—even though most of these products are exported to America by U.S. companies, including GE (Taiwan's biggest exporter), IBM, Hewlett-Packard, and Mattel. Such trade restrictions could have wiped out any cost savings from subcontracting or operating in Taiwan. To avoid rough treatment from the U.S. administration, Taiwan eventually increased the value of its currency, a move that made offshore imports originating in Taiwan more expensive.

U.S. companies could become gypsies, moving from one location to another as the cost of protectionism rises. U.S. retailers and clothing importers, for example, have embarked on systematic island-hopping, moving from one island to another to bypass limits on clothing imports. As soon as a new source of merchandise is found, the U.S. government moves in and imposes quotas, forcing the American importers to move on to other islands. This could be an acceptable short-term strategy, but sooner or later you run out of islands.

You may get trapped. Once a company moves its manufacturing operations to a developing country, the host government may begin to pressure management to transfer more advanced technologies or to support local spin-off industries. In many instances, the host countries insist on domestic content, technology transfer, and domestic equity positions that eventually lead to independent production capabilities. The company is often trapped: if it wants to stay in that country, it has no choice but to accede.

Mexico is a case in point. In early 1985, it rejected IBM's plan to build a plant there to produce microcomputers. But when IBM agreed to increase its plant investment from $6.1 million to $91 million, to buy parts built in Mexico, and to export 92% of its production, the government reversed itself. In the auto industry, Mexico has a 60% domestic content requirement for cars produced for the domestic market and a 30% domestic content requirement for cars destined for export. In addition, foreign businesses are limited to 40% ownership of joint ventures in auto parts.

Consider also India. In 1973, India passed a new law, the Foreign Exchange Regulation Act, under which foreign companies operating in India had to dilute their equity positions. When in 1977 the government asked IBM to dilute its equity to 74% and Coca-Cola to 40%, both companies decided to leave India rather than comply. Coca-Cola didn't want to disclose its syrup formula, and IBM didn't want to lose control of its marketing operations. India didn't miss the two companies: Burroughs and ICL are now doing IBM's work, and an Indian soft drink company called "77" has taken over Coke's market. But IBM and Coke no doubt miss India.

You'll lose valuable friends at home. When companies move operations overseas, life at home changes. Labor unions, resenting the loss of domestic jobs, are less likely to cooperate on other fronts. Their dissatisfaction is particularly important because U.S. companies need their help if they are to become more competitive. As UAW President Owen Bieber put it in a 1986 speech, "If we can't get support from the main players in the industry on our public policy agenda, the question might be asked why we should continue to work with them on the productivity side."

Labor dissatisfaction can also be expensive. In November 1986, the UAW struck GM's Delco Electronics plant in Kokomo, Indiana over a plan to boost outsourcing from Mexico. After a seven-day strike, GM canceled the plans. The National Association of Machinists and Aerospace Workers has proposed a "Rebuilding America" program that would force companies to contribute 1% of after-tax profits to a fund used to create new industries to replace those that leave the country. Similarly, the Teamsters union has proposed a plan that would require U.S. companies making products abroad for import back to the States to pay their foreign workers at least the going U.S. wage or forfeit the privilege of access to the U.S. marketplace. American companies paying less than the prevailing U.S. hourly compensation would have to put the difference into a fund for retraining U.S. workers.

Pressure can come from society as a whole. As more companies go offshore, more jobs are lost and the trade deficit worsens. Growing unhappiness over these conditions can create pressure on the government to intervene and force companies to assume part of the social costs they are generating. The government might, for instance, pass legislation forcing companies to give their workers "early" notification of plant closings or to assume responsibility for the training of their laid-off workers.

Offshore manufacturing has another effect of political significance: companies that may have lobbied collectively five years ago may become divided on issues of protectionism. That is, those who import most of their products and components have different concerns from their industry counterparts that manufacture in the United States. The whole industry loses clout. The semiconductor industry experienced such a split. In June 1985, Micron Technology Inc. of Idaho filed an antidumping petition against seven Japanese producers of 64K DRAM chips. The Semiconductor Industry Association, however, did not support the move because some of its members—like Motorola and Texas Instruments—produce in Japan. The association's official policy is to improve member access to the Japanese market.

The auto industry is another divided industry. GM, the industry's leader in forging international alliances, has vigorously opposed protectionism. Ford and Chrysler, on the other hand, have repeatedly asked for surcharges on Japanese imports. Similarly, in the textile industry, apparel manufacturers and big retail stores have paid no attention to the "Crafted with Pride in U.S.A." campaign that the textile industry and labor unions are promoting. Why should they, when 20% of their brand-name products are imported?

Of course, offshore manufacturing isn't wrong in every case. Indeed, there are legitimate reasons to locate overseas—to take advantage of certain natural resources, to expand export markets, or to be more responsive to local markets. But managers should question the assumption that it is always right. Chances are, in their eagerness to save money on labor, many companies are giving up more than they bargained for, not the least of which is their future competitive position.

Companies must recognize that offshore manufacturing does not constitute a long-term strategy. At best, it is merely a short-term tactical move that buys time for companies to restore their competitive health at home. Unless they break away from old traditions and look at their business as a total package, American companies cannot expect to become world competitors.

Appendix: The Race to Manufacture Offshore

It's a fact that the electronics, textile, machine tool, subcompact auto, and other industries are moving their manufacturing operations abroad. The evidence is all around us. Although no one set of statistics accounts for all the forms of offshore manufacturing—be it setting up plants abroad, purchasing from a foreign subsidiary or joint venture, subcontracting from a foreign company, or buying from foreign companies through market transactions—the available data are persuasive.

The best information on products manufactured or assembled abroad is a set of numbers from the U.S. International Trade Commission on imports entering under tariff items 806.30 and 807.00. These provisions permit the portion of the product made of U.S. components to enter the United States duty free. A quick glance at the 806 and 807 statistics shows a dramatic rise in the value of offshore-manufactured imports (the accompanying table of selected years illustrates the trend).

Offshore imports rose continually from $953 million in 1966 to $36.5 billion in 1986, despite fluctuations in the dollar. Their share of U.S.-manufactured imports nearly doubled in the same period.

Most of these imports are in three price-sensitive industries: autos (59% of the total in 1985), electronics (15%), and textiles (3%). Most of the auto industry's investments have been in Europe, Japan, Canada, and Mexico. The electronics industry has invested mostly in East Asia, while the textile investments are concentrated in Latin America and the Caribbean.

These figures grossly underestimate the true extent of the phenomenon. They exclude, for example, products of a U.S. company manufactured abroad containing only foreign components. Such items are considered ordinary imports and don't fall under the 806 and 807 provisions. Similarly, products of a foreign company under contract with a U.S. business enter as ordinary imports. And much of what a U.S. affiliate abroad ships to its domestic parent does not appear in the 806 and 807 statistics. (Note that at least 35% of U.S. imports and exports from 1977 to 1980 were intracompany.[4])

Obviously, U.S. companies are augmenting their overseas facilities: capital expenditures by majority-owned foreign affiliates of U.S. manufacturing companies climbed from $12 billion in 1978 to $17 billion in 1986. Meanwhile, U.S. manufacturing capacity utilization fell from 84.2% to 78.8%.

Aggregate statistics aside, evidence abounds. In 1974, some 70,000 workers were employed in 450 plants along the Mexican border under the in-bond, or *maquiladora*, program. By 1986, the figures had grown to 300,000 workers and 1,100 factories. The value added by these plants grew from $300 million to more than $1.3 billion in those 12 years. American businesses, operating 865 of these factories, account for most of the production.

In 1985, U.S. companies like RCA, Motorola, and Texas Instruments employed more than half the 73,000 people working for the electronics industry in Malaysia and sent back to America more than $300 million worth of semiconductors. In Mexico, the three U.S. automakers accounted for more than 55% of Mexico's total car production in 1986, and all three were planning to expand there. U.S. companies' imports from South Korea, Taiwan, Mexico, and Brazil are estimated to rise from 100,000 units in 1984 to 500,000 in 1988.

The Growth of 806 and 807 Imports

Year	Total Value of 806 and 807 Imports (in millions of dollars)	Percentage of Total U.S. Imports	Percentage of U.S.-Manufactured Imports
1966	$ 953.0	3.7%	6.4%
1967	1,035.1	3.8	6.5
1969	1,838.8	5.1	8.0
1970	2,208.2	5.5	8.5
1973	4,247.1	6.0	9.4
1975	5,162.4	5.3	10.1
1978	9,735.3	5.5	9.1
1982	18,275.5	7.4	12.1
1983	21,845.7	8.1	12.8
1985	30,535.1	9.0	12.3
1986	36,469.9	9.9	12.4
1987	39,820.1†	10.0	12.9

Sources: U.S. Tariff Commission, *Economic Factors Affecting the Use of Items 807.00 and 806.30 of the Tariff Schedules of the United States*, Publication 339 (Washington, D.C.: USTC, September 1970); U.S. International Trade Commission, *Imports Under Items 806.30 and 807.00 of the Tariff Schedules of the United States, 1982–85*, Publication 1920, and *The Use and Economic Impact of TSUS Items 806.30 and 807.00*, Publication 2053 (Washington, D.C.: USITC, December 1986 and January 1988); and U.S. Department of Commerce, *Survey of Current Business*, various issues.

† Projected figure.

Notes

1. See, for example, William J. Abernathy, Kim B. Clark, and Alan M. Kantrow, "The New Industrial Competition," *Harvard Business Review*, September–October 1981, p. 68.
2. Dennis J. Encarnation, "Cross-Investment: A Second Front of Economic Rivalry," *California Management Review*, Winter 1987, p. 38.
3. Kenichi Ohmae, *Triad Power* (New York: Free Press, 1985), p. 5.
4. Jane Sneddon Little, "Intrafirm Trade and U.S. Protectionism: Thoughts Based on a Small Survey," *New England Economic Review*, January–February 1986, p. 42.

PART

III

Improving Competitiveness through Systems and Policies

1
Why Some Factories Are More Productive Than Others

Robert H. Hayes and Kim B. Clark

The battle for attention is over. The time for banging drums is long past. Everyone now understands that manufacturing provides an essential source of competitive leverage. No longer does anyone seriously think that domestic producers can outdo their competitors by clever marketing only—"selling the sizzle" while cheating on quality or letting deliveries slip. It is now time for concrete action on a practical level: action to change facilities, update processing technologies, adjust work-force practices, and perfect information and management systems.

But when managers turn to these tasks, they quickly run up against a stumbling block. Namely, they do not have adequate measures for judging factory-level performance or for comparing overall performance from one facility to the next. Of course, they can use the traditional cost-accounting figures, but these figures often do not tell them what they really need to know. Worse, even the best numbers do not sufficiently reflect the important contributions that managers can make by reducing confusion in the system and promoting organizational learning.

Consider the experience of a U.S. auto manufacturer that discovered itself with a big cost disadvantage. The company put together a group to study its principal competitor's manufacturing operations. The study generated reams of data, but the senior executive in charge of the activity still felt uneasy. He feared that the group was getting mired in details and that things other than managerial practices—like the age of facilities and their location—might be the primary drivers of performance. How to tell?

Similarly, a vice president of manufacturing for a specialty chemical producer had misgivings about the emphasis his company's system for evaluating plant managers placed on variances from standard costs. Differences in these standards made comparisons across plants difficult. What was more troubling, the system did not easily capture the trade-offs among factors of production or consider the role played by capital equipment or materials. What to do?

Another manufacturer—this time of paper products—found quite different patterns of learning in the same departments of five of its plants scattered across the United States. Although each department made much the same products using similar equipment and materials, they varied widely in performance over a period of years. Why such differences?

Our point is simple: before managers can pinpoint what's needed to boost manufacturing performance, they must have a reliable way of ascertaining why some factories are more productive than others. They also need a dependable metric for identifying and measuring such differences and a framework for thinking about how to improve their performance—and keep it improving. This is no easy order.

These issues led us to embark on a continuing, multiyear study of 12 factories in 3 companies (see the appendix for details on research methodology). The study's purpose is to clarify the variables that influence productivity growth at the micro level.

The first company we looked at, which employs a highly connected and automated manufacturing process, we refer to as the Process Company. Another, which employs a batch approach based on a disconnected line-flow organization of work, we refer to as the Fab (fabrication-assembly) Company. The third, which uses several different batch processes to make components for sophisticated electronic systems, is characterized by very rapid changes in both product and process. We refer to it as the Hi-Tech Company. All five factories of the Process Company and three of the four factories of the Fab Company are in the United States (the fourth is just across the border in Canada). Of the three factories belonging to the Hi-Tech Company, one is in the United States, one in Europe, and one in Asia.

In none of these companies did the usual profit-and-loss statements—or the familiar monthly operating reports—provide adequate, up-to-date information about factory performance. Certainly, managers routinely evaluated such performance, but the metrics they used made their task like that of watching a distant activity through a thick, fogged window. Indeed, the measurement systems in place at many factories obscure and even alter the details of their performance.

A Fogged Window

Every plant we studied employed a traditional standard cost system: the controller collected and reported data each month on the actual costs incurred during the period for labor, materials, energy, and depreciation, as well as on the costs that would have been incurred had workers and equipment performed at predetermined "standard" levels. The variances from these standard costs became the basis for problem identification and performance evaluation. Other departments in the plants kept track of head counts, work-in-process inventory, engineering changes, the value of newly installed equipment, reject rates, and so forth.

In theory, this kind of measurement system should take a diverse range of activities and summarize them in a way that clarifies what is going on. It should act like a lens that brings a blurry picture into sharp focus. Yet, time and again, we found that these systems often masked critical developments in the factories and, worse, often distorted management's perspective.

Each month, most of the managers we worked with received a blizzard of variance reports but no overall measure of efficiency. Yet this measure is not hard to calculate. In our study, we took the same data generated by plant managers and combined them into a measure of the total factor productivity (TFP)—the ratio of total output to total input (see the appendix for more details on TFP).

This approach helps dissipate some of the fog—especially because our TFP data are presented in constant dollars instead of the usual current dollars. Doing so cuts through the distortions produced by periods of high inflation. Consider the situation at Fab's Plant 1, where from 1974 to 1982 output fluctuated between $45 million and $70 million—in nominal (current dollar) terms. In real terms, however, there was a steep and significant decline in unit output. Several executives initially expressed disbelief at the magnitude of this decline because they had come to think of the plant as a "$50 million plant." Their traditional accounting measures had masked the fundamental changes taking place.

Another advantage of the TFP approach is that it integrates the contributions of all the factors of production into a single measure of total input. Traditional systems offer no such integration. Moreover, they often overlook important factors. One of the plant managers at the Process Company gauged performance in a key department by improvements in labor hours and wage costs. Our data showed that these "improvements" came largely from the substitution of capital for labor. Conscientious efforts to prune labor content by installing equipment—without developing the management skills and systems needed to realize its full potential—proved shortsighted. The plant's TFP (which, remember, takes into account both labor and capital costs) improved very little.

This preoccupation with labor costs, particularly direct labor costs, is quite common—even though direct labor now accounts for less than 15% of total costs in most manufacturing companies. The managers we studied focused heavily on these costs; indeed, their systems for measuring direct labor were generally more detailed and extensive than those for measuring other inputs that were several times more costly. Using sophisticated bar-code scanners, Hi-Tech's managers tracked line operators by the minute but had difficulty identifying the number of manufacturing engineers in the same department. Yet these engineers accounted for 20% to 25% of total cost—compared with 5% for line operators.

Just as surprising, the companies we studied paid little attention to the effect of materials consumption on productivity. Early on, we asked managers at one of the Fab plants for data on materials consumed in production during each of a series of months. Using these data to estimate materials productivity gave us highly erratic values.

Investigation showed that this plant, like many others, kept careful records of materials purchased but not of the direct or indirect materials actually consumed in a month. (The latter, which includes things like paper forms, showed up only in a catchall manufacturing overhead account.) Further, most of the factories recorded materials transactions only in dollar, rather than in physical, terms and did not readily adjust their standard costs figures when inflation or substitution altered materials prices.

What managers at Fab plants called "materials consumed" was simply an estimate derived by multiplying a product's standard materials cost—which itself assumes a constant usage of materials—by its unit output and adding an adjustment based on the current variation from standard materials prices. Every year or half-year, managers would reconcile this estimated consumption with actual materials usage, based on a physical count. As a result, data on actual materials consumption in any one period were lost.

Finally, the TFP approach makes clear the difference between the data that managers see and what those data actually measure. In one plant, the controller argued that our numbers on engineering changes were way off base. "We don't have anything like this level of changes," he claimed. "My office signs off on all changes that go through this place, and I can tell you that the number you have here is wrong." After a brief silence, the engineering manager spoke up. He said that the controller reviewed only very large (in dollar terms) engineering changes and that our data were quite accurate. He was right. The plant had been tracking all engineering changes, not just the major changes reported to the controller.

A Clear View

With the foglike distortions of poor measurement systems cleared away, we were able to identify the real levers for improving factory performance. Some, of course, were structural—that is, they involve things like plant location or plant size, which lie outside the control of a plant's managers. But a handful of managerial policies and practices consistently turned up as significant. Across industries, companies, and plants, they regularly exerted a powerful influence on productivity. In short, these are the managerial actions that make a difference.

INVEST CAPITAL

Our data show unequivocally that capital investment in new equipment is essential to sustaining growth in TFP over a long time (that is, a decade or more). But they also show that capital investment all too often reduces TFP for up to a year. Simply investing money in new technology or systems guarantees nothing. What matters is how their introduction is managed, as well as the extent to which they support and reinforce continual improvement throughout a factory. Managed right, new investment supports cumulative, long-term productivity improvement and process understanding—what we refer to as "learning."

The Process Company committed itself to providing new, internally designed equipment to meet the needs of a rapidly growing product. Over time, as the company's engineers and operating managers gained experience, they made many small changes in product design, machinery, and operating practices. These incremental adjustments added up to major growth in TFP.

Seeking new business, the Fab company redesigned an established product and purchased the equipment needed to make it. This new equipment was similar to the plant's existing machinery, but its introduction allowed for TFP-enhancing changes in work flows. Plant managers discovered how the new configuration could accommodate expanded production without a proportional increase in the work force. These benefits spilled over: even the older machinery was made to run more efficiently.

In both cases, the real boost in TFP came not just from the equipment itself but also from the opportunities it provided to search for and apply new knowledge to the overall production process. Again, managed right, investment unfreezes old assumptions, generates more efficient concepts and designs for a production system, and expands a factory's skills and capabilities.

Exhibit I shows the importance of such learning for long-term TFP growth at one of Fab's plants between 1973 and 1982. TFP rose by 96%. Part of this increase, of course, reflected changes in utilization rates and the introduction of new technology. Even so, roughly two-thirds (65%) of TFP growth was learning-based, and fully three-fourths of that learning effect (or 49% of TFP growth) was related to capital investment. Without capital investment, TFP would have increased, but at a much slower rate.

Such long-term benefits incur costs; in fact, the indirect costs associated with introducing new equipment can be staggering. In Fab's Plant 1, for example, a $1 million investment in new equipment imposed *$1.75 million* of additional costs on the plant during its first year of operation! Had the plant cut these indirect costs by half, TFP would have grown an additional 5% during that year.

Everyone knows that putting in new equipment usually causes problems. Everyone expects a temporary drop in efficiency as equipment is installed and workers learn to use it. But managers often underestimate the costly ripple effects of new equipment on inventory, quality, equipment utilization, reject rates, downtime, and material waste. Indeed, these indirect costs often exceed the direct cost of the new equipment and can persist for more than a year after the equipment is installed.

Here, then, is the paradox of capital investment. It is essential to long-term productivity growth, yet in the short run, if poorly managed, it can play havoc with TFP. It is risky indeed for a company to try to "invest its way" out of a productivity problem. Putting in new

Exhibit I.   Capital investment, learning, and productivity growth in Fab Company's Plant 2 (1973–1982)

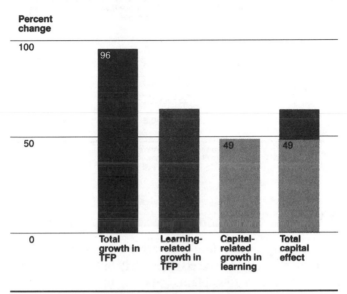

These estimates are based on a regression analysis of TFP growth. We estimated learning-related changes by using both a time trend and cumulative output. The capital-related learning effect represents the difference between the total learning effect and the effect that remained once capital was introduced into the regression. The total capital effect is composed of a learning component and a component reflecting technical advance.

equipment is just as likely to create confusion and make things worse for a number of months. Unless the investment is made with a commitment to continual learning—and unless performance measures are chosen carefully—the benefits that finally emerge will be small and slow in coming. Still, many companies today are trying to meet their competitive problems by throwing money at them—new equipment and new plants. Our findings suggest that there are other things they ought to do first, things that take less time to show results and are much less expensive.

Exhibit II.   Impact of waste on TFP in Process Company plants

Plant/ department	Average waste rate	Effect on TFP of a 10 % reduction in waste rate	Degree of uncertainty*
1-C	11.2 %	+1.2 %	.009
2-C	12.4	+1.8	.000
3-C	12.7	+2.0	.000
4-C	9.3	+3.1	.002
5-C	8.2	+0.8	.006

*The probability that waste rate reductions have a zero or negative impact on TFP.

REDUCE WASTE

We were not surprised to find a negative correlation between waste rates (or the percentage of rejects) and TFP, but we were amazed by its magnitude. In the Process plants, changes in the waste rate (measured by the ratio of waste material to total cost, expressed as a percentage) led to dramatic operating improvements. As Exhibit II shows, reducing the percentage of waste in Plant 4's Department C by only one-tenth led to a 3% improvement in TFP, conservatively estimated.

The strength of this relationship is more surprising when we remember that a decision to boost the production throughput rate (which ought to raise TFP because of the large fixed components in labor and capital costs) also causes waste ratios to increase. In theory, therefore, TFP and waste percent should increase together. The fact that they do not indicates the truly powerful impact that waste reduction has on productivity.

GET WIP OUT

The positive effect on TFP of cutting work-in-process (WIP) inventories for a given level of output was much greater than we could explain by reductions in working capital. Exhibit III documents the relationship between WIP reductions and TFP in the three companies.

Exhibit III.   Impact of work-in-process reductions on TFP

Company	Plant/ department	Effect on TFP of a 10 % reduction in WIP	Degree of uncertainty*
Hi-Tech	1-A	+1.15%	.238
	1-B	+1.18	.306
	1-C	+3.73	.103
	1-D	+9.11	.003
Process	1-H	+1.63%	.001
	2-H	+4.01	.000
	3-H	+4.65	.000
	4-H	+3.52	.000
	5-H	+3.84	.000
Fab	1	+2.86%	.000
	2	+1.14	.000
	3	+3.59	.002

*The probability that work-in-process reductions have a zero or negative impact on TFP.

Although there are important plant-to-plant variations, all reductions in WIP are associated with increases in TFP. In some plants, the effect is quite powerful; in Department D of Hi-Tech's Plant 1, reducing WIP by one-tenth produced a 9% rise in TFP.

These data support the growing body of empirical evidence about the benefits of reducing WIP. From studies of both Japanese and American companies, we know that cutting WIP leads to faster, more reliable delivery times, lowers reject rates (faster production cycle times reduce inventory obsolescence and make possible rapid feedback when a process starts to misfunction), and cuts overhead costs. We now know it also drives up TFP.

The trouble is, simply pulling work-in-process inventory out of a factory will not, by itself, lead to such improvements. More likely, it will lead to disaster. WIP is there for a reason, usually for many reasons; it is a symptom, not the disease itself. A long-term program for reducing WIP must attack the reasons for its being there in the first place: erratic process yields, unreliable equipment, long production changeover and set-up times, ever-changing production schedules, and suppliers who do not deliver on time. Without a cure for these deeper problems, a factory's cushion of WIP is often all that stands between it and chaos.

Reducing Confusion

Defective products, mismanaged equipment, and excess work-in-process inventory are not only problems in themselves. They are also sources of confusion. Many things that managers do can confuse or disrupt a factory's operation: erratically varying the rate of production, changing a production schedule at the last minute, overriding the schedule by expediting orders, changing the crews (or the workers on a specific crew) assigned to a given machine, haphazardly adding new products, altering the specifications of an existing product through an engineering change order (ECO), or monkeying with the process itself by adding to or altering the equipment used.

Managers may be tempted to ask, "Doesn't what you call confusion—changing production schedules, expediting orders, shifting work crews, adding or overhauling equipment and changing product specifications—reflect what companies inevitably have to do to respond to changing customer demands and technological opportunities?"

Our answer to this question is an emphatic, No! Responding to new demands and new opportunities requires change, but it does not require the confusion it usually creates. Much of our evidence on confusion comes from factories that belong to the same company and face the same external pressures. Some plant managers are better than others at keeping these pressures at bay. The good ones limit the number of changes introduced at any one time and carefully handle their implementation. Less able managers always seem caught by surprise, operate haphazardly, and leapfrog from one crisis to the next. Much of the confusion in their plants is internally generated.

While confusion is not the same thing as complexity, complexity in a factory's operation usually produces confusion. In general, a factory's mission becomes more complex—and its focus looser—as it becomes larger, as it adds different technologies and products, and as the number and variety of production orders it must accommodate grow. Although the evidence suggests that complexity harms performance, each company's factories were too similar for us to analyze the effects

Exhibit IV. Impact of engineering change orders on TFP in three Fab Company plants

Plant	Mean level of ECOs per month	Number of ECOs in lowest month	Number of ECOs in highest month	Effect on TFP of increasing number of ECOs from 5 to 15 per month
1	16.5	1	41	− 2.8 %
2	12.2	2	43	4.6
3	7.0	1	19	−16.6

of complexity on TFP. But we could see that what managers did to mitigate or fuel confusion within factories at a given level of complexity had a profound impact on TFP.

Of the sources of confusion we examined, none better illustrated this relationship with TFP than engineering change orders. ECOs require a change in the materials used to make a product, the manufacturing process employed, or the specifications of the product itself. We expected ECOs to lower productivity in the short run but lead to higher TFP over time. Exhibit IV, which presents data on ECO activity in three Fab plants, shows its effects to be sizable. In Plant 2, for example, increasing ECOs by just ten per month reduced TFP by almost 5%. Moreover, the debilitating effects of ECOs persisted for up to a year.

Our data suggest that the average level of ECOs implemented in a given month, as well as the variation in this level, is detrimental to TFP. Many companies would therefore be wise to reduce the number of ECOs to which their plants must respond. This notion suggests, in turn, that more pressure should be placed on engineering and marketing departments to focus attention on only the most important changes—as well as to design things right the first time.

Essential ECOs should be released in a controlled, steady fashion rather than in bunches. In the one plant that divided ECOs into categories reflecting their cost, low-cost ECOs were most harmful to TFP. More expensive ECOs actually had a positive effect. The reason: plant managers usually had warning of major changes and, recognizing that they were potentially disruptive, carefully prepared the ground by warning supervisors, training workers, and bringing in engineers. By contrast, minor ECOs were simply dumped on the factory out of the blue.

VALUE OF LEARNING

If setting up adequate measures of performance is the first step toward getting full competitive leverage out of manufacturing, identifying factory-level goals like waste or WIP reduction is the second. But without making a commitment to ongoing learning, a factory will gain no more from these first two steps than a one-time boost in performance. To sustain the leverage of plant-level operations, managers must pay close attention to—and actively plan for—learning.

We are convinced that a factory's learning rate—the rate at which its managers and operators learn to make it run better—is at least of equal importance as its current level of productivity. A factory whose TFP is lower than another's, but whose rate of learning is higher, will eventually surpass the leader. Confusion, as we have seen, is especially harmful to TFP. Thus the two essential tasks of factory management are to create clarity and order (that is, to prevent confusion) and to facilitate learning.

But doesn't learning always involve a good deal of experimentation and confusion? Isn't there an inherent conflict between creating clarity and order and facilitating learning? Not at all.

Confusion, like noise or static in an audio system, makes it hard to pick up the underlying message or figure out the source of the problem. It impedes learning, which requires controlled experimentation, good data, and careful analysis. It chews up time, resources, and energy in efforts to deal with issues whose solution adds little to a factory's performance. Worse, engineers, supervisors, operators, and managers easily become discouraged by the futility of piecemeal efforts. In such environments, TFP lags or falls.

Reducing confusion and enhancing learning do not conflict. They make for a powerful combination—and a powerful lever on competitiveness. A factory that manages change poorly, that does not have its processes under control, and that is distracted by the noise in its systems learns too slowly, if at all, or learns the wrong things.

In such a factory, new equipment will only create more confusion, not more productivity. Equally troubling, both managers and workers in such a factory will be slow to believe reports that a sister plant—or a competitor's plant—can do things better than they can. If the evidence is overwhelming, they will simply argue, "It can't work here. We're different." Indeed they are much different—and less productive too.

'WHERE THE MONEY IS'

Many companies have tried to solve their data-processing problems by bringing in computers. They soon learned that computerizing a poorly organized and error-ridden information system simply creates more problems: garbage in, garbage out. That lesson, learned so long ago, has been largely forgotten by today's managers, who are trying to improve manufacturing performance by bringing in sophisticated new equipment without first reducing the complexity and confusion of their operations.

Spending big money on hardware fixes will not help if managers have not taken the time to simplify and clarify their factories' operations, eliminate sources of error and confusion, and boost the rate of learning. Of course, advanced technology is important, often essential. But there are many things that managers must do first to prepare their organizations for these new technologies.

When plant managers are stuck with poor measures of how they are doing and when a rigid, by-the-book emphasis on standards, budgets, and exception reports discourages the kind of experimentation that leads to learning, the real levers on factory performance remain hidden. No amount of capital investment can buy heightened competitiveness. There is no way around the importance of building clarity into the system, eliminating unnecessary disruptions and distractions, ensuring careful process control, and nurturing in-depth technical competence. The reason for understanding why some factories perform better than others is the same reason that Willie Sutton robbed banks: "That's where the money is."

Appendix: Research Methods

There are three basic approaches for identifying the effects of management actions and policies on factory-level productivity: first, a longitudinal analysis, which looks at a single factory over a long time; second, a cross-sectional analysis, which compares the performance (at the same time) of two or more factories that make similar products and have similar manufacturing processes; and third, a combined approach, which collects several years' worth of data for factories having a variety of structural characteristics and uses statistical analysis to identify the effects of what managers do. We have used all three methods.

For each factory, we gathered data on a monthly basis for at least one-and-a-half years and usually for more than five. In several cases, we were able to track performance over a nine-year period; in more than half the cases, our data go back to the factory's start-up. To our knowledge, this is the first attempt to explore in such depth the sources of productivity growth at the factory level in the United States, and our data base is the most comprehensive yet compiled.

We developed our central performance measure, total factor productivity, by first calculating each factory's monthly partial factor productivities—that is, by dividing its output in turn by labor, materials, capital, and energy (for both outputs and inputs, we used 1982 dollars to eliminate the impact of inflation). To calculate a factory's total monthly output, we multiplied the quantity of each of the products it made in any month by that product's 1982 standard cost. To estimate labor input, we relied on total hours of work in each major employee classification (direct labor, indirect labor, and so forth); to estimate capital input, we used the book value of assets adjusted for inflation; and to estimate materials input, we deflated the dollar values of materials consumption by a materials price index based on 1982 dollars.

We then combined these partial measures into an index of overall total factor productivity (TFP). Because of the large fixed component in capital as well as labor cost, each factory's TFP is quite sensitive to changes in production volume and to the timing of major capital investments. To separate the movements in TFP linked to changes in production capacity from those linked to changes in operating efficiency, we included an estimate of capacity utilization in all regression analyses.

The Figure shows the quite different productivity experience at the Process Company's five plants. Hi-Tech's plants enjoyed rapid growth in output and productivity, but some of the Process and Fab plants had declining productivity and (in one case) declining output. All the Hi-Tech plants learned at a very high rate, although productivity growth in the early months was anything but fast or smooth, and some plants seemed to learn faster than others. Moderate growth and learning characterized the Fab Company's plants 2, 3, and 4; at Plant 1, however, volume declined, and TFP growth was flat or negative during much of the time we studied it.

This disparity in performance is not limited to comparisons across companies. Even within a company, productivity growth differed significantly across plants—even where each produced identical products and faced the same market and technological conditions. We cannot explain these differences by reference to technology, product variety, or market demands— they have to do with management.

Figure.   *Productivity at Process Company plants*

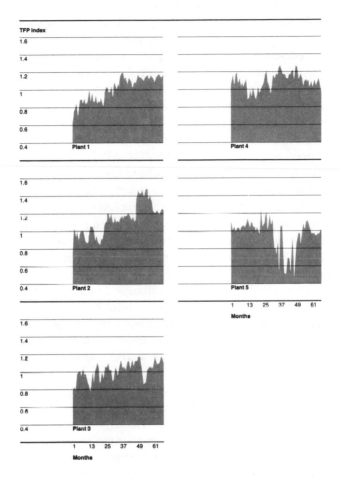

Once we developed the data on TFP, we discussed each factory's results with its management. Some of the anomalies we found resulted from errors in the data provided us; others were caused by certain events (the advent of the deer-hunting season, for example, or a year-end peak in purchased materials). We made no attempt to relate monthly TFP figures to managerial variables until each factory's managers understood our method of calculating TFP and agreed that the patterns we found fairly represented their factory's behavior.

After developing credible TFP estimates, we had to identify and measure those managerial policies that might have an impact on TFP. The Table lists these policies and describes the measures we used to capture them.

Using multiple linear regression analysis, we first examined the effect of these policy variables on TFP in the same factory over time. Early findings, coupled with discussions with a number of managers, suggested that the simple ratios and averages we were using did not adequately capture the phenomena we were trying to understand. Actions like overhauling older equipment, training workers, and implementing an engineering change order are similar in nature to investments—that is, they will likely cause short-term inefficiencies. To test the long-term effects of such actions, we included lagged variables, which allowed us to estimate that effect on TFP of management actions taken in previous months.

Other management activities may have little effect on productivity unless they are held at a certain level for several months. Boosting the amount spent on maintaining equipment, for example, does not do much if sustained for only one month. In these cases, we looked at the relationship between TFP and a five-month moving average of relevant management variables.

For still other activities—a profound change, say, in production rates—it matters greatly if the change is highly unusual or is part of a pattern of widely fluctuating rates. For each of these variables, we examined the relationship between TFP and the variable's average absolute deviation (using the five-month moving average as the estimated mean value for the variable).

A last, brief note about the importance of combining statistical analysis with ongoing field research. We found immense value in discussing our findings with the managers involved. We expected, for example, that equipment maintenance and workforce training would share a positive relationship to productivity growth. Our plant data, however, revealed a consistently negative relationship: high expenditures on maintenance and training, even in lagged forms, generally were associated with *low* TFP. When we talked about this with plant managers in all three companies, we discovered that they used maintenance and training as *corrective* measures. That is, they boosted maintenance in response to equipment problems; when the problems were solved, they reduced it. By themselves, the data would not allow us to separate corrective from preventive maintenance, or even from the costs of modifying or rebuilding equipment.

Table.   *Managerial policies*

Policy category	Indicators
Equipment	Average age of equipment
	Average maintenance expense as a percentage of equipment book value
Quality	Process waste; yield as a percentage of total input materials
	Intermediate and final reject rates
	Customer return rates
Inventory	Work-in-process as a percentage of total materials or production cost
Work force	Average age and education of workers
	Hours of overtime per week
	Absenteeism rate
	Hiring and layoff rates
	Avarage hours of training per employee
Policies affecting confusion	Fluctuations in production volume
	Number of product types produced
	Number of production orders scheduled
	Number of schedule changes as a percentage of number of production orders scheduled
	Number and type of engineering change orders
	Introduction of new processing equipment

2
Quality on the Line

David A. Garvin

When it comes to product quality, American managers still think the competitive problem much less serious than it really is. Because defining the term accurately within a company is so difficult (is quality a measure of performance, for example, or reliability or durability), managers often claim they cannot know how their product quality stacks up against that of their competitors, who may well have chosen an entirely different quality "mix." And since any comparisons are likely to wind up as comparisons of apples with oranges, even a troubling variation in results may reflect only a legitimate variation in strategy. Is there, then, a competitive problem worth worrying about?

I have recently completed a multiyear study of production operations at all but one of the manufacturers of room air conditioners in both the United States and Japan (details of the study are given in Appendix A). Each manufacturer uses a simple assembly-line process; each uses much the same manufacturing equipment; each makes an essentially standardized product. No apples versus oranges here: the comparison is firmly grounded. And although my data come from a single industry, both that industry's manufacturing process and its managers' range of approaches to product quality give these findings a more general applicability.

The shocking news, for which nothing had prepared me, is that the

Author's note: I thank Professor Robert Stobaugh for his helpful comments on an earlier draft, the Division of Research at the Harvard Business School for financial support, and the Nomura School of Advanced Management in Tokyo for arranging and coordinating my trip to Japan.

failure rates of products from the highest-quality producers were between 500 and 1,000 times less than those of products from the lowest. The "between 500 and 1,000" is not a typographical error but an inescapable fact. There is indeed a competitive problem worth worrying about.

Measuring Quality

Exhibit I presents a composite picture of the quality performance of U.S. and Japanese manufacturers of room air conditioners. I have measured quality in two ways: by the incidence of "internal" and of "external" failures. Internal failures include all defects observed (either during fabrication or along the assembly line) before the product leaves the factory; external failures include all problems incurred in the field after the unit has been installed. As a proxy for the latter, I have used the number of service calls recorded during the product's first year of warranty coverage because that was the only period for which U.S. and Japanese manufacturers offered comparable warranties.

Measured by either criterion, Japanese companies were far superior to their U.S. counterparts: their average assembly-line defect rate was almost 70 times lower and their average first-year service call rate nearly 17 times better. Nor can this variation in performance be attributed simply to differences in the number of minor, appearance-related defects. Classifying failures by major functional problems (leaks, electrical) or by component failure rates (compressors, thermostats, fan motors) does not change the results.

More startling, on both internal and external measures, the poorest Japanese company typically had a failure rate less than half that of the best U.S. manufacturer. Even among the U.S. companies themselves, there was considerable variation. Assembly-line defects ranged from 7 to 165 per 100 units—a factor of 20 separating the best performer from the worst—and service call rates varied by a factor of 5.

For ease of analysis, I have grouped the companies studied according to their quality performance (see the Appendix B). These groupings illustrate an important point: quality pays. Exhibit II, for example, presents information on assembly-line productivity for each of these categories and shows that the highest-quality producers were also those with the highest output per man-hour. On the basis of the number of direct labor hours actually worked on the assembly line, productivity at the best U.S. companies was five times higher than at the worst.

Exhibit I. *Quality in the room air conditioning industry (1981–1982*)*

	Internal failures				External failures			
	Fabrication: coil leaks per 100 units	Assembly-line defects per 100 units			Service call rate per 100 units under first-year warranty coverage			
		Total	Leaks	Electrical	Total	Compressors	Thermostats	Fan motors
Median								
United States	4.4	63.5	3.1	3.3	10.5†	1.0	1.4	.5
Japan	< .1	.95	.12	.12	.6	.05	.002	.028
Range								
United States	.1-9.0	7-165	1.3-54	.9-34	5.3-26.5	.5-3.4	.4-3.6	.2-2.6
Japan	.03-.4	.15-3.0	.0015-.5	.0015-1.0	.04-2.0	.002-.1	0-.03	.001-.2

*Although most companies reported total failure rates for 1981 or 1982, complete data on component failure rates were often available only or earlier years. For some U.S. companies, 1979 or 1980 figures were employed. Because there was little change in U.S. failure rates during this period, the mixing of data from different years should have little effect.

†Service call rates in the United States normally include calls where no product problems were found ("customer instruction" calls); those in Japan do not. I have adjusted the U.S. median to exclude these calls; without the adjustments, the median U.S. service call rate would be 11.4 per 100 units. Figures for the range should be adjusted similarly, although the necessary data were not available from the U.S. companies with the highest and lowest service call rates.

Exhibit II. Quality and productivity

Grouping of companies by quality performance	Units produced per assembly-line direct labor man-hour actual hours*		Units produced per assembly-line direct labor man-hour standard output†	
	Median	Range	Median	Range
Japanese manufacturers	NA‡	NA	1.8	1.4-3.1
Best U.S. plants	1.7	1.7§	1.7	1.4-1.9
Better U.S. plants	.9	.7-1.0	1.1	.8-1.2
Average U.S. plants	1.0	.6-1.2	1.1	1.1-1.7
Poorest U.S. plants	.35	.35§	1.3	.8-1.6

*Direct labor hours have been adjusted to include only those workers involved in assembly (i.e. where inspectors and repairmen were classified as direct labor, they have been excluded from the totals).

†Computed by using the average cycle time to derive a figure for hourly output, and then dividing by the number of assembly-line direct laborers (excluding inspectors and repairmen) to determine output per man-hour.

‡NA = not available.

§In this quality grouping, man-hour data were only available from a single company.

Measuring productivity by "standard output" (see Exhibit II) blurs the picture somewhat. Although the Japanese plants maintain a slight edge over the best U.S. plants, categories of performance tend to overlap. The figures based on standard output, however, are rather imperfect indicators of productivity—for example, they fail to include overtime or rework hours and so overstate productivity levels, particularly at the poorer companies, which devote more of their time to correcting defects. Thus, these figures have less significance than do those based on the number of hours actually worked.

Note carefully that the strong association between productivity and quality is not explained by differences in technology or capital intensity, for most of the plants employed similar manufacturing techniques. This was especially true of final assembly, where manual operations, such as hand brazing and the insertion of color-coded wires, were the norm. Japanese plants did use some automated transfer lines and packaging equipment, but only in compressor manufacturing and case welding was the difference in automation significant.

The association between cost and quality is equally strong. Reducing field failures means lower warranty costs, and reducing factory defects cuts expenditures on rework and scrap. As Exhibit III shows, the Japanese manufacturers incurred warranty costs averaging 0.6% of sales; at the best American companies, the figure was 1.8%; at the worst 5.2%.

In theory, low warranty costs might be offset by high expenditures on defect prevention: a company could spend enough on product pretesting or on inspecting assembled units before shipment to wipe out any gains from improved warranty costs. Figures on the total costs of quality, however, which include expenditures on prevention and inspection as well as the usual failure costs of rework, scrap, and warranties, lead to the opposite conclusion. In fact, the total costs of quality incurred by Japanese producers were less than one-half the failure costs incurred by the best U.S. companies.

The reason is clear: failures are much more expensive to fix after a unit has been assembled than before. The cost of the extra hours spent pretesting a design is cheap compared with the cost of a product recall; similarly, field service costs are much higher than those of incoming inspection. Among manufacturers of room air conditioners, the Japanese—even with their strong commitment to design review, vendor selection and management, and in-process inspection—still have the lowest overall quality costs.

Nor are the opportunities for reduction in quality costs confined to this industry alone. A recent survey[1] of U.S. companies in ten man-

Exhibit III. *Quality and costs*

Grouping of companies by quality performance	Warranty costs as a percentage of sales*		Total cost of quality (Japanese companies) and total failure costs (U.S. companies) as a percentage of sales†	
	Median	Range	Median	Range
Japanese manufacturers	.6%	.2-1.0%	1.3%	.7-2.0%
Best U.S. plants	1.8	1.1-2.4	2.8	2.7-2.8
Better U.S. plants	2.4	1.7-3.1	3.4	3.3-3.5
Average U.S. plants	2.2	1.7-4.3	3.9	2.3-5.6
Poorest U.S. plants	5.2%	3.3-7.0%	>5.8%	4.4->7.2%

*Because most Japanese air conditioners are covered by a three-year warranty while most U.S. units are covered by a warranty of five years, these figures somewhat overstate the Japanese advantage. The bias is unlikely to be serious, however, because second- to fifth-year coverage in the United States and second- to third-year coverage in Japan are much less inclusive—and therefore, less expensive—than first-year coverage. For example, at U.S. companies second- to fifth-year warranty costs average less than one-fifth of first-year expenses.

†Total cost of quality is the sum of all quality-related expenditures, including the costs of prevention, inspection, rework, scrap, and warranties. The Japanese figures include expenditures in all of these categories, while the U.S. figures, because of limited data, include only the costs of rework, scrap, and warranties (failure costs). As a result, these figures understate total U.S. quality costs relative to those of the Japanese.

ufacturing sectors found that total quality costs averaged 5.8% of sales—for a $1 billion corporation, some $58 million per year primarily in scrap, rework, and warranty expenses. Shaving even a tenth of a percentage point off these costs would result in an annual saving of $1 million.

Other studies, which use the PIMS data base, have demonstrated a further connection among quality, market share, and return on investment.[2] Not only does good quality yield a higher ROI for any given market share (among businesses with less than 12% of the market, those with inferior product quality averaged an ROI of 4.5%, those with average product quality an ROI of 10.4%, and those with superior product quality an ROI of 17.4%); it also leads directly to market share gains. Those businesses in the PIMS study that improved in quality during the 1970s increased their market share five to six times faster than those that declined—and three times faster than those whose quality remained unchanged.

The conclusion is inescapable: improving product quality is a profitable activity. For managers, therefore, the central question must be: What makes for successful quality management?

Sources of Quality

Evidence from the room air conditioning industry points directly to the practices that the quality leaders, both Japanese and American, have employed. Each of these areas of effort—quality programs, policies, and attitudes; information systems; product design; production and work force policies; and vendor management—has helped in some way to reduce defects and lower field failures.

PROGRAMS, POLICIES, AND ATTITUDES

The importance a company attaches to product quality often shows up in the standing of its quality department. At the poorest performing plants in the industry, the quality control (QC) manager invariably reported to the director of manufacturing or engineering. Access to top management came, if at all, through these go-betweens, who often had very different priorities from those of the QC manager. At the best U.S. companies, especially those with low service call rates, the quality department had more visibility. Several companies had vice presidents of quality; at the factory level each head of QC reported directly to the plant manager. Japanese QC managers also reported directly to their plant managers.

Of course, reporting relationships alone do not explain the observed differences in quality performance. They do indicate, however, the seriousness that management attaches to quality problems. It's one thing to say you believe in defect-free products, but quite another to take time from a busy schedule to act on that belief and stay informed. At the U.S. company with the lowest service call rate, the president met weekly with all corporate vice presidents to review the latest service call statistics. Nobody at that company needed to ask whether quality was a priority of upper management.

How often these meetings occurred was as important as their cast of characters. Mistakes do not fix themselves; they have to be identified, diagnosed, and then resolved through corrective action. The greater the frequency of meetings to review quality performance, the fewer undetected errors. The U.S. plants with the lowest assembly-line defect rates averaged ten such meetings per month; at all other U.S. plants, the average was four. The Japanese companies reviewed defect rates daily.

Meetings and corrective action programs will succeed, however, only if they are backed by genuine top-level commitment. In Japan, this commitment was deeply ingrained and clearly communicated. At four of the six companies surveyed, first-line supervisors believed product quality—not producing at low cost, meeting the production schedule, or improving worker productivity—was management's top manufacturing priority. At the other two, quality ranked a close second.

The depth of this commitment became evident in the Japanese practice of creating internal consumer review boards. Each of the Japanese producers had assembled a group of employees whose primary function was to act as typical consumers and test and evaluate products. Sometimes the products came randomly from the day's production; more frequently, they represented new designs. In each case, the group had final authority over product release. The message here was unmistakable: the customer—not the design staff, the marketing team, or the production group—had to be satisfied with a product's quality before it was considered acceptable for shipment.

By contrast, U.S. companies showed a much weaker commitment to product quality. At 9 of the 11 U.S. plants, first-line supervisors told me that their managers attached far more importance to meeting the production schedule than to any other manufacturing objective. Even the best performers showed no consistent relationship between failure rates and supervisors' perceptions of manufacturing priorities.

What commitment there was stemmed from the inclusion (or absence) of quality in systems of performance appraisal. Two of the three companies with the highest rates of assembly-line defects paid their workers on the basis of total output, not defect-free output. Is it any wonder these employees viewed defects as being of little consequence? Not surprisingly, domestic producers with low failure rates evaluated both supervisors and managers on the quality of output—supervisors, in terms of defect rates, scrap rates, and the amount of rework attributable to their operations; managers, in terms of service call rates and their plants' total costs of quality.

These distinctions make good sense. First-line supervisors play a pivotal role in managing the production process, which is responsible for internal failures, but have little control over product design, the quality of incoming materials, or other factors that affect field performance. These require the attention of higher level managers, who can legitimately be held responsible for coordinating the activities of design, purchasing, and other functional groups in pursuit of fewer service calls or reduced warranty expenses.

To obtain consistent improvement, a formal system of goal setting is necessary.[3] Only three U.S. plants set annual targets for reducing field failures. Between 1978 and 1981, these three were the only ones to cut their service call rates by more than 25%; most of the other U.S. plants showed little or no change. All the Japanese companies, however, consistently improved their quality—in several cases, by as much as 50%—and all had elaborate companywide systems of goal setting.

From the corporate level at these companies came vague policy pronouncements ("this year, let the customer determine our quality"), which were further defined by division heads ("reduced service call rates are necessary if we are to lower costs") and by middle managers ("compressor failures are an especially serious problem that must be addressed"). Actual quantitative goals ("improve compressor reliability by 10%") were often set by foremen or workers operating through quality control circles. The collaborative nature of this goal-setting process helped these targets earn wide support.

At the final—or first—level of goal setting, specificity matters. Establishing an overall target for an assembly-line defect rate without specifying more detailed goals by problem category, such as leaks or electrical problems, is unlikely to produce much improvement. A number of U.S. plants have tried this approach and failed. Domestic producers with the lowest defect rates set their overall goals last. Each inspection point along the assembly line had a target of its own, which was agreed on by representatives of the quality and manufacturing departments. The sum of these individual targets established the overall goal for the assembly line. As a result, responsibility for quality became easier to assign and progress easier to monitor.

INFORMATION SYSTEMS

Successful monitoring of quality assumes that the necessary data are available, which is not always true. Without specific and timely information on defects and field failures, improvements in quality are seldom possible. Not surprisingly, at the poorest U.S. companies information on defects and field failures was virtually nonexistent. Assembly-line defects and service call rates were seldom reported. "Epidemic" failures (problems that a large proportion of all units had in common) were widespread. Design flaws remained undetected. At one domestic producer, nearly a quarter of all 1979–1981 warranty expenses came from problems with a single type of compressor.

Other companies reported more extensive quality information—daily and weekly defect rates as well as quarterly and, occasionally, monthly service call rates. These variations in the level of reporting detail correlated closely with differences in quality performance. Among average U.S. performers, for example, quality reports were quite general. Data on assembly line defects gave no breakdowns by inspection point; data on field failures were for entire product lines, not for separate models. Without further refinement, such data cannot isolate quality problems.

A 10% failure rate for a product line can mean a number of things: that all models in the line fail to perform 10% of the time, with no single problem standing out; that several models have a 5% failure rate and one a 30% rate, which suggests a single problem of epidemic proportions; or anything in between. There is no way of distinguishing these cases on the basis of aggregate data alone. What is true of goal setting is equally true of reporting systems: success requires mastering the details.

The best U.S. companies reported defect rates for each inspection point on the assembly line and field failure rates by individual model. The Japanese not only collected information that their U.S. counterparts ignored, such as failure rates in the later years of a product's life;

they also insisted on extreme precision in reporting. At one company, repairmen had to submit reports on every defective unit they fixed. In general, it was not unusual for Japanese managers to be able to identify the 30 different ways in which Switch X had failed on Model Y during the last several years. Nor did they have to wait for such information.

Service call statistics in the United States took anywhere from one month to one year to make the trip from the field to the factory; in Japan, the elapsed time averaged between one week and one month. Differences in attitude are part of the explanation. As the director of quality at one Japanese company observed, field information reached his company's U.S. subsidiaries much more slowly than it did operations in Japan—even though both employed the same system for collecting and reporting data.

PRODUCT DESIGN

Room air conditioners are relatively standardized products. Although basic designs in the United States have changed little in recent years, pressures to improve energy efficiency and to reduce costs have resulted in a stream of minor changes. On the whole, these changes have followed a common pattern: the initiative came from marketing; engineering determined the actual changes to be made and then pretested the new design; quality control, manufacturing, purchasing, and other affected departments signed off; and, where necessary, prototypes and pilot production units were built.

What did differ among companies was the degree of design and production stability. As Exhibit IV indicates, the U.S. plants with the lowest failure rates made far fewer design changes than did their competitors.

Exhibit IV conveys an important message. Variety, at least in America, is often the enemy of quality. Product proliferation and constant design change may keep the marketing department happy, but failure rates tend to rise as well. By contrast, a limited product line ensures that workers are more familiar with each model and less likely to make mistakes. Reducing the number of design changes allows workers to devote more attention to each one. Keeping production level means less reliance on a second shift staffed by inexperienced employees.

The Japanese, however, have achieved low failure rates even with relatively broad product lines and rapidly changing designs. In the room air conditioning industry, new designs account for nearly a third

Exhibit IV. *Quality and product stability*

Grouping of companies by quality performance	Median number of design changes per year	Median number of models	Median number of design changes per model*	Median percentage that peak production exceeded low production†
Japanese manufacturers	NA‡	80	NA	170%
Best U.S. plants	43	56	.8	27
Better U.S. plants	150	81	1.9	63
Average U.S. plants	400	126	3.2	50
Poorest U.S. plants	133	41	3.2	100%

*Column 1 divided by column 2.

†The figures in this column were derived by dividing each plant's largest daily output for the year by its smallest (non-zero) output for the year.

‡NA = not available.

of all models offered each year, far more than in the United States. The secret: an emphasis on reliability engineering and on careful shakedowns of new designs before they are released.

Reliability engineering is nothing new; it has been practiced by the aerospace industry in this country for at least 20 years. In practice, it involves building up designs from their basic components, determining the failure probabilities of individual systems and subsystems, and then trying to strengthen the weak links in the chain by product redesign or by incorporating more reliable parts. Much of the effort is focused up front, when a product is still in blueprint or prototype form. Managers use statistical techniques to predict reliability over the product's life and subject preliminary designs to exhaustive stress and life testing to collect information on potential failure modes. These data form the basis for continual product improvement.

Only one American maker of room air conditioners practiced reliability engineering, and its failure rates were among the lowest observed. All of the Japanese companies, however, placed considerable emphasis on these techniques. Their designers were, for example, under tremendous pressure to reduce the number of parts per unit; for a basic principle of reliability engineering is that, everything else being equal, the fewer the parts, the lower the failure rate.

Japanese companies worked just as hard to increase reliability through changes in components. They were aided by the Industrial Engineering Bureau of Japan's Ministry of International Trade and Industry (MITI), which required that all electric and electronic components sold in the country be tested for reliability and have their ratings on file at the bureau. Because this information was publicly available, designers no longer needed to test components themselves in order to establish reliability ratings.

An emphasis on reliability engineering is also closely tied to a more thorough review of new designs before units reach production. American manufacturers usually built and tested a single prototype before moving to pilot production; the Japanese often repeated the process three or four times.

Moreover, all affected departments—quality control, purchasing, manufacturing, service, and design engineering—played an active role at each stage of the review process. American practice gave over the early stages of the design process almost entirely to engineering. By the time other groups got their say, the process had gained momentum, schedules had been established, and changes had become difficult to make. As a result, many a product that performed well in the laboratory created grave problems on the assembly line or in the field.

PRODUCTION AND WORK FORCE POLICIES

The key to defect-free production is a manufacturing process that is "in control"—machinery and equipment well maintained, workplaces clean and orderly, workers well trained, and inspection procedures suited to the rapid detection of deviations. In each of these areas, the Japanese were noticeably ahead of their American competitors.

Training of the labor force, for example, was extensive, even for employees engaged in simple jobs. At most of the Japanese companies, preparing new assembly-line workers took approximately six months, for they were first trained for all jobs on the line. American workers received far less instruction (from several hours to several days) and were usually trained for a single task. Not surprisingly, Japanese workers were much more adept at tracking down quality problems originating at other work stations and far better equipped to propose remedial action.

Instruction in statistical quality control techniques supplemented the other training offered Japanese workers. Every Japanese plant relied heavily on these techniques for controlling its production process. Process control charts, showing the acceptable quality standards of various fabrication and assembly-line operations, were everywhere in general use. Only one U.S. plant—the one with the lowest defect rate—had made a comparable effort to determine the capabilities of its production process and to chart the results.

Still, deviations will occur, and thorough and timely inspection is necessary to ferret them out quickly. Japanese companies therefore employed an inspector for every 7.1 assembly-line workers (in the United States the ratio was 1:9.5). The primary role of these inspectors was to monitor the production process for stability; they were less "gatekeepers," weeding out defective units before shipment, than providers of information. Their tasks were considered especially important where manual operations were common and where inspection required sophisticated testing of a unit's operating characteristics.

On balance, then, the Japanese advantage in production came less from revolutionary technology than from close attention to basic skills and to the reduction of all unwanted variations in the manufacturing process. In practice, this approach can produce dramatic results. Although new model introductions and assembly-line changeovers at American companies boosted defect rates, at least until workers became familiar with their new assignments, Japanese companies experienced no such problems.

Before every new model introduction, Japanese assembly-line workers were thoroughly trained in their new tasks. After-hours seminars explained the product to the work force, and trial runs were common. During changeovers, managers kept workers informed of the models slated for production each day, either through announcements at early morning meetings or by sending assembled versions of the new model down the line 30 minutes before the change was to take place, together with a big sign saying "this model comes next." American workers generally received much less information about changeovers. At the plant with the highest defect rate in the industry, communication about changeovers was limited to a single small chalkboard, listing the models to be produced each day, placed at one end of the assembly line.

The Japanese system of permanent employment also helped to improve quality. Before they are fully trained, new workers often commit unintentional errors. Several American companies observed that their workers' inexperience and lack of familiarity with the product line contributed to their high defect rates. The Japanese, with low absenteeism and turnover, faced fewer problems of this sort. Japanese plants had a median turnover of 3.1%; the comparable figure for U.S. plants was two times higher. Even more startling were the figures on absenteeism: a median of 3.1% for American companies and *zero* for the Japanese.

In addition, because several of the U.S. plants were part of larger manufacturing complexes linked by a single union, they suffered greatly from "bumping." A layoff in one part of the complex would result in multiple job changes as workers shifted among plants to protect seniority rights. Employees whose previous experience was with another product would suddenly find themselves assembling room air conditioners. Sharp increases in defects were the inevitable result.

VENDOR MANAGEMENT

Without acceptable components and materials, no manufacturer can produce high-quality products. As computer experts have long recognized, "garbage in" means "garbage out." Careful selection and monitoring of vendors is therefore a necessary first step toward ensuring reliable and defect-free production.

At the better U.S. companies, the quality department played a major role in vendor selection by tempering the views of the engineering ("do their samples meet our technical specifications") and purchasing ("is that the best we can do on price") departments. At the very best companies, however, purchasing departments independently ranked quality as their primary objective. Buyers received instruction in the concepts of quality control; at least one person had special responsibility for vendor quality management; goals were set for the quality of incoming components and materials; and vendors' shipments were carefully monitored.

Purchasing departments at the worst U.S. companies viewed their mission more narrowly: to obtain the lowest possible price for technically acceptable components. Site visits to new vendors were rarely made, and members of the purchasing department seldom got involved in the design review process. Because incoming inspection was grossly understaffed (at one plant, two workers were responsible for reviewing 14,000 incoming shipments per year), production pressures often allowed entire lots to come to the assembly line uninspected. Identification of defective components came, if at all, only after they had been incorporated into completed units. Inevitably, scrap and rework costs soared.

In several Japanese companies incoming materials arrived directly at the assembly line without inspection. New vendors, however, first had to pass rigorous tests: their products initially received 100% inspection. Once all problems were corrected, sampling inspection became the norm. Only after an extended period without a rejection were vendors allowed to send their products directly to the assembly line. At the first sign of deterioration in vendor performance, more intensive inspection resumed.

In this environment, inspection was less an end in itself than a means to an end. Receiving inspectors acted less as policemen than as quality consultants to the vendor. Site visits, for example, were mandatory when managers were assessing potential suppliers and continued for as long as the companies did business together. Even more revealing, the selection of vendors depended as much on management philosophy, manufacturing capability, and depth of commitment to quality as on price and delivery performance.

Closing the Gap

What, then, is to be done? Are American companies hopelessly behind in the battle for superior quality? Or is an effective counterattack possible?

Although the evidence is still fragmentary, there are a number of encouraging signs. In 1980, when Hewlett-Packard tested 300,000 semiconductors from three U.S. and three Japanese suppliers, the Japanese chips had a failure rate one-sixth that of the American chips. When the test was repeated two years later, the U.S. companies had virtually closed the gap. Similar progress is evident in automobiles. Ford's Ranger trucks, built in Louisville, Tennessee, offer an especially dramatic example. In just three years, the number of "concerns" registered by the Louisville plant (the automaker's measure of quality deficiencies as recorded at monthly audits) dropped to less than one-third its previous high. Today, the Ranger's quality is nearly equal that of Toyota's SR5, its chief Japanese rival.

But in these industries, as with room air conditioners, quality improvement takes time. The "quick fix" provides few lasting gains. What is needed is a long-term commitment to the fundamentals— working with vendors to improve their performance, educating and training the work force, developing an accurate and responsive quality information system, setting targets for quality improvement, and demonstrating interest and commitment at the very highest levels of management. With their companies' futures on the line, managers can do no less. (See Appendix B.)

Appendix A: Research Methods

This article is based mainly on data collected in 1981 and 1982 from U.S. and Japanese manufacturers of room air conditioners. I selected that industry for study for a number of reasons: it contains companies of varying size and character, which implies a wide range of quality policies and performance; its products are standardized, which facilitates intercompany comparisons; and it employs a simple assembly-line process, which is representative of many other mass production industries.

Nine of the ten U.S. companies in the industry and all seven of the Japanese companies participated in the study. They range in size from small air conditioning specialists with total sales of under $50 million to large home appliance manufacturers with annual sales of more than $200 million in this product line alone. Taken together, they account for approximately 90% of U.S. industry shipments and 100% of Japanese industry shipments. I have collected data separately for each plant (two of the American companies operate two plants apiece; otherwise, each company employs only a single plant). Of the 18 plants studied, 11 are American and 7 Japanese.

Once U.S. companies had agreed to participate in the study, I sent them a questionnaire requesting background information on their product line, production practices, vendor management practices, quality policies, and quality performance. I then visited them all in order to review the questionnaire results, collect additional data, tour the factories, and conduct interviews with key personnel. The interviews were open-ended and unstructured, although I posed similar questions at each company. A typical visit included interviews with managers in the quality, manufacturing, purchasing, engineering, and service departments, as well as several hours spent walking the production floor.

Preliminary analysis of the interviews and questionnaires showed that companies neither employed the same conventions in reporting data nor answered questions in the same degree of detail. I therefore sent each company its own set of follow-up questions to fill in these gaps and to make the data more comparable across companies. In addition, I requested each company to administer a brief questionnaire on quality attitudes to each of its first-line production supervisors.

I followed a similar approach with the Japanese manufacturers, although time constraints limited the amount of information that I could collect. All questionnaires were first translated into Japanese and mailed to the participating companies. Six of the seven companies completed the same basic quality questionnaire as did their American counterparts; the same companies also administered the survey on quality attitudes to a small number of their first-line supervisors. With the aid of a translator, I conducted on-site interviews at all the companies and toured six of the plants.

Appendix B: Classifying Plants By Quality Performance

To identify patterns of behavior, I first grouped U.S. plants into categories according to their quality performance on two dimensions—internal quality (defect rates in the factory) and external quality (failure rates in the field).

Table A presents the basic data on external quality. I measured field performance in two ways: by the service call rate for units under first-year warranty coverage (the total number of service calls recorded in 1981 divided by the number of units in the field with active first-year warranties) and by the service call rate for units under first-year warranty coverage less "customer instruction calls" (only those service calls that resulted from a faulty unit, not from a customer who was using the unit improperly or had failed to install it correctly).

Table A.   Field performance for U.S. plants in 1981

Plant	Service call rate, first year warranty coverage		Service call rate less "customer instruction" calls	
	Percentage	Rank	Percentage	Rank
1	5.3%	1	< 5.3%	1
2	8.7	2	< 8.7	2,3
3	9.2	3	5.6	2,3
4	10.5	4	9.8	5
5	11.1	5	9.3	4
6	11.4	6	10.5	6
7	12.6	7	10.5	6
8	16.2	8	11.8	8
9	17.5	9	13.8	9
10	22.9	10	< 22.9	10
11	26.5%	11	< 26.5%	11

	Ranking of plants on field performance external quality		
	Good	Average	Poor
Plant number	1, 2, 3	4, 5, 6, 7, 8	9, 10, 11

The second measure was necessary because companies differed in their policies toward customer instruction calls. Some reimbursed repairmen for these calls without argument; others did their best to eliminate such calls completely. An accurate assessment of product performance required the separation of these calls from problems that reflect genuinely defective units.

I classified plants on the basis of their rankings on the second of the two measures in Table A, and then grouped them according to their actual levels of field failures. In most cases, the dividing lines were clear, although there were some borderline cases. Plant 8, for example, had a total service call rate well above the industry median, yet after subtracting customer instruction calls, its failure rate differed little from the other average performers. Because this second figure more accurately reflects the rate of product malfunction, I treated Plant 8 as having average, rather than poor, external quality. A number of companies with high failure rates did not break out customer instruction calls. I have treated them as having poor external quality because their customer instruction calls would have to have been two or three times as frequent as the highest rate recorded in 1981 for them to have warranted an average ranking.

I followed a similar procedure in classifying plants on internal quality. Because companies differed in how they defined and recorded defects (some noted every single product flaw; others were interested only in major malfunctions), I employed several indexes to ensure consistency. The results are displayed in Table B. I ranked companies first by their total assembly-line defect rates (every defect recorded at every station along the assembly line divided by the number of units produced) and then by the number of defects requiring off-line repair. The second index compensates for the different definitions just noted, for it more accurately reflects the incidence of serious problems. Minor adjustments and touch-ups can generally be made without pulling a unit off the line; more serious problems normally require off-line repair. Measured on this basis, the high total defect rates of Plants 1 and 9 appear to be much less of a problem.

Because several companies had to estimate the off-line repair rate, I used a third index, the number of repairmen per assembly-line direct laborer, to measure defect seriousness. The proportion of the work force engaged in repair activities, including workers assigned to separate rework lines and to rework activities in the warehouse, is likely to correlate well with the incidence of serious defects, for more serious problems usually require more time to correct and necessitate a larger repair staff. This measure provides important additional information, confirming the conclusions about Plant 1 (its high total defect rate appears to include a large number of minor problems) but contradicting those about Plant 9 (its large number of repairmen suggests that defects are, in fact, a serious problem, despite the small proportion of units requiring off-line repair).

I assigned plants to groups using much the same procedure as before. I first computed a composite ranking for each plant by averaging together the three rankings of Table B. Dividing lines between groups followed the absolute levels of the indexes for each plant. Once again, some judgment was involved, particularly for Plants 4, 5, and 9. Plants 5 and 9 were borderline cases, candidates for ranking as either average or poor internal quality. I classified the former as average, even though its overall rank was low, because its absolute scores on the first two measures were quite close to the median. I classified the latter as poor because its absolute scores on both the first and the third measures were so high. Plant 4 presented a different problem, for it provided no information at all on assembly-line defects. Rather than classifying the plant on the basis of the third index alone, I employed supplementary data. Based on its defect rate at the

Table B.   Internal quality for U.S. plants in 1981

Plant	Assembly-line defects per 100 units		Assembly-line defects per 100 units requiring off-line repair		Repairman per assembly-line direct laborer	
	Number	Rank	Number	Rank	Number	Rank
1	150	9	34	5,6	.06	3
2	7	1	7	1	.05	2
3	10	2	10	3	.04	1
4	NA*	NA	NA	NA	.09	8
5	57	5	47	7	.13	9
6	70	6	67	8	.06	3
7	26	4	7	1	.08	6
8	8	3	11	4	.08	6
9	>100	7	> 30	5,6	.16	11
10	165	10	165	10	.13	9
11	135	8	> 68	9	.07	5

*NA = not available.

Ranking of plants on internal quality

Good	Average	Poor
Plant number: 2, 3, 7, 8	1, 4(?), 5, 6	9, 10, 11

Table C. *Classification of plants on internal and external quality*

		External quality			
		Poor	Fair	Good	Excellent
Poor U.S. plants	Internal quality				
Average U.S. plants	Poor	Plants 9, 10, 11			
Better U.S. plants	Fair		Plants 4, 5, 6	Plant 1	
Best U.S. plants	Good		Plants 7, 8	Plants 2, 3	
	Excellent				All Japanese plants

end-of-the-line quality audit and its rework and scrap costs as a percentage of sales, both of which were quite close to figures reported by other companies with average internal quality, Plant 4 showed up as an average performer.

Table C combines the results of the previous two tables. Overall quality rankings appear for each plant. In most cases, success on internal quality implied success on external measures, although the correlation is not perfect, as Plants 1, 7, and 8 demonstrate. The Japanese plants are in a category of their own, for on both internal and external measures they are at least twice as good as the best U.S. plant.

Notes

1. "Quality Cost Survey," *Quality*, June 1977, p. 20.
2. Sidney Schoeffler, Robert D. Buzzell, and Donald F. Heany, "Impact of Strategic Planning on Profit Performance," *Harvard Business Review* March–April 1974, p. 137; and Robert D. Buzzell and Frederik D. Wiersema, "Successful Share-Building Strategies," *Harvard Business Review* January–February 1981, p. 135.
3. For a summary of evidence on this point, see Edwin A. Locke et al., "Goal Setting and Task Performance: 1969–1980," *Psychological Bulletin*, vol. 90, no. 1, p. 125.

3
Robust Quality

Genichi Taguchi and Don Clausing

When a product fails, you must replace it or fix it. In either case, you must track it, transport it, and apologize for it. Losses will be much greater than the costs of manufacture, and none of this expense will necessarily recoup the loss to your reputation. Taiichi Ohno, the renowned former executive vice president of Toyota Motor Corporation, put it this way: Whatever an executive thinks the losses of poor quality are, they are actually six times greater.

How can manufacturing companies minimize them? If U.S. managers learn only one new principle from the collection now known as Taguchi Methods, let it be this: Quality is a virtue of design. The "robustness" of products is more a function of good design than of on-line control, however stringent, of manufacturing processes. Indeed—though not nearly so obvious—an inherent lack of robustness in product design is the primary driver of superfluous manufacturing expenses. But managers will have to learn more than one principle to understand why.

Zero Defects, Imperfect Products

For a generation, U.S. managers and engineers have reckoned quality losses as equivalent to the costs absorbed by the factory when it builds defective products—the squandered value of products that cannot be shipped, the added costs of rework, and so on. Most managers think losses are low when the factory ships pretty much what it builds; such is the message of statistical quality control and other traditional quality control programs that we'll subsume under the seductive term "Zero Defects."

Of course, customers do not give a hang about a factory's record of staying "in spec" or minimizing scrap. For customers, the proof of a product's quality is in its performance when rapped, overloaded, dropped, and splashed. Then, too many products display temperamental behavior and annoying or even dangerous performance degradations. We all prefer copiers whose copies are clear under low power; we all prefer cars designed to steer safely and predictably, even on roads that are wet or bumpy, in crosswinds, or with tires that are slightly under or overinflated. We say these products are robust. They gain steadfast customer loyalty.

Design engineers take for granted environmental forces degrading performance (rain, low voltage, and the like). They try to counter these effects in product design—insulating wires, adjusting tire treads, sealing joints. But some performance degradations come from the interaction of parts themselves, not from anything external happening to them. In an ideal product—in an ideal anything—parts work in perfect harmony. Most real products, unfortunately, contain perturbations of one kind or another, usually the result of a faulty meshing of one component with corresponding components. A drive shaft vibrates and wears out a universal joint prematurely; a fan's motor generates too much heat for a sensitive microprocessor.

Such performance degradations may result either from something going wrong in the factory or from an inherent failure in the design. A drive shaft may vibrate too much because of a misaligned lathe or a misconceived shape; a motor may prove too hot because it was put together improperly or yanked into the design impetuously. Another way of saying this is that work-in-progress may be subjected to wide variations in factory process and ambience, and products may be subjected to wide variations in the conditions of customer use.

Why do we insist that most degradations result from the latter kind of failure, design failures, and not from variations in the factory? Because the ambient or process variations that work-in-process may be subjected to in the factory are not nearly as dramatic as the variations that products are subjected to in a customer's hands—obvious when you think about it, but how many exponents of Zero Defects do? Zero Defects says, The effort to reduce process failure in the factory will simultaneously reduce instances of product failure in the field. We say, The effort to reduce product failure in the field will simultaneously reduce the number of defectives in the factory.

Still, we can learn something interesting about the roots of robustness and the failures of traditional quality control by confronting Zero Defects on its own ground. It is in opposition to Zero Defects that Taguchi Methods emerged.

Robustness as Consistency

According to Zero Defects, designs are essentially fixed before the quality program makes itself felt; serious performance degradations result from the failure of parts to mate and interface just so. When manufacturing processes are out of control, that is, when there are serious variations in the manufacture of parts, products cannot be expected to perform well in the field. Faulty parts make faulty connections. A whole product is the sum of its connections.

Of course, no two drive shafts can be made *perfectly* alike. Engineers working within the logic of Zero Defects presuppose a certain amount of variance in the production of any part. They specify a target for a part's size and dimension, then tolerances that they presume will allow for trivial deviations from this target. What's wrong with a drive shaft that should be 10 centimeters in diameter actually coming in at 9.998?

Nothing. The problem—and it is widespread—comes when managers of Zero Defects programs make a virtue of this necessity. They grow accustomed to thinking about product quality in terms of acceptable deviation from targets—instead of the consistent effort to hit them. Worse, managers may specify tolerances that are much too wide because they assume it would cost too much for the factory to narrow them.

Consider the case of Ford vs. Mazda (then known as Toyo Koygo), which unfolded just a few years ago. Ford owns about 25% of Mazda and asked the Japanese company to build transmissions for a car it was selling in the United States. Both Ford and Mazda were supposed to build to identical specifications; Ford adopted Zero Defects as its standard. Yet after the cars had been on the road for a while, it became clear that Ford's transmissions were generating far higher warranty costs and many more customer complaints about noise.

To its credit, Ford disassembled and carefully measured samples of transmissions made by both companies. At first, Ford engineers thought their gauges were malfunctioning. Ford parts were all in-spec, but Mazda gearboxes betrayed no variability at all from targets. Could *that* be why Mazda incurred lower production, scrap, rework, and warranty costs?[1]

That was precisely the reason. Imagine that in some Ford transmissions, many components near the *outer limits* of specified tolerances—that is, fine by the definitions of Zero Defects—were randomly assembled together. Then, many trivial deviations from the target tended to "stack up." An otherwise trivial variation in one part exacerbated a variation in another. Because of deviations, parts interacted with greater friction than they could withstand individually or with greater vibration than customers were prepared to endure.

Mazda managers worked consistently to bring parts in on target. Intuitively, they took a much more imaginative approach to on-line quality control than Ford managers did; they certainly grasped factory conformance in a way that superseded the pass/fail, in-spec/out-of-spec style of thinking associated with Zero Defects. Mazda managers worked on the assumption that robustness begins from meeting exact targets *consistently*—not from always staying within tolerances. They may not have realized this at the time, but they would have been even better off missing the target with perfect consistency than hitting it haphazardly—a point that is illuminated by this simple analogy:

Sam and John are at the range for target practice. After firing ten shots, they examine their targets. Sam has ten shots in a tight cluster just outside the bull's-eye circle. John, on the other hand, has five shots in the circle, but they are scattered all over it—as many near the perimeter as near dead center—and the rest of his shots are similarly dispersed around it (see Exhibit I).

Zero Defects theorists would say that John is the superior shooter because his performance betrays no failures. But who would you really rather hire on as a bodyguard?

Sam's shooting is consistent and virtually predictable. He probably knows why he missed the circle completely. An adjustment to his sights will give many perfect bull's-eyes during the next round. John has a much more difficult problem. To reduce the dispersion of his shots, he must expose virtually all the factors under his control and find a way to change them in some felicitous combination. He may decide to change the position of his arms, the tightness of his sling, or the sequence of his firing: breathe, aim, slack, and squeeze. He will have little confidence that he will get all his shots in the bull's-eye circle next time around.

When extrapolated to the factory, a Sam-like performance promises greater product robustness. Once consistency is established—no mean feat, the product of relentless attention to the details of design and

Exhibit I.

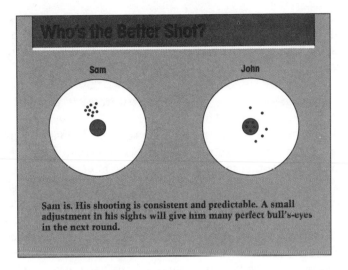

Who's the Better Shot?

Sam   John

Sam is. His shooting is consistent and predictable. A small adjustment in his sights will give him many perfect bull's-eyes in the next round.

process both—adjusting performance to target is a simple matter: stack-up can be entirely obviated. If every drive shaft is .005 centimeters out, operators can adjust the position of the cutting tool. In the absence of consistent performance, getting more nearly on target can be terribly time-consuming.

But there is another side to this. There is a much higher probability of catastrophic stack-up from random deviations than from deviations that show consistency. Assuming that no part is grossly defective, a product made from parts that are all off target in exactly the same way is more likely to be robust than a product made from parts whose deviations are in-spec but unpredictable. We have statistical proofs of this, but a moment's reflection should be enough. If all parts are made consistently, the product will perform in a uniform way for customers and will be more easily perfected in the next version. If all parts are made erratically, some products will be perfect, and some will fall apart.

So the case against Zero Defects begins with this: Robustness derives from consistency. Where deviation is consistent, adjustment to the target is possible; catastrophic stack-up is more likely from scattered deviation within specifications than from consistent deviation outside. This regard for consistency, for being on target, has a fascinating and practical application.

The Quality Loss Function

Analysis of Ford's *overall* losses as compared with Mazda's suggests that when companies deviate from targets, they run an increasingly costly risk of loss. Overall loss is quality loss plus factory loss. The more a manufacturer deviates from targets, the greater its losses.

From our experience, quality loss—the loss that comes after products are shipped—increases at a geometric rate. It can be roughly quantified as the Quality Loss Function (QLF), based on a simple quadratic formula. Loss increases by the square of deviation from the target value, $L=D^2C$, where the constant is determined by the cost of the countermeasure that the factory might use to get on target.

If you know what to do to get on target, then you know what this action costs per unit. If you balk at spending the money, then with every standard deviation from the target, you risk spending more and more. The greater the deviation from targets, the greater the compounded costs.

Let's say a car manufacturer chooses not to spend, say, $20 per transmission to get a gear exactly on target. QLF suggests that the manufacturer would wind up spending (when customers got mad) $80 for two standard deviations from the target ($20 multiplied by the square of two), $180 for three, $320 for four, and so forth.

This is a simple approximation, to be sure, not a law of nature. Actual field data cannot be expected to vindicate QLF precisely, and if your corporation has a more exacting way of tracking the costs of product failure, use it. But the tremendous value of QLF, apart from its bow to common sense, is that it translates the engineer's notion of deviation from targets into a simple cost estimate managers can use. QLF is especially helpful in the important early stages of new product development, when tolerances are set and quality targets are established.

Sony Televisions: Tokyo versus San Diego

The compelling logic of QLF is best illustrated by the performance of Sony televisions in the late 1970s. The case demonstrates how engineering data and economic data can (and should) be seen in tandem.

Sony product engineers had ascertained that customers preferred pictures with a particular color density, let's call it a nominal density of 10. As color density deviated from 10, viewers became increasingly dissatisfied, so Sony set specification limits at no less than 7 and no more than 13.

Sony manufactured TV sets in two cities, San Diego and Tokyo. Sets shipped from San Diego were uniformly distributed within specs, which meant that a customer was as likely to buy a set with a color density of 12.6 as one with a density of 9.2. At the same time, a San Diego set was as likely to be near the corporate specification limits of 13 or 7 as near the customer satisfaction target of 10. Meanwhile, shipments from Tokyo tended to cluster near the target of 10, though at that time, about 3 out of every 1,000 sets actually fell outside of corporate standards.

Akio Morita, the chairman of Sony, reflected on the discrepancy this way: "When we tell one of our Japanese employees that the measurement of a certain part must be within a tolerance of plus or minus five, for example, he will automatically strive to get that part as close to zero tolerance as possible. When we started our plant in the United States, we found that the workers would follow instructions perfectly. But if we said make it between plus or minus five, they would get it somewhere near plus or minus five all right, but rarely as close to zero as the Japanese workers did."

If Morita were to assign grades to the two factories' performances, he might say that Tokyo had many more As than San Diego, even if it did get a D now and then; 68% of Tokyo's production was in the A range, 28% in the B range, 4% in the C range, and 0.3% in the D range. Of course, San Diego made some out-of-spec sets; but it didn't ship its Fs. Tokyo shipped everything it built without bothering to check them. Should Morita have preferred Tokyo to San Diego?

The answer, remember, must be boiled down to dollars and cents, which is why the conventions of Zero Defects are of no use here. Suppose you bought a TV with a color density of 12.9, while your neighbor bought one with a density of 13.1. If you watch a program on his set, will you be able to detect any color difference between yours and his? Of course not. The color quality does not present a striking problem at the specification limit of 13. Things do not suddenly get more expensive for the San Diego plant if a set goes out at 13.1.

The losses start mounting when customers see sets at the target value of 10. Then, anything much away from 10 will seem unsatisfactory, and customers will demand visits from repairpeople or will demand replacement sets. Instead of spending a few dollars per set to adjust them close to targets, Sony would have to spend much more to make good on the sets—about two-thirds of the San Diego sets—

that were actually displeasing customers. (Dissatisfaction certainly increases more between 11.5 and 13 than between 10 and 11.5.)

What Sony discovered is that you gain virtually nothing in shipping a product that just barely satisfies the corporate standard over a product that just fails. San Diego shipped marginal sets "without defects," but their marginal quality proved costly.

Using QLF, Sony might have come up with even more striking figures. Say the company estimated that the cost of the countermeasure required to put every set right—an assembly line countermeasure that puts every set at a virtual 10—was $9. But for every San Diego set with a color density of 13 (three standard deviations from the target), Sony spent not $9 but $81. Total quality loss at San Diego should have been expected to be *three times* the total quality loss at the Tokyo factory.

Deviation: Signal to Noise

If Zero Defects doesn't work, what does? We have said that quality is mainly designed in, not controlled from without. In development work, engineers must discipline their decisions at virtually every step by comparing expected quality loss with known manufacturing cost. On the other hand, the reliability of QLF calculations is pretty obviously restricted by the accuracy of more preliminary measures. It is impossible to discern any loss function properly without first setting targets properly.

How *should* design engineers and manufacturing managers set targets? Let us proceed slowly, reconsidering what engineers do when they test components and subassemblies and how they establish what no particular part "wants to be" in the context of things that get in its way.

When Sony engineers designed their televisions, they assumed that discriminating customers would like a design that retained a good picture or "signal" far from the station, in a lightning storm, when the food processor was in use, and even when the power company was providing low voltage. Customers would be dismayed if the picture degraded every time they turned up the volume. They would reject a TV that developed snow and other annoying "noises" when afflicted by nasty operating conditions, which are themselves considered noises.

In our view, this metaphorical language—signal as compared with noise—can be used to speak of all products, not just televisions. The signal is what the product (or component or subassembly) is trying to deliver. Noises are the interferences that degrade signal, some of them coming from outside, some from complementary systems within the product. They are very much like the factors we spoke of as accounting for variations in product performance—environmental disturbances as well as disturbances engendered by the parts themselves.

And so it seems reasonable to define robustness as the virtue of a product with a high signal-to-noise ratio. Customers resent being told, "You were not expected to use our product in high humidity or in below-freezing temperatures." They want good performance under actual operating conditions—which are often less than perfect. We all assume that a product that performs better under adverse conditions will be that much more durable under normal conditions.

Signal-to-noise ratios are designed into products before the factory ramps up. The strength of a product's signal—hence, its robustness—is primarily the responsibility of the product designers. Good factories are faithful to the intention of the design. But mediocre designs will always result in mediocre products.

Choosing Targets: Orthogonal Arrays

How, then, do product designers maximize signal-to-noise ratios? World-class companies use a three-step decision-making process:

1. They define the specific objective, selecting or developing the most appropriate signal and estimating the concomitant noise.
2. They define feasible options for the critical design values, such as dimensions and electrical characteristics.
3. They select the option that provides the greatest robustness or the greatest signal-to-noise ratio.

This is easier said than done, of course, which is why so many companies in Japan, and now in the United States, have moved to some form of simultaneous engineering. To define and select the correct signals and targets is no mean feat and requires the expertise of all product specialists. Product design, manufacturing, field support, and marketing—all of these should be worked out concurrently by an interfunctional team.

Product designers who have developed a "feel" for the engineering of particular products should take the lead in such teams. They can get away with only a few, limited experiments, where new people would have to perform many more. Progressive companies make an effort to keep their product specialists working on new versions rather than bump them up to management positions. Their compensation schemes reward people for doing what they do best.

But the virtues of teamwork beg the larger question of how to develop an efficient experimental strategy that won't drain corporate resources as you work to bring prototypes up to customer satisfaction. Intuition is not really an answer. Neither is interfunctionality or a theory of organization. Product designers need a scientific way to get at robustness. They have depended too long on art.

The most practical way to go about setting signal-to-noise ratios builds on the work of Sir Ronald Fisher, a British statistician whose brilliant contributions to agriculture are not much studied today. Most important is his strategy for systematic experimentation, including the astonishingly sensible plan known as the "orthogonal array."

Consider the complexity of improving a car's steering. Customers want it to respond consistently. Most engineers know that steering responsiveness depends on many critical design parameters—spring stiffness, shock absorber stiffness, dimensions of the steering and suspension mechanisms, and so on—all of which might be optimized to achieve the greatest possible signal-to-noise ratio.

It makes sense, moreover, to compare the initial design value to both a larger and a smaller value. If spring stiffness currently has a nominal value of 7, engineers may want to try the steering at 9 and at 5. One car engineer we've worked with established that there are actually 13 design variables for steering. If engineers were to compare standard, low, and high values for each critical variable, they would have 1,594,323 design options.

Proceed with intuition? Over a million possible permutations highlight the challenge—that of a blind search for a needle in a haystack—and steering is only one subsystem of the car. In Japan, managers say that engineers "like to fish with one rod"; engineers are optimistic that "the next cast will bring in the big fish"—one more experiment and they'll hit the ideal design. Naturally, repeated failure leads to more casts. The new product, still not robust to customers' conditions, is eventually forced into the marketplace by the pressures of time, money, and diminishing market share.

To complete the optimization of robustness most quickly, the search strategy must derive the maximum amount of information from a few trials. We won't go through the algebra here, but the key is to develop a system of trials that allows product engineers to analyze the *average* effect of change in factor levels under different sets of experimental conditions.

And this is precisely the virtue of the orthogonal array. It balances the levels of performance demanded by customers against the many variables—or noises—affecting performance. An orthogonal array for 3 steering performance levels—low, medium, and high—can reduce the experimental possibilities to 27. Engineers might subject each of the 27 steering designs to some combination of noises, such as high/low tire pressure, rough/smooth road, high/low temperature. After all of the trials are completed, signal-to-noise values may be used to select the best levels for each design variable.

If, for example, the average value for the first nine trials on spring stiffness is 32.4, then that could characterize level one of spring stiffness. If the average value for the second group of trials is 26.7, and the average for the third group 28.9, then we would select level one as the best value for spring stiffness. This averaging process is repeated to find the best level for each of the 13 design variables.

The orthogonal array is actually a sophisticated "switching system" into which many different design variables and levels of change can be plugged. This system was conceived to let the relatively inexperienced designer extract the *average* effect of each factor on the experimental results, so he or she can reach reliable conclusions despite the large number of changing variables.

Of course, once a product's characteristics are established so that a designer can say with certainty that design values—that is, optimized signal-to-noise ratios—do not interact at all, then orthogonal arrays are superfluous. The designer can instead proceed to test each design variable more or less independently, without concern for creating noise in other parts or subassemblies.

System Verification Test: The Moment of Truth

After they've maximized signal-to-noise ratios and optimized design values, engineers build prototypes. The robustness of the complete product is now verified in the System Verification Test (SVT)—perhaps the most critical event during product development.

In the SVT, the first prototypes are compared with the current benchmark product. Engineers subject both the prototype and the benchmark to the same extreme conditions they may encounter in actual use. Engineers also measure the same critical signal-to-noise ratios for all contenders. It is very important for the new product to surpass the robustness of the benchmark product. If the ideal nominal voltage is 115 volts, we want televisions that will have a signal of 10 even when voltage slips to a noisy 100 or surges to an equally noisy 130. Any deviations from the perfect signal must be considered in terms of QLF, that is, as a serious financial risk.

The robust product, therefore, is the one that minimizes the average of the square of the deviation from the target—averaged over the different customer-use conditions. Suppose you wish to buy a power supply and learn that you can buy one with a standard deviation of one volt. Should you take it? If the mean value of output voltage is 1,000 volts, most people would think that, on average, an error of only one volt is very good. However, if the average output were 24 volts, then a standard deviation of one seems very large. We must always consider the ratio of the mean value divided by the standard deviation.

The SVT gives a very strong indication, long before production begins, of whether customers will perceive the new product as having world-class quality and performance. After the new design is verified to have superior robustness, engineers may proceed to solve routine problems, fully confident that the product will steadily increase customer loyalty.

Back to the Factory

The relationship of field to factory proves to be a subtle one—the converse of what one might expect. We know that if you control for variance in the factory, you reduce failure in the field. But as we said at the outset, a concerted effort to reduce product failure in the field will simultaneously reduce the number of defectives in the factory.

Strive to reduce variances in the components of the product and you will reduce variances in the production system as a whole. Any strengthening of a design—that is, any marked increase of a product's signal-to-noise ratio—will simultaneously reduce a factory's quality losses.

Why should this be so? For many reasons, most importantly the symmetries between design for robustness and design for manufacture. Think of how much more robust products have become since the introduction of molded plastics and solid-state circuitry. Instead of serving up many interconnected wires and tubes and switches—any one of which can fail—engineers can now imprint a million transistors on a virtually indestructible chip. Instead of joining many components together with screws and fasteners, we can now consolidate parts into subassemblies and mount them on molded frames that snap together.

All of these improvements greatly reduce opportunities for noise interfering with signal; they were developed to make products robust. Yet they also have made products infinitely more manufacturable. The principles of designing for robustness are often indistinguishable from the principles of designing for manufacture—reduce the number of parts, consolidate subsystems, integrate the electronics.

A robust product can tolerate greater variations in the production system. Please the customer and you will please the manufacturing manager. Prepare for variances in the field and you will pave the way for reducing variations on the shop floor. None of this means the manufacturing manager should stop trying to reduce process variations or to achieve the same variations with faster, cheaper processes. And there are obvious exceptions proving the rule—chip production, for example, where factory controls are ever more stringent—though it is hard to think of exceptions in products such as cars and consumer electronics.

The factory is a place where workers must try to meet, not deviate from, the nominal targets set for products. It is time to think of the factory as a product with targets of its own. Like a product, the factory may be said to give off an implicit signal—the consistent production of robust products—and to be subject to the disruptions of noise—variable temperatures, degraded machines, dust, and so forth. Using QLF, choices in the factory, like choices for the product, can be reduced to the cost of deviation from targets.

Consider, for instance, that a cylindrical grinder creates a cylindrical shape more consistently than a lathe. Product designers have argued for such dedicated machines; they want the greatest possible precision. Manufacturing engineers have traditionally favored the less precise lathe because it is more flexible and it reduces production cost. Should management favor the more precise cylindrical grinder? How do you compare each group's choice with respect to quality loss?

In the absence of QLF's calculation, the most common method for establishing manufacturing tolerances is to have a concurrence meeting. Design engineers sit on one side of the conference room, manufacturing engineers on the opposite side. The product design engineers start chanting "Tighter Tolerance, Tighter Tolerance, Tighter Tolerance," and the manufacturing engineers respond with "Looser Tolerance, Looser Tolerance, Looser Tolerance." Presumably, the factory would opt for a lathe if manufacturing chanted louder and longer. But why follow such an irrational process when product design people and manufacturing people *can* put a dollar value on quality precision?

Management should choose the precision level that minimizes the total cost, production cost plus quality loss—the basics of QLF. Managers can compare the costs of competing factory processes by adding the manufacturing cost and the average quality loss (from expected deviations) of each process. They gain economical precision by evaluating feasible alternative production processes, such as the lathe and cylindrical grinder. What would be the quality loss if the factory used the lathe? Are the savings worth the future losses?

Similar principles may be applied to larger systems. In what may be called "process parameter design," manufacturers can optimize production parameters—spindle speed, depth of cut, feed rate, pressure, temperature—according to an orthogonal array, much like the spring stiffness in a steering mechanism. Each row of the orthogonal array may define a different production trial. In each trial, engineers produce and measure several parts and then use the data to calculate the signal-to-noise ratio for that trial. In a final step, they establish the best value for each production parameter.

The result? A robust process—one that produces improved uniformity of parts and often enables managers to simultaneously speed up production and reduce cycle time.

How Much Intervention?

Finally, there is the question of how much to intervene *during* production.

Take the most common kind of intervention, on-line checking and adjusting of machinery and process. In the absence of any operator monitoring, parts tend to deviate progressively from the target. Without guidance, different operators have widely varying notions of (1) how often they should check their machines and (2) how big the discrepancy must be before they adjust the process to bring the part value back near the target.

By applying QLF, you can standardize intervention. The cost of checking and adjusting has always been easy to determine; you simply have to figure the cost of downtime. With QLF, managers can also figure the cost of *not* intervening, that is, the dollar value to the company of reduced parts variation.

Let's go back to drive shafts. The checking interval is three, and the best adjustment target is 1/1,000th of an inch. If the measured discrepancy from the target is less than 1/1,000th of an inch, production continues. If the measured discrepancy exceeds this, the process is adjusted back to the target. Does this really enable operators to keep the products near the target in a way that minimizes total cost?

It might be argued that measuring every third shaft is too expensive. Why not every tenth? There is a way to figure this out. Say the cost of intervention is 30 cents, and shafts almost certainly deviate from the target value every fifth or sixth operation. Then, out of every ten produced, at least four bad shafts will go out, and quality losses will mount. If the seventh shaft comes out at two standard deviations, the cost will be $1.20; if the tenth comes out at three standard deviations, the cost will be $2.70; and so on. Perhaps the best interval to check is every fourth shaft or every fifth, not every third. If the fourth shaft is only one standard deviation from the target value, intervention is probably not worth the cost.

The point, again, is that these things can and should be calculated. There isn't any reason to be fanatical about quality if you *cannot* justify your fanaticism by QLF. Near the target, production should continue without adjustment; the quality loss is small. Outside the limit, the process should be adjusted before production continues.

This basic approach to intervention can also be applied to preventive maintenance. Excessive preventive maintenance costs too much. Inadequate preventive maintenance will increase quality loss excessively. Optimized preventive maintenance will minimize total cost.

In Japan, it is said that a manager who trades away quality to save a little manufacturing expense is "worse than a thief"—a little harsh, perhaps, but plausible. When a thief steals $200 from your company, there is no net loss in wealth between the two of you, just an exchange of assets. Decisions that create huge quality losses throw away social productivity, the wealth of society.

QLF's disciplined, quantitative approach to quality builds on and enhances employee involvement activities to improve quality and productivity. Certainly, factory-focused improvement activities do not by and large increase the robustness of a product. They can help realize it, however, by reducing the noise generated by the complex interaction of shop-floor quality factors—operators, operating methods, equipment, and material.

Employees committed to hitting the bull's-eye consistently cast a sharper eye on every feature of the factory environment. When their ingenuity and cost-consciousness are engaged, conditions change dramatically, teams prosper, and valuable data proliferate to support better product and process design. An early, companywide emphasis on robust product design can even reduce development time and smooth the transition to full-scale production.

Too often managers think that quality is the responsibility of only a few quality control people off in a factory corner. It should be evident by now that quality is for everyone, most of all the business's strategists. It is only through the efforts of every employee, from the CEO on down, that quality will become second nature. The most elusive edge in the new global competition is the galvanizing pride of excellence.

Note

1. See Lance A. Ealey's admirable account of this case in *Quality by Design: Taguchi Methods® and U.S. Industry* (Dearborn, Mich.: ASI Press, 1988), pp. 61–62.

4

Made in U.S.A.: A Renaissance in Quality

Joseph M. Juran

Let me clear up for good one bit of chauvinist nonsense.

In the minds of some journalists and industrialists, Japan's world leadership in product quality is the result of the lectures given four decades ago by two Americans—W. Edwards Deming and Joseph M. Juran. Had Deming and I not given those lectures, these people insist, Japanese goods would still be of stone-age quality.

In my view, there is not a shred of truth in such assertions. Had Deming and I stayed home, the Japanese would have achieved world quality leadership all the same. We did provide a jump start, without which the Japanese would have been put to more work and the job might have taken longer, but they would still be ahead of the United States in the quality revolution.

Let me explain what I think actually happened in Japan following World War II, what we now know about the subject of quality that we didn't know then, and why I think the United States is finally, four decades later, on the brink of its own quality revolution.

It surprises many people that Japanese companies wanted to listen to quality experts after World War II, but, in fact, the Japanese were no strangers to the concept of quality in manufacturing despite the poor quality of their exports. It was just that Japanese priorities before the war were far different from ours in the West.

At the outbreak of World War II, there were three levels of quality in Japan. At the low end, prewar consumer exports were wretched.

Author's note: The author wishes to acknowledge the contribution of Dr. A. Blanton Godfrey, chairman and CEO of Juran Institute, Inc.

As the only Japanese products to which most Westerners had access, however, they became the basis for Japan's reputation as a producer of shoddy goods. Around the world, *Made in Japan* had come to mean poor quality or worse.

The reason was that instead of putting their efforts into consumer-export goods, for years the Japanese had harnessed most of their capital and their best managers, engineers, and materials to the country's imperial ambitions. As a result, military hardware, the second level of Japanese quality, was quite competitive with that of the Western powers. In fact, Japanese torpedoes were superior to ours, and Japan's Zero Fighter shot down a lot of U.S. planes in the early stages of the war.

At the top of the quality pyramid was the ancient Japanese tradition of fine craftsmanship in handmade goods. When Dutch and Portuguese explorers reached the Japanese islands on their sixteenth-century voyages of discovery, they found that certain Japanese craft products—including swords, paper, lacquerware, copper, and woodblock prints—were superior to anything known in Europe.

Even before the war, in other words, the Japanese had achieved competitive and even superior quality in certain areas. But they had never tried to achieve it in the large-scale manufacture of consumer products. The result was that quality, or rather its absence, was the highest postwar hurdle faced by Japanese companies in their attempt to sell goods on the world market. But the shock of losing the war had opened their minds to the need for change, so they were willing to listen to Western experts. They also researched Western literature on quality. In fact, that's how they stumbled onto me. In 1951, I had published the first edition of my *Quality Control Handbook*, and, shortly thereafter, it appeared in translation in Japan. The Japanese decided that the person who wrote it was someone they should hear more from.

In 1954, I accepted an invitation from the Japanese Federation of Economic Organizations (the Keidanren) and the Japanese Union of Scientists and Engineers to come to Japan and speak. I gave the Japanese no secrets. What I told them was what I had been telling audiences in the United States for years. The difference was not what I said but whose ears heard it.

No one was more surprised than I when the people who attended my first two-day lectures in Japan turned out to be CEOs—70 at each session, 140 in all—from the largest manufacturing companies in the country. After those sessions, two additional groups, each consisting of 150 senior Japanese managers, spent two weeks with me. When I gave such lectures in the United States, the audiences consisted of engineers and quality control managers. Never before my 1954 trip to Japan, and never since, has the industrial leadership of a major power given me so much of its attention. Once in the United States, just a few months ago, I faced an audience of 70 leading CEOs, but that was for one hour.

What did I tell the Japanese? Two things. First, I described the state of the art of quality management as it stood in 1954. It wasn't very sophisticated by today's standards. As a matter of fact, in some of my recent research into the history of quality, I've been surprised to see how many earlier civilizations had reached roughly the same conclusions we had reached four decades ago. What we knew about managing for quality then, and what I covered with the Japanese, was how to manufacture products to design specifications and then how to inspect them for defects so that as few flawed products as possible would find their way into buyers' hands. The Egyptians did as much 5,000 years ago when they employed inspectors to check the work of the masons who dressed stones for the pharaohs' pyramids. The ancient Chinese set up a separate department of the central government to establish quality standards and maintain them.

But the Japanese didn't have to buy me a plane ticket to learn about quality inspections. That was in the book. They did get their money's worth with the second idea I passed onto them, however. The idea was something that I had been working on since 1924, when I began my first job as an engineer at Western Electric, the manufacturing arm of the Bell System.

Back then I was a bright youngster and a pretty good chess player, and I thought I could match strides with anyone in analyzing problems. One early problem I was asked to analyze concerned a tiny circuit breaker that Western Electric made by the million. The inspectors regularly scrapped about 15% of these circuit breakers because they didn't meet the specification for electrical resistance. The local production supervisor and I worked together to eliminate this waste.

One critical component of the circuit breaker was a wire-wound coil. I measured up many reels of the supply wire and found that the electrical resistance was very uniform within any given reel but that the variation from one reel to another was considerable. We got rid of that variable by measuring out from each reel a length of wire equal in resistance to the mean of the specification limits and then cutting up the entire reel into pieces of that same length. Now, despite reel-to-reel variation, all lengths of wire were uniform in resistance. To my surprise, the result was only a slight drop in the defect rate. We were still scrapping more than 10% of the product because it failed to meet the resistance specification.

My next step was to measure and plot the resistance of the finished circuit breakers. I found that though they were quite uniform, the average resistance was not at the mean of the specification but was shifted toward the minimum. A closer look at the manufacturing process located the difficulty. The workers were soldering the wire to the units at a point about two inches from the end of the wire and then cutting off the excess. All we had to do was provide two more inches to the specified length of each piece of wire before it was cut. When we were done, a defect-prone process had become virtually defect-free.

I was fascinated by the experience. We had analyzed the manufacturing process to find the sources of our problems and then fixed them, which had the effect of increasing our production of these little circuit breakers by approximately 15% without extra machines, extra people, or extra material. In other words, by improving the production process, we had not only improved the quality of the circuit breakers, we had also lowered the cost of producing them. I went to my boss and said, "I know that problems like this exist throughout the plant. Why don't we search them out and fix every one of them?"

He agreed with me that this would be a wonderful thing to do, but he said that process improvement wasn't our job. "We're the inspection department," I remember him saying, "and our job is to look at these things after they're made and find the bad ones. Making them right in the first place is the job of the production department. They don't want us telling them how to do their job, just as we don't want them telling us how to do ours." And that's where it ended. So the opportunity to build a means of continually improving quality into the production structure ran into the kind of organizational barrier that I would encounter again and again in U.S. industry: production was the job of one unit, quality of another unit, and no one was in charge of process improvement.

I talked to the Japanese about these organizational barriers to quality management, and I suggested that they try to find ways to institutionalize programs within their companies that would yield continuous quality improvement. That is exactly what they did. Around those programs, the Japanese built a quality revolution.

I don't use the word revolution carelessly. The Japanese understood what I was getting at with my suggestion that quality could mean more than just inspecting for defective products and manufacturing to specification. They pursued a larger role for quality—a strategic role—and soon I, the expert, was learning from my students. To launch their quality revolution, here's what the Japanese did:

> The senior executives of Japanese companies took personal charge of managing for quality.
>
> The executives trained their entire managerial hierarchies in how to manage for quality. (The seed courses for this training were the lectures I gave in 1954.)
>
> Japanese companies went into quality improvement at a revolutionary pace and maintained that pace year after year.
>
> The companies trained their engineers to use statistical methods for quality control. (The seed courses for this training were Deming's 1950 lectures.)
>
> The companies provided their work forces with the means to participate in quality improvement. The method that they came up with was a Japanese invention: the Quality Control Circle.
>
> The companies enlarged their business plans to include quality goals. This concept is more recent in origin, but it has been growing, and the trend seems irreversible.

Each of these actions was unprecedented in industrial history. Together, they added up to a massive change in direction, one that refutes the chauvinistic notion that two Americans were somehow solely responsible for the quality revolution in Japan.

On the contrary, the unsung heroes of the Japanese quality revolution were the Japanese managers.

By 1966, 12 years after my first visit to Japan, the quality of Japanese products still hadn't risen to U.S. or European levels. However, the annual rate of quality improvement in Japan already exceeded the rate in the West. Witnessing this change, I sounded a warning at a European conference held in Stockholm that year. "The Japanese," I said, "are headed for world quality leadership and will attain it in the next two decades because no one else is moving there at the same pace."

The warning went unheeded. To the West, it was simply inconceivable, even laughable, that Japan of all countries could become the world's quality leader. This was the country that had sold us toys that fell apart on Christmas morning and light bulbs that burned out when they were first screwed into their sockets.

Yet understanding why a quality revolution took place in Japan still doesn't explain why a similar quality revolution did *not* take place in the United States. Many of our company managers and engineers listened to similar lectures. The difference was not a result of quality secrets given only to the Japanese. Our companies could have taken every step the Japanese companies took. They failed to take those steps because they saw no reason to do so.

During the 1950s, U.S. products were generally competitive with European and superior to Japanese products. The Europeans, and especially the Japanese, held an advantage in price because of their lower labor costs. U.S. manufacturers responded to this price competition. Whenever possible, they lowered their own labor costs by shifting production to low labor-cost areas like Mexico, Puerto Rico, or the Far East. They also turned to Washington for help, asking for tariffs, quotas, and laws against dumping. They appealed to consumers' patriotism, urging them to "Buy American." In these and other ways, U.S. companies tried to compete with the Japanese on price. Meanwhile, the rise in Japanese quality caught them completely off-guard.

U.S. companies were ambushed for two reasons. The first had to do with their cultural bias. The American mind-set saw the Japanese as copyists rather than innovators. Japan might compete on price but never on quality.

The other reason U.S. companies failed to see superior Japanese quality coming was that they lacked the proper instruments on their corporate dashboards. The indicators they were watching didn't measure quality. The Japanese indicators did.

During the postwar decades, Japanese practice diverged from that of the West. In their anxiety to change their quality reputation, Japanese companies evolved means of measuring customer satisfaction, competitive quality, performance of major processes (such as cycle time for product development), and more. These measures found a place on the corporate instrument panel and contributed to CEO decision making. In some Japanese companies, the annual quality audit is called the president's audit because the company president personally presides over the presentation meeting.

In contrast, U.S. corporate dashboards did not evolve measures of quality. U.S. companies, widely perceived as being among the world's quality leaders, were not anxious to tamper with their quality reputation. In fact, American CEOs had long been detached from the quality function, which had become the responsibility of designated quality managers. CEOs focused instead on financial reports, and their decisions reflected that focus. Xerox Corporation is probably the best example of how a financially powerful company allowed itself to be taken completely by surprise.

In the 1950s and 1960s, Xerox had a lock on a key industrial process: copying documents. The Xerox process outperformed every other method: scribes, carbon paper, ditto ink, mimeograph. Everybody wanted Xerox copies, and nobody could get them except by leasing a Xerox machine. The company was growing, and Xerox executives could look at their instruments and see sales, costs, and profits at a glance. But they had no meter showing customer satisfaction. If they had, it would have set off a vital alarm.

The Xerox machines malfunctioned or broke down regularly, and Xerox executives knew it. They could have sent their designers back to the drawing board to redesign the machines so they wouldn't fail. Instead, they created a field-service force they could dispatch to restore service. As far as Xerox executives were concerned, that solved the problem. In fact, their financial instruments told them that the service department actually earned a profit, which only served as further evidence that they had made the right decision.

Xerox's customers didn't agree. They didn't want repairs; they wanted machines that didn't break down in the first place, because while they were waiting for the service technician, they couldn't get out their reports. But Xerox customers had no alternative. They could make copies by the Xerox process only by leasing Xerox machines. Moreover, some customers leased extra machines to give them backup, and according to Xerox's financial readouts, that made the company's service decision look even smarter.

This situation set the stage for the entry of competition, and the Japanese rushed in. They skirted the patents. They developed machines that didn't break down so often. Their copies were better, and their cost per copy was lower. The effect on market share became so devastating that Xerox's very survival came into question.

I was drawn into the Xerox picture when sales began to hemorrhage. The entire senior staff cleared a day to discuss quality with me. As I conferred with engineers and managers, it soon emerged that while facts on quality were abundant, some essential summaries were not reaching the decision makers.

One such summary concerned the specific failure-prone features of the copy machines. For each service call, the service department logged the *failure mode*, or outward symptom, of the problem. To show the frequency of each failure mode, engineers summarized these data in tables much like those that show the frequency of different human maladies.

When I singled out one popular Xerox copier and asked for a list of public enemies one to ten, it was promptly provided. The enemy lists for predecessor models were also readily available. However, when I then placed these lists side by side, lo and behold, they were identical! In other words, features that had been clearly identified as likely to fail had nevertheless consistently been carried over into the new machines, model after model, like genetic disorders.

Xerox had no lack of design engineers who might have corrected these problems, but it was largely product managers who decided what the design engineers should spend their time working on. Since the chief mission of product managers was to sell more copiers, they prodded the designers to come up with new product features that would translate into increasing new sales. The continuing cancer of failure-prone features—a prime cause of the hemorrhage in sales to Xerox's old customers—had a lower priority despite the threat it posed to the very survival of the company.

I concluded that this disparity in priorities was directly traceable to the content of the information package available to Xerox's senior managers. Summarized data on sales and sales growth were displayed on senior managers' instrument panels, and the managerial reward system gave generous weight to sales volume. In contrast, the senior management dashboard lacked summarized information on field failures, their effect on customer relations, the performance of competing machines, the growing cancer of failure-prone features, and the extent of customer defections.

The Xerox scenario has become a familiar one in the United States. We have seen industry after industry fall victim to Japanese ambush. In the 1950s, there were about 30 American-owned companies making color televisions in the United States. By the 1980s, we were down to one.

The most publicized example took place in the auto industry. Japanese cars were of such poor quality in the 1950s that they were virtually unsalable in the United States. By contrast, consumers held U.S. cars in relatively high regard. In addition, U.S. quality kept improving, though at a pedestrian pace.

But then the Japanese automakers adopted the concept of quality improvement, applied it at an unprecedented rate, and kept at it year after year. In 1975, by my estimate, after more than two decades of work, the Japanese caught up with and surpassed U.S. automakers in product quality. (See Exhibit I.) U.S. automakers didn't know it in 1975, but the Japanese had already left them in the dust. And what was true in the automobile industry was true in many other industries as well.

I had a revealing glimpse into Western automakers' perceptions of Japanese quality while I was preparing the third edition of my *Quality*

Exhibit I.

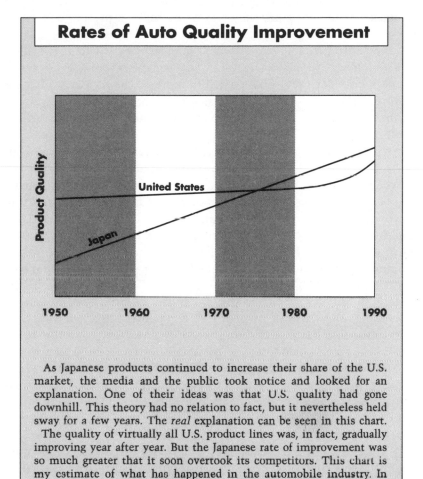

Rates of Auto Quality Improvement

As Japanese products continued to increase their share of the U.S. market, the media and the public took notice and looked for an explanation. One of their ideas was that U.S. quality had gone downhill. This theory had no relation to fact, but it nevertheless held sway for a few years. The *real* explanation can be seen in this chart.

The quality of virtually all U.S. product lines was, in fact, gradually improving year after year. But the Japanese rate of improvement was so much greater that it soon overtook its competitors. This chart is my estimate of what has happened in the automobile industry. In some industries, the lines crossed much earlier. In other industries, the lines have not yet crossed.

Control Handbook. I had approached Shoichiro Toyoda, then senior managing director and later CEO of Toyota Motor Company, asking if he would be willing to write a chapter on quality in the automobile industry. He graciously agreed, but he asked that before publication I get a critique of his manuscript from Western experts on auto quality.

I honored his request by securing commentaries from managers at

Chrysler, Volvo, FIAT, Ford, and Leyland-Authi. The Western managers were interested but skeptical. One of them wrote, "If they really do what he says they do, they should be making pretty good cars." The year was 1972.

It was during the 1970s that U.S. managers began to revise their views of Japanese quality. In fact, they began traveling to Japan to discover how Japanese quality had become so good. Many of these visitors expressed astonishment on seeing the facilities because, as some of them put it, "The Japanese use the same equipment, the same input materials, the same manufacturing processes that we use!"

What the visitors failed to see were differences of a less obvious sort. The Japanese had thrown overboard the old idea of using inspection to weed out defects and had adopted new quality concepts instead. They focused on customer needs rather than on mere conformity to specifications. They put senior managers in charge of quality. They implemented a revolutionary rate of quality improvement. To give top priority to quality, they virtually redesigned their companies. To lock in annual quality improvement, they broke down organizational barriers of the kind that had frustrated me at Western Electric in the mid-1920s and that persist to this day in too many U.S. companies.

As the quality crisis deepened, U.S. companies launched initiatives to improve *their* quality. Of hundreds of such initiatives in the 1970s and 1980s, most failed. Most of these failures could be traced to the ignorance of otherwise intelligent senior managers about quality. For decades, these managers had delegated quality to a quality department. Disengaged from the quality function, they never acquired the training and experience needed to set appropriate quality goals and develop a plan of action for achieving them.

Worse yet, CEOs tried to delegate the entire responsibility for their quality action plans to middle managers. They thought they could make the right speeches, establish broad goals, and leave everything else to subordinates. American CEOs didn't understand that quality was no longer one problem among many; it was now *the* problem. They didn't realize that fixing quality meant fixing whole companies, a task that can't be delegated.

The effort to delegate action on quality was a fatal error. The 1970s and 1980s slipped by, matters grew worse, and all we gained from these widespread failures were lessons learned about what does not work.

During the 1970s and 1980s, I was dismayed at the spectacle of so many U.S. companies flailing away in vain, attempting to reach quality leadership through strategies that were doomed to failure. But from around 1990, I began to grow more optimistic.

The good news, after all, is that some U.S. companies did attain world-class quality during the 1980s. There were no more than perhaps 50 of these quality successes—a tiny part of the U.S. economy—but they nevertheless demonstrated that it could be done.

In the course of the 1980s, some people expressed the view that the United States was doomed to remain at second-class quality levels. Western culture, they said, is less well-suited than Japanese culture to the disciplines of quality improvement. But our most successful companies have demolished that contention. Motorola is one example; it has become a leading seller of communications equipment in Japan. Xerox is another. It has come from behind to recapture much of the market share it had lost.

Our need is not to redesign our culture. Our need is to intensify what these companies have shown us we can do.

Some mighty forces now drive this scaling up of effort. The most powerful is an intense new global competition in quality. This competition has produced a major shift in world economic priorities. While the twentieth century has been the Century of Productivity, the twenty-first century will be the Century of Quality.

Another powerful driver is Japan's success. They were the early winners in this new competition; their reward has been promotion to the status of economic superpower.

In the United States, an added driver is the Malcolm Baldrige National Quality Award. Less than five years old, this award has already greatly raised the visibility of quality as an essential discipline. The National Institute of Standards and Technology (NIST) administers the award. It also publicizes winners' quality results and methods. NIST receives about 200,000 requests annually for the application forms, but fewer than 200 companies actually apply. Companies use the great majority of those forms to conduct self-audits and learn where they stand with respect to the Baldrige criteria. For example, AT&T now conducts annual internal quality audits based on the Baldrige criteria.

And there are other drivers. Companies that have attained world-class quality have begun requiring their suppliers to move toward world-class quality as well. In this way, quality criteria spread gradually within the entire supplier chain. The forces driving quality extend even to academia. At least one major company has told its chief sources of college graduates, "In the future, we will send our recruiters to only those schools that are willing to embark on Total Quality Management."

The new impetus for quality will be limited only by the pace at which our CEOs accept responsibility for their *nondelegable* roles. There are seven steps that a responsible CEO must take to achieve quality in any organization. They are strikingly similar to the steps that CEOs already routinely take in managing for financial results. To lead a revolution in managing for quality, every CEO must:

> Set up and serve on the company's quality council, the quality equivalent of the finance committee.
>
> Establish corporate quality goals, including quality improvement goals, and make them a part of the business plan.
>
> Make provision for training the entire company hierarchy in managing for quality.
>
> Establish the means to measure quality results against quality goals.
>
> Review results against goals on a regular basis.
>
> Give recognition for superior quality performance.
>
> Revise the reward system to respond to the changes demanded by world-class quality.

In the spring of 1993, I addressed a meeting of the Business Roundtable in Washington, D.C.

On this occasion, the Roundtable had convened 70 CEOs for a day devoted to the subject of quality, the first time in its history that the Roundtable had set aside an entire day for that subject. The agenda included several speakers in addition to reports on research projects that the Roundtable had commissioned. It also included focus groups on various quality topics. It showed every sign of being a watershed event in the history of the quality movement in the United States, which was certainly the hope of the members who had organized it. I had been invited to give the opening address.

For me, it was also a first. I have met with many American CEOs while consulting for their companies, but this was the first time that I had ever addressed so many of them en masse.

My mind went back to the training courses I gave four decades ago to those hundreds of Japanese executives who spent so much time with me on my first visit to Japan. One of the sponsors of those training courses was the Keidanren. Like the Business Roundtable, the Keidanren is among the most influential organizations in its country, and its membership includes the CEOs of a number of major companies.

As I spoke, I couldn't help wondering whether the Americans would follow up on their first quality conference as effectively as the Japanese have over the last 40 years.

The critical variable in Japanese quality leadership is the extent of active participation by senior managers. The same will be true in the United States. We were once among the world's quality leaders and then lost that leadership primarily because our senior managers were isolated from the quality function. We will regain that leadership, rung by rung, when our senior managers carry out the quality-management roles that they cannot afford to delegate. Only then can *Made in U.S.A.* become a symbol once again of world-class quality.

5
Getting Control of Just-in-Time

Uday Karmarkar

Like all good revolutions, just-in-time manufacturing is producing revolutionaries who don't know when to stop. It is also producing overreactions from people determined to make them stop. Consider the curiously vexed debate about how to get materials to, and work in process through, the shop floor.

Pick up virtually any manufacturing magazine these days and there will be some articles and pages of advertisements by consultants extolling the virtues of JIT over such computer-driven control systems as materials requirements planning (MRP) or materials resource planning (MRP II)—as if JIT principles were opposed to MRP and to the use of computers. One recent ad put the choice this starkly: "JIT vs. MRP II—JIT is the key to your survival!"

MRP, proponents of JIT explain, is merely a "push" technique. An MRP II program promises manufacturing managers more precision than it can deliver, requires unnecessary information, and demands more formal discipline than the shop floor needs. In contrast, JIT people seem especially drawn to such computerless, "pull" techniques as kanban, the system used extensively in Japan's auto and electronics industries. For JIT, presumably, human pull is good, computer push is bad.

What must be particularly confusing to manufacturing managers who get wind of this debate is that kanban systems are used most successfully by the same Japanese and American corporations that are famous for spearheading the use of advanced computer automation—Toyota or Hewlett-Packard, for example. In crucial respects, MRP II aims to be a JIT system, while kanban cannot. Worst of all, doesn't kanban look suspiciously like the old order point, order quantity (OP, OQ) system that MRP once discredited and replaced?

This debate needs clarity, and then it needs to end. The idealized conception of the shop floor one gets from some extreme JIT advocates—a line, inherently flexible, inventoryless, even computerless, replenished by infinitely responsive suppliers—may actually prevent manufacturing managers from using the tools they need to run their operations. JIT principles should certainly not preempt the use of MRP II. Indeed, most advanced manufacturing companies find that they require a hybrid system of shop floor control systems—tailored systems, including innovative pull systems like kanban, as well as time-tested, computer-driven push systems like MRP II. (See Exhibit I.)

At the same time, shop floor managers should know just when MRP II is an unnecessary burden and when kanban can't work—when push comes to shove and pull comes to tug. All managers can learn interesting strategic lessons from their choices. The question of how to manage inventory cuts quickly to the basics of manufacturing in an age of intense global competition: How much automation is enough? How should the factory respond to customers? How much can you load on workers? How do you deal with orders? What is waste? The shop floor is still a microcosm of the whole business.

Pulling and Pushing at JIT

The basic difference between pull and push is that a pull system initiates production as a reaction to present demand, while push initiates production in anticipation of future demand. Thus a fast food restaurant like McDonald's runs on a pull system, while a catering service operates a push system.

At McDonald's, the customer orders a hamburger, the server gets one from the rack, the hamburger maker keeps an eye on the rack and makes new burgers when the number gets too low. The manager orders more ground beef when the maker's inventory gets too low. In effect, the customer's purchase triggers the pull of materials through the system; the customer initiates a chain of demand.

In a push system, the caterer estimates how many steaks or lobsters are likely to be ordered in any given week. He reckons roughly how long it takes to broil a steak or serve a party of four; he figures out how many meals he can accommodate and commits to buying what he needs in advance. He can account for the special event that he knows is scheduled to take place in midweek. In other words, the caterer gets a picture of production in his mind and pushes materials to where he expects them to be needed.

What Is JIT Anyway? When you drop everything to take care of a walk-in client, you are reacting, implicitly, to a pull system. When you plan for a meeting, you are in the push mode. What does either method have to do with JIT?

Nothing directly. Think of JIT as a statement of objectives. It underscores the importance of lead-time management in all aspects of manufacturing. It asserts that incremental reductions in lead times are crucial indices of manufacturing improvement. JIT presumes that to achieve such reductions the system should deliver to every operator, in any conversion process, whatever he or she needs just when it is needed. It saves the money tied up in downstream inventories, protecting against long lead times. Shorter lead times mean improved responsiveness and flexibility.

JIT promises to preempt the delays and confusion associated with the stack-up of materials. Correspondingly, it saves the money that would otherwise go into indirect labor for storing and moving work-in-process (WIP) inventory and storing and handling buffer stock.

An analogy to commuter traffic may be useful. Say a thousand cars have to get through the Lincoln Tunnel every ten minutes. Wouldn't it be ideal for the economy (and sanity) of New Yorkers if each driver left home at precisely the right time to fall into the line at the entrance, so each car entered, one after another, like cars in a train? Would New Yorkers need six-lane divided highways leading to the tunnel if they could enforce this JIT ideal?

To be sure, there are a number of established materials control techniques—pull techniques—associated with JIT, particularly as Japanese companies have realized it. There are synchronized deliveries from proximate suppliers, who can also deliver more or less as production needs fluctuate. There are floor layouts and kanban systems in which materials are constrained to flow consecutively along predictable paths and at a pace determined, in effect, by the last operator in the chain.

These pull techniques, excellent as they are, should not, however, be confused with JIT's governing principles. JIT aims to manage lead times and eliminate waste. There is nothing inherent in push systems that makes them incompatible with JIT. On the contrary. The goal is to get drivers to leave home at just the right time to take their places

Exhibit 1.

Tailored Production Controls

	Materials Planning	Control Stage Order Release	Shop Floor
Pull: Continuous Flow	1 JIT	2 Rate Based	3 JIT-Pull
Hybrid Push-Pull: Batch, Repetitive	4 JIT-MRP	5 Pull or MRP	6 Pull
Hybrid Push-Pull: Batch, Dynamic	7 MRP	8 MRP	9 Pull or Order Scheduling
Push: Custom Engineering	10 MRP	11 Order Scheduling	12 Operation Scheduling

Low ◀——— Lead-Time Variability ———▶ High

Exhibit I. (continued)

Continuous Flow: The production process is dedicated to one or a few similar products. Production is continuous and level so that the lead time for production is uniform and predictable. Some examples are assembly lines, transfer lines, and dedicated-flow lines.

1. Since production rates are uniform and predictable, material can be delivered to the process in a JIT manner.

2. Work orders are not required since production is level. A blanket order specifying a "going rate" is adequate. Occasionally, if the production mix is changed, the rates may be changed, but these changes are infrequent.

3. The predictability of the process and the production rate make it possible to design for smooth JIT materials flow on the shop floor. If there are points at which small inventories are accumulated for quality control or accounting purposes, they can be replenished in a pull manner.

Batch, Repetitive: Parts of the process may resemble a continuous-flow system while others involve multiple products produced in batches. Lead times are fairly constant and predictable. The product mix is relatively constant but may have variations from month to month. Typical is production of parts and components for a high-volume end product – such as cars or electronics.

4. Some parts and materials that are used uniformly can be delivered in a JIT manner. In other cases, with long lead time items, MRP is required to plan purchasing, delivery, and coordination between plants.

5. Since lead times are predictable, MRP works well but so do pull methods – and they are cheaper. MRP may be required for master scheduling when work orders are generated; inventory must be managed, and work centers must coordinate.

6. Work on the shop floor flows relatively smoothly, and pull systems can be used to move work on the shop floor. If MRP systems are used, the trick is to coordinate pull on the floor with MRP work orders. One simplifying device is to combine several levels of the bill of materials into fewer levels so that the points of coordination with MRP are minimized. Tandem hybrid systems work well.

Exhibit I. (continued)

Batch, Dynamic: Production is in batches, and the output mix and volume can vary; many customers come in with their orders on a weekly and monthly basis. The load on the facility changes; bottlenecks can shift, with backlogs appearing here and there; lead times become variable. Examples are parts and product manufacturers supplying several customers, factories supplying retail outlets with multiple parts, and medium- and low-volume plants.

7. As production mix and volumes change, many different materials and parts are required; departments must coordinate production. MRP becomes essential to match purchasing with production and coordinate parts fabrication and assembly. Production volumes can be smaller than lots likely to be purchased. Inventories build up and must be tracked.

8. Output varies too much for pull systems to work well. Look ahead, and build what will be needed. Even if MRP's timing isn't perfect, it does all the bookkeeping on quantities, inventory availability, and requirements, net of inventories.

9. At the shop floor level, work orders must be tracked. In some early common operations such as metal pressing, blanking, or molding, volumes may be high enough and level enough to use a pull system. Work orders, generating a master schedule, tie together purchasing, parts, subassemblies, assemblies, and customer orders. All are "pegged" and tracked with the MRP system.

Custom Engineering: With low-volume, complex engineered products or with custom manufacturing, there is no regularity in production patterns. The load on the facility can vary widely; what took two weeks when ordered in January might take four months in June. Queues and congestion are a major concern, and lead-time management requires a high level of analysis and detail. Examples of such facilities are machine tool manufacturers, custom-equipment builders, and products with a high option and custom content.

10. There is no regularity in materials usage; some materials may be ordered only after a customer order is received. MRP is invaluable as an information management tool. It books orders, maintains bills, whether custom or standard, and coordinates customer orders, shop orders, and purchasing orders.

11. The factory runs on work orders generated by MRP. But MRP's poor understanding of lead times and capacity limits means that the order releases are of little use for good time and delivery performance. MRP still plays a role, however, in maintaining information about materials and inventory availability and coordination between departments.

12. Scheduling systems (OPT, CLASS, MIMI) that can handle the complexity of detailed operational scheduling are only just appearing. They are too complex and costly for smaller shops.

at the tunnel entrance. JIT advocates shouldn't care whether the signal to leave comes as a computerized call or as a wave from the next-door neighbor.

The Limits of Pull. There is no denying that pull systems are very effective in disciplining production to meet demand just-in-time and, in certain environments, are more effective than push systems. But are pull systems inherently JIT? No pull system, in fact, can constrain workers consciously to produce just-in-time for some future event—because pull systems do not recognize future events. The inventory level triggers production; the pull system aims to fill up depleted inventory—whether it's Big Macs or machined parts.

Pull systems are fine if your McDonald's franchise is downtown with a steady daily stream of customers. But if you're next to a football stadium, how can a pull system alone prepare you for the day of a game? Similarly, it's easy to see how implausible a pull system would be in solving the Lincoln Tunnel's JIT problem. Wouldn't it be more sensible to stagger the cars according to some kind of push system—say, "blue cars leave at 7:45"—than to expect all commuters acting individually to leave for work in perfect synchrony?

There is a paradox here. JIT advocates admire pull systems and look askance at computer-governed push systems like MRP. Yet the latter inherently aims to be a JIT system, while pull systems do not really recognize the future events you are supposed to be just-in-time for. This confusion has a history.

Forty years ago, the most common control system was OP, OQ, a pull system that seeks to exploit the presumed efficiencies of batch manufacturing. It was not known for its quick responsiveness to customers. Inventory managers determined the point below which materials and parts should not fall, and clerks ordered stock whenever it fell below that point. You put a line in a pail of bolts; when you exposed the line, you ordered more bolts. The order was based on average demand, and the fixed trigger point for releasing an order was based on typical behavior.

These techniques were more or less suitable for managing retail operations, though even in those settings there were problems like the McDonald's franchise on the day of a game. If you ran a garage, for example, it would be tough to restock snow tires quickly after a big blizzard because every tire store would hit its order point and there would be a flood of reorders. The OP, OQ system would not react and place an early order when a blizzard was forecast.

If OP, OQ could be annoying to retailers, it could be disastrous to manufacturers. For want of a part, whole lines were shut down. And job lot orders, when they finally did come in, often forced manufacturers to tie up cash in more stock than they needed. Nor did OP, OQ integrate all information that was available when initiating production: How long does it take to build a product? What is likely external demand? In fact, parts and components are often built for in-house demand rather than for outside customers, and their requirements are well-known.

Managers often took obviously inappropriate action because of the old OP, OQ method. Demand surges invariably caused shortages; small shortages triggered production of parts even when people knew there would be no near-term demand for the part. Against this flawed system, MRP—the first generation of what is now MRP II—had obvious merit and won wide acceptance very quickly.[1]

MRP to the Rescue. The concept behind MRP was straightforward, and MRP II is no real departure. In the same way that the caterer plans and conceives the whole week's production, the MRP system explodes the entire manufacturing operation into discrete parts making up the whole. It then projects demand, the time it would take to meet it, and the materials needed.

The key to MRP is that you have to tell it the lead time to manufacture a part, component, or assembled product. If parts production is intended to support, say, final assembly of a telephone, MRP orders only the parts that are actually going into the phones you expect to sell—not some preset job lot determined by "efficient scale."

So instead of building according to a fixed inventory position of various parts, MRP mandates building to the scheduled delivery of the final product. That, at least, is the theory. The best feature of MRP is its demonstrated capacity to work through the bills-of-materials relationships by which parts and subassemblies become the final product. MRP calculations start at the end items to be shipped and proceed stage by stage through bills of materials, releasing orders for the various parts or assemblies, according to a predetermined quantity and timing. The process then automatically repeats for the next level of parts going into each planned component or assembly.

Penetration of MRP methods into manufacturing has been substantial, especially in industries characterized by complex bills of materials, large numbers of open orders, and many needs for materials coordination among plants, vendors, and customers. Indeed, MRP has become so much the standard for materials management that it has led to the professionalization of the task, as exemplified by the American Production and Inventory Control Society. At the same time, owing to the heavy computer demands of MRP, systems managers and MIS departments have taken over a good deal of manufacturing management.

Push Comes to Shove

MRP II—more exact than MRP before it—initiates production of various components, releases orders, and offsets inventory reductions. MRP II grasps the final product by its parts, orders their delivery to operators, keeps track of inventory positions in all stages of production, and determines what is needed to add to existing inventories. What more could JIT ask?

A major barrier to MRP, though, is the cost of hardware and software for a complex computerized system—no minor barrier especially to smaller producers. And even more important are the costs of training and implementation. You have to teach your workers a lot that they don't know about computers. And in order to enter the right data and the right relationships, you have to spend a great deal of time finding out things about your system that you don't presently know: How should parts be timed to be put together just the way you want them? How long will it take for delivery of all the critical parts?

MRP does not conflict with JIT, but MRP must assume a fixed production environment with fixed lead times. Even with the best intentions, people who set up MRP systems base them on established and often flawed methods of conceiving conversion processes—methods that could be full of inefficiencies and that could be easily improved if workers were not constrained by MRP expectations.

In this context, the professionalization of materials control is a handicap, not a benefit. MRP standards have become a kind of orthodoxy, so people resist the introduction of new methods to the shop floor. New methods can threaten the positions of MIS managers, materials managers, MRP vendors, consultants, and educators who have become attached to the standards.

Of the many standard assumptions made by MRP, the fixed lead times are the most troublesome. Why is MRP so susceptible to getting lead times wrong? The best answer is that production lead times vary depending on the degree of congestion or loading within the shop. The fallacy in MRP is that its releases produce the very conditions that determine lead times, but these lead times have already been taken as known and fixed in making the releases. Consider again the cars traveling to the tunnel. The time it takes for any one car depends on traffic conditions and starting times. Change the pattern of departures, and you change the load on the system and the time it takes.

There is another way of looking at this. A single lead-time number must suffice in MRP for all situations faced on the floor. Consequently, the number has to be set high enough to cover all variations up to the worst case. If an order is ever late, people have an incentive to increase the planned lead time in the system so that the delay does not occur again. A commuter who might encounter an accident or traffic jam will leave early to protect against such contingencies. Similarly, orders will usually be released too early and will often complete early, thereby increasing inventories in the system.

Incentives for Improvement. Perhaps the most pernicious aspect of MRP is the removal of any responsibility for lead-time reduction from the shop floor. How can there be incentives to reduce lead times if there are no rewards for completing work faster than MRP's fixed standards say?

Another big problem with MRP is its unnecessarily complex and centralized nature. MRP II systems plan and coordinate materials flow and produce order releases to the shop floor. But in many situations, the shop floor can be more flexible than MRP II.

For example, an assembly group might want to change its build schedule because parts aren't available for some current schedule. Yet change is stymied because the appropriate paperwork is unavailable and won't be available until the next run of the MRP system—say, next week. It often makes no practical sense to run an MRP plan every day. It takes time to collect and distribute all the data involved. Also, a good-size MRP system can tie up the central computer for hours. The same computer might be used for everything from word processing to payroll and general ledger accounting. Yet some shops would be better off working in just such short cycles.

Some MRP enhancements have addressed these problems. MRP vendors have created "shop floor control" modules—actually monitors, not controllers, which track progress on the shop floor. The resource management tools in MRP II analyze capacity and resource loading. Perhaps the best known of these systems is "rough-cut capacity planning." This method analyzes the load that MRP order releases create on the shop floor. If this load exceeds the capacity of a work center, the implication is that the work in the shop will not get done within the time allowed. The human planner must now find some way to cure the problem diagnosed. Sophisticated techniques for evaluating the lead-time consequences of MRP releases are also available now, including order release methods (X-FLO, for example), scheduling techniques (OPT, CLASS, MIMI), and simulations (FACTOR).

While helpful, these methods increase MRP costs and can be subject to the same criticisms as the system they are meant to restore: they remove responsibility and incentives from the shop floor and they are only as good as the information put into them.

Does Pull Ever Come to Tug?

If MRP superseded OP, OQ, the kanban method is often prescribed as a JIT technique that overcomes the deficiencies of MRP. Presumably, if you set up a production system that works like a bucket brigade, you can forget about providing incentives for continual improvement or gathering what may prove to be incorrect information. The team will discipline itself according to the next customer's needs.

To the extent that kanban works like a bucket brigade, it is indeed a JIT system. Everyone in the chain takes about the same amount of time to pass a bucket, and the system can work without any inventories of buckets between people. If the output end slows down, the whole chain will react and slow down; if it speeds up, the chain will react and speed up as much as possible, until limited by the slowest bucket passer.

Nor is kanban just warmed-over OP, OQ. With kanban systems, workers can see clearly the value of lead-time reduction. Unlike other pull systems, kanban combines production control with inventory control. The interaction between lead times and inventory levels becomes obvious to everybody on the line.

Moreover, the production supervisor owns the inventories that are produced; they are not pushed into other hands. He or she is thus forced to recognize that increasing the lead time of manufacturing increases WIP as well as finished inventory. This is completely unlike conventional pull systems like OP, OQ in which the inventory management function is separated from production or replenishment.

Indeed, the kanban method of posting circulating work orders makes the current work commitment of the manufacturing cell immediately obvious to everybody in the cell. Planning setups in advance, therefore, or opportunistically consolidating batches to save setups can become routine. The mix changes and demand surges that call for personnel reassignments become more transparent.

Kanban has another virtue that JIT people like. The fixed pool of cards in a kanban cell reduces the extent to which demand fluctuations are passed on by the cell to other upstream cells. The cards provide an upper bound that filters out extreme variations. At the same time, the system disciplines the downstream customer by punishing wide fluctuations or demand surges. A sudden surge will not be satisfied until the limited number of cards circulate many times. This encourages uniform demand and level schedules on the downstream side.

Kanban Is Reactive. Kanban is not without difficulties, though, which show up especially when it is forced to operate in complex operations where variations are too great or too intractable to be disciplined easily. Toyota's kanbans discipline suppliers, but a supplier's kanban cannot discipline Toyota.

The kanban method works best where there is a uniform flow—a level-loaded, synchronous, or balanced system. It does *not* plan well. JIT enthusiasts should realize that when a kanban system is implemented in an environment full of variations in supply and demand, it is even less likely than MRP to operate in a stockless manner—that is, without a burdensome amount of WIP. Variability causes the same extreme problems that it does in other pull systems. Extra cards or containers—buffers, for example—have to be introduced to cover variability and avoid back orders. Nothing in a kanban system magically reduces inventory levels due to some internal rule or formula.

Since the system is reactive, changes in demand level percolate slowly from stage to stage. Even if it is perfectly obvious that demand is rising, there is no standard way to prepare for the situation. Some U.S. assemblers that work with Japanese suppliers using pull systems have commented that if there is a steep change in demand levels, the suppliers take from three to six months to adjust to it and encounter plenty of problems until the system reaches smooth operation again.

Tailored Controls, Hybrid Systems

Where does all this leave us? Which system should the manufacturing manager choose? The simple fact is that there is no need to choose between push or pull. These methods are not mutually exclusive, and each has its pros and cons. The best solution is often a hybrid that uses the strengths of both approaches.

Pull methods tend to be cheaper because they do not require computerization—hardware or software. They leave control and responsibility at a local level and offer attractive incentives for lead-time management. MRP systems are good at materials planning and coordination and provide a natural hub for interfunctional communication and data management. When it comes to work release, they are good at computing quantities even if they are weak on timing. A successful hybrid system can use each approach to its best advantage.

The key to tailoring production control lies in understanding how the nature of the production process drives the choice of control method. The accompanying exhibit summarizes various manufacturing control methods and process characteristics. For a continuous-flow process, ongoing materials planning is not essential and JIT supply techniques work well. Order releases do not change from week to week, so a rate-based approach can be used. At the shop floor level, JIT materials-flow discipline combined with pull release—kanban, for example—is effective.

In a repetitive manufacturing environment with fairly stable but varying schedules, materials planning can be a combination of MRP II and JIT methods. Order release may require MRP calculations if changes are frequent or if it is necessary to coordinate with long lead times or complex materials supply and acquisition. Pull methods work well on the shop floor.

As we move to more dynamic, variable contexts—like job shop manufacturing—MRP becomes invaluable for planning and release. Pull techniques cannot cope with increasing demand and lead-time variability. Shop floor control requires higher levels of tracking and scheduling sophistication. Materials flow is too complex for strict JIT.

Finally, in very complex environments, even job release requires sophisticated push methods. Where these are too expensive, the only option is to live with poor time performance, large inventories, and plenty of tracking and expediting.

The Best of Both. The dividing line between push and pull is obviously not sharp. In many situations, the two can coexist and are complementary. Most important, it is perfectly possible to take elements of one system and add them to the other. If pull systems have natural lead-time reduction incentives and push systems do not, for example, there is nothing to prevent managers from instituting a program of incentives in the context of a push system. Given the importance of lead-time reduction, in fact, it is crucial for managers to measure lead-time performance and provide feedback on response and turn-around times to each work center and shop. Though MRP systems do little to encourage good lead-time performance directly, managers can introduce measurement and incentive schemes based on MRP's data collection capabilities.

There is nothing to stop managers from compensating for the deficiencies of pull systems either. Pull systems, for instance, have no means of lot tracking—pegging lots to specific customers. But customers may want to keep track of their orders, and there may be special regulatory or quality control reasons for maintaining a lot's identity. So why not add lot tracking and data collection systems to a kanban line, leaving the release function as a pull system? (One simple and effective approach is to accumulate the information physically, with the lot itself as it moves through various process stages, and then record it electronically at inventory points in the process.)

Theoretically, there is no limit on the variety of control methods that can be developed. Most are hybrids. Attempts to implement pure push systems are usually accompanied by the growth of some informal, reactive pull procedures. The most common, alas, is the "hot list," by which assembly tells manufacturing what parts it wants most on a given day.

In a way, such informal procedures are only piggybacking on the official MRP system, using short-term release information that MRP has not yet processed. The trouble with any informal procedure, however, is that it is very unsystematic; it may be based on assembly's guess of what it can get from parts and does not take into account the actual position of open orders in parts. Moreover, it undermines the credibility of the official system. Since there can be no coordination between the two, disbelief in the official system becomes self-fulfilling. Instead of such informal overrides of MRP II, consider one of the following hybrids:

JIT-MRP. There are now several modifications of existing MRP II systems, which add pull elements and remove some of the problems connected with the system's lack of responsiveness. Some such modifications are "synchro-MRP," "rate-based MRP II," and "JIT-MRP." These systems are appropriate for continuous-flow or level-repetitive processes, where production is at a level rate and lead times are constant. In these situations, the order release and inventory management functions are of little value. The facility can be designed to operate in a JIT manner so that any material that enters the facility flows along predictable paths and leaves at predictable intervals. Work is released by a pull mechanism, so there is no WIP buildup on the floor.

Such a JIT-MRP line produces to meet a daily or weekly build rate rather than build to specific individual work orders. This means that inventory position isn't necessary for release calculations. Inventory levels can be adequately calculated after the fact on a so-called "back-flush" or "post-deduct" basis by subtracting to allow for production that has already taken place. In short, MRP serves mainly for materials coordination, materials planning, and purchasing and not for releasing orders. The shop floor is operated as a JIT flow system.

Tandem Push-Pull. In a repetitive batch environment where lead times are fairly stable, either an MRP or a pull approach can achieve order release. MRP would be best for purchase planning of items with long lead times. Actual build routines closely correspond with the MRP II schedule, yet the timing of subassembly and assembly releases can be eliminated to allow the shop floor to change rapidly in response to short-term demand pull. Subassembly and assembly are flexible, short-cycle processes that can easily be run on a pull basis.

In this common situation, push and pull systems can simply be juxtaposed—MRP II to ensure parts availability based on end-item schedules and kanban for actual subassembly and assembly releases. MRP can be run only as frequently as necessary for parts purchasing and planning. Since the floor schedules can change quickly, the MRP database will always be playing catch-up with actual part withdrawals. This approach has been particularly successful in subassembly and assembly environments in which manufacturing cycle times are much shorter than parts purchasing and fabrication lead times.

Requirement-driven Kanban. Consider another situation where individual cells within the manufacturing chain can be run with kanban control, although MRP II runs much of the rest of the process. This can occur where final assembly schedules are unstable with respect to volume and mix, yet certain portions of the production process see fairly steady demand. A plastics injection molding cell that makes the same bottle for different shampoos is a good example. The MRP system can predict requirements for plastic parts quite well; kanban could run the injection molding cell.

One approach for such a case is to use MRP II to plan the number of cards in the cell on the basis of the gross requirements for all the parts produced by the cell. The MRP system doesn't have to monitor the inventory level in the cell or match demand with available inven-

tories since the system doesn't make order releases. The gross requirements are an aggregate forecast of demand from the cell. Of course,
as the gross requirements increase, additional cards are introduced
into the cell in advance of the demand increase. They are withdrawn
as the requirement level drops. MRP thus plays the role of planning
adviser to the cell, setting the budget level in terms of the number of
cards but not specifying the "expenditure" or release of the cards.

Many component manufacturing shops supplying subassembly and
assembly operations, where the mix may change substantially but the
total volume does not vary much, can use this approach. Other users
are builders of common components or subassemblies like motors,
similar components like PCBs, and metal-forming operations like blanking, shearing, and pressing.

Dynamic Kanban. Pull methods like OP, OQ typically do have some
push component, such as seasonal expectations. Forecasts of demand
patterns can be used to set new values for the order quantity and for
the order point. In this manner, the otherwise passive pull system is
able to anticipate predictable changes.

Similarly, the card quantity in a kanban system can be altered in
response to regular changes in demand forecasts—not only seasonal
variations but obvious trends or planned promotions. In these cases,
the forecast can be used to calculate the number of cards necessary to
support the changed level of demand. The cards become a planning
parameter driven by forecasts of activity.

Looking Ahead to CIM

There are no panaceas for manufacturing management problems. A
single approach will not suffice for all situations. Managers have to
design and refine solutions. Kanban itself, like so many JIT techniques,
evolved over many years.

I believe that future advances in pull systems will most likely accommodate even more computerized and automated factory environments. The challenge will be to create incentives for process improvements in the automated factory. Expert systems will have important
roles in troubleshooting and diagnosing problems, sometimes even
substituting for shop floor supervisors.

The fastest growing area for push methods is "factory management
systems"—new methods oriented toward shop floor management rather
than materials planning. These new systems monitor manufacturing

and collect production data and merge with technologies like smart cards and bar coding. Even newer techniques of scheduling and cell management are leading to a bottom-up style of factory management. Indeed, as information technology evolves further, push techniques, like the pull approaches, will tend to decentralize control to the local, cell level.

In today's manufacturing settings, we are witnessing a drift toward the ultimate JIT factory, in which the needs of a JIT cell are perfectly coordinated with the output of all others and matched to customers' varying demands. Expressed in those terms, that's the ultimate CIM factory too.

Note

1. Early *Harvard Business Review* coverage included Jeffrey G. Miller and Linda G. Sprague, "Behind the Growth in Materials Requirements Planning," September–October 1975, p. 83.

6

Making Supply Meet Demand in an Uncertain World

Marshall L. Fisher, Janice H. Hammond, Walter R. Obermeyer, and Ananth Raman

Thanks to global competition, faster product development, and increasingly flexible manufacturing systems, an unprecedented number and variety of products are competing in markets ranging from apparel and toys to power tools and computers. Despite the benefits to consumers, this phenomenon is making it more difficult for manufacturers and retailers to predict which of their goods will sell and to plan production and orders accordingly.

As a result, inaccurate forecasts are increasing, and along with them the costs of those errors. Manufacturers and retailers alike are ending up with more unwanted goods that must be marked down—perhaps even sold at a loss—even as they lose potential sales because other articles are no longer in stock. In industries with highly volatile demand, like fashion apparel, the costs of such "stockouts" and markdowns can actually exceed the total cost of manufacturing.[1]

To address the problem of inaccurate forecasts, many managers have turned to one or another popular production-scheduling system. But quick-response programs, just-in-time (JIT) inventory systems, manufacturing resource planning, and the like are simply not up to the task. With a tool like manufacturing resource planning, for example, a manufacturer can rapidly change the production schedule stored in its computer when its original forecast and plan prove incorrect. Creating a new schedule doesn't help, though, if the supply chain has already been filled based on the old one.

Similarly, quick response and JIT address only part of the overall picture. A manufacturer might hope to be fast enough to produce in direct response to demand, virtually eliminating the need for a forecast. But in many industries, sales of volatile products tend to occur in a concentrated season, which means that a manufacturer would need an unjustifiably large capacity to be able to make goods in response to actual demand. Using quick response or JIT also may not be feasible if a company is dependent on an unresponsive supplier for key components. For example, Dell Computer Corporation developed the capability to assemble personal computers quickly in response to customers' orders but found that ability constrained by component suppliers' long lead times.

We think that manufacturers and retailers alike can greatly reduce the cost of forecasting errors by embracing *accurate response*, a new approach to the entire forecasting, planning, and production process. We believe that companies can improve their forecasts and simultaneously redesign their planning processes to minimize the impact of inaccurate forecasts. Accurate response provides a way to do both. It entails figuring out what forecasters can and cannot predict well, and then making the supply chain fast and flexible so that managers can postpone decisions about their most unpredictable items until they have some market signals, such as early-season sales results, to help correctly match supply with demand.

This approach incorporates two basic elements that other forecasting and scheduling systems either totally or partially lack. First, it takes into account missed sales opportunities. Forecasting errors result in too little or too much inventory. Accurate response measures the costs per unit of stockouts and markdowns, and factors them into the planning process. Most companies do not even measure how many sales they have lost, let alone consider those costs when they commit to production.

Second, accurate response distinguishes those products for which demand is relatively predictable from those for which demand is relatively unpredictable. It does this by using a blend of historical data and expert judgment.

Those two elements help companies rethink and overhaul not only every important aspect of their supply chains—including the configuration of their supplier networks, schedules for producing and delivering unfinished materials, transportation, and the number and location of warehouses—but also the designs of their products. Armed with the knowledge of which products have predictable demand and which do not, they can then take different approaches to manufacturing each class of product. Those in the relatively predictable category should be made the furthest in advance in order to reserve greater manufacturing capacity for making unpredictable items closer to the selling season. Such a strategy enables companies to make smaller quantities of the unpredictable products in advance, see how well the different goods fare early in the selling period, and then use that information to determine which products to make more of.

Accurate response thus enables companies to use the power of flexible manufacturing and shorter cycle times much more effectively. And the capability to do a better job of matching supply and demand produces savings that drop straight to the bottom line. One supplier in the fashion-ski-apparel business, Aspen, Colorado-based Sport Obermeyer, Ltd., has slashed its mismatch costs in half by using accurate response.

By dramatically reducing mismatch costs, this approach also gives companies the option of taking a further action: lowering prices. Currently, suppliers, distributors, and retailers alike build mismatch costs into their prices. In other words, they try to make consumers pay more to cover the cost of inaccurate forecasts.

Clearly, companies that make or sell products with long lifetimes and steady sales do not need to make such changes to their forecasting and planning systems. Forecasts for those products are likely to be consistently close to the mark, and in any case, the long lifetimes of such products greatly reduce the cost of any forecast inaccuracy. But for companies that deal with products that are new or highly seasonal, or have short lifetimes, the accurate response approach is essential. Any manufacturer whose capacity is constrained during peak production periods can benefit from making better use of its off-peak capacity. And any retailer that has difficulty predicting demand can likewise benefit by learning which products to order in bulk before the selling season and which to order in increments during the season.

The Growing Need to Face Demand Uncertainty

A few companies are already using some of the techniques incorporated in accurate response. The Timberland Company, the fast-growing New Hampshire-based shoe manufacturer, for example, has developed a sophisticated production-planning system linked to a sales-tracking system that updates demand forecasts. Those systems, along with efforts to reduce lead times in obtaining leather from tanners, have enabled the company to reduce stockout and markdown costs significantly.

L.L. Bean, the Maine outdoor-sporting-goods company, has started to use its understanding of uncertainty to drive its inventory-planning decisions. As a direct marketer, Bean finds it easy to capture stockout data. Having discovered that forecasts for its continuing line of "never out" products are much more accurate than those for its new products, Bean estimates demand uncertainty differently for each category and then uses those estimates in making product-supply decisions.

But most companies still treat the world as if it were predictable. They base production planning on forecasts of demand made far in advance of the selling season to provide ample time for efficient production and distribution. And when that approach results in shortages of some products, and in pipelines filled with obsolete components and finished goods because anticipated hot sellers have bombed, it is generally seen as a forecasting problem. Everyone unfairly blames the forecasters.

The real problem, though, is that most companies do a poor job of incorporating demand uncertainty into their production-planning processes. They are aware of demand uncertainty when they create a forecast—witness the widespread reliance on safety stocks—but they design their planning processes as if that initial forecast truly represented reality. They do this for two reasons. First, it's complicated to factor multiple demand scenarios into planning; most companies simply don't know how to do it. Second, the dramatic increase in demand unpredictability is fairly recent, so most companies haven't yet changed their planning systems to adapt to it. The result, as shown by the sharp increase in department store markdowns in the past two decades, has been catastrophic. (See Exhibit I.)

All this is somewhat ironic given the advances during the past 15 years that have ostensibly made it easier to identify and supply ever-smaller market niches. Point-of-sale scanners have provided a flood of data on consumers' buying patterns. And by reducing the cost of making smaller quantities of products, flexible manufacturing has enabled companies to make a much wider variety of goods—all with the goal of giving customers exactly what they want. Even industries that traditionally have not been considered fashion driven have been affected. The number of new-product introductions in the U.S. food industry, for example, has exploded in recent years, from 2,000 in 1980 to 18,000 in 1991.

But frequent introductions of new products have two side effects that most companies are not prepared to address. For one, they reduce the average lifetime of products; more of them are either at the begin-

Exhibit I.

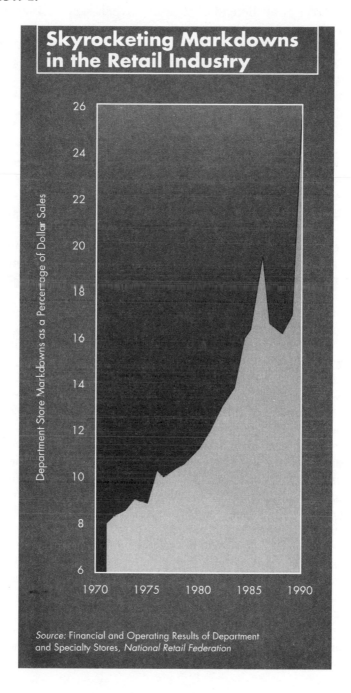

Skyrocketing Markdowns in the Retail Industry

Source: Financial and Operating Results of Department and Specialty Stores, *National Retail Federation*

ning of their life (when prediction is tough because there is no demand history) or at the end of their life (when keeping inventory is expensive because the products will soon become obsolete). For another, as products proliferate, demand is divided over a growing number of stock-keeping units (SKUs). Even if manufacturers and retailers can forecast aggregate demand figures with some certainty, it is becoming increasingly difficult to predict how that demand will be distributed among the many SKUs they sell. To visualize this effect, compare the relative difficulty of predicting who will win a baseball game (the aggregate result) with the difficulty of predicting who will score more runs in each inning (the result at an SKU level).

Consider the problems General Motors' Cadillac division faced after redesigning its Seville and Eldorado models. Based on initial demand forecasts for its 1992 line, General Motors allocated half the capacity of its Detroit-Hamtramck plant to those two models; the remaining capacity was slated to produce Buicks and Oldsmobiles. However, demand for the Sevilles and Eldorados quickly exceeded supply: GM's underproduction of the two models led to the loss of thousands of potential customers. Scrambling to meet the growing demand, GM changed its allocation and devoted 86% of the plant's capacity to the Cadillac models. Eventually, the company allocated all of the plant's production capacity to the Seville and Eldorado. But the damage had already been done.

In the computer industry, which is contending with considerable product proliferation, short product life cycles, and a limited history of specific customer demand, undersupply and oversupply problems are endemic. And in retailing, consolidation in many segments has given the surviving businesses much more power over suppliers—power they have not been shy about using to reduce their own vulnerability to an unpredictable market. Kmart, for example, told a number of its toy suppliers last July that it would in effect buy products from them on a consignment basis: the toy manufacturers were expected to send products to Kmart distribution centers based on Kmart's orders, but Kmart would not actually purchase the products unless and until they were sent from the distribution center to a Kmart store. Products not selling up to expectations would be returned from the distribution center to the manufacturer.

Black & Decker Corporation lost tens of millions of dollars in sales in less than one year because of increased retailer demands, notes Al Strumar, the company's former vice president of advanced manufacturing technology. In the power tool industry, stiff competition has meant an increased variety of products and a need for faster delivery. Also, to some extent, power tools have become fashion items that compete with ties and compact discs for Father's Day and Christmas gift purchases. As a result, a few years ago, some of Black & Decker's largest retailer customers began pushing the company to deliver smaller orders more frequently—on a just-in-time basis. Those customers also established a policy of canceling any order that could not be shipped 100% complete and on time. Black & Decker couldn't meet those exacting requirements using its traditional planning methods. Top managers' attention has subsequently turned to making plants fast and flexible so that the company can respond to rapid changes in market preferences.

How Accurate Response Developed at Sport Obermeyer

Any company that chooses to implement accurate response should obviously tailor the approach to its own situation. But the case of Sport Obermeyer provides a good example of how it can be done. In fact, the insights that emerged from our analysis of Sport Obermeyer formed the foundation for the accurate response approach.

In the fashion skiwear business, demand is heavily dependent on a variety of factors that are difficult to predict—weather, fashion trends, the economy—and the peak of the retail selling season is only two months long. Even so, Sport Obermeyer has been able to eliminate almost entirely the cost of producing skiwear that customers don't want and of not producing skiwear that they do want by using accurate response. The company estimates that by implementing this approach, it has increased its profits by between 50% and 100% over the last three years.

Founded in 1950 by German-born aeronautical engineer and ski instructor Klaus Obermeyer, Sport Obermeyer is a leading supplier in the U.S. fashion-ski-apparel market. Its products are manufactured by a joint venture in the Far East and by independent manufacturers located in the Far East, Europe, the Caribbean, and the United States. With sales of approximately $30 million in 1992, Sport Obermeyer had a commanding 45% share of the children's market and an 11% share of the adult market.

Nearly all of Sport Obermeyer's products are newly designed each year to include changes in style, fabric, and color. And until the mid-1980s, the company's design-and-sales cycle was relatively straightforward: design the product, make samples, and show samples to retailers in March; place production orders with suppliers in March and April after receiving retail orders; receive goods at Sport Obermeyer's distribution center in September and October; and then ship them immediately to retail outlets. That approach worked well for more than 30 years: production commitments were based on firm orders, and fall delivery provided ample time for efficient manufacturing.

In the mid-1980s, however, several factors rendered the approach obsolete. First, as Sport Obermeyer's sales volume grew, the company began to hit manufacturing constraints during the peak skiwear-production period. It was unable to book sufficient production with high-quality-skiwear manufacturers during the critical summer months to allow all of its volume to be produced after it had received firm retail orders. As a result, it began booking production the previous November, or about a year before the goods would be sold, based on speculation about what retailers would order.

Second, the pressure to reduce manufacturing costs and increase variety compelled Sport Obermeyer to develop a more complex supply chain. (Today a parka sold in the United States might be sewn in China from fabrics and findings—zippers, snaps, buckles, and thread—sourced from Japan, South Korea, and Germany.) Such a supply chain supported increased variety and improved production efficiency but greatly increased lead times. Finally, and most important, Sport Obermeyer successfully launched a line of children's fashion skiwear. Dealers began demanding earlier delivery, because a substantial portion of sales in the booming children's category had begun to take place in August, during the back-to-school season.

To contend with lengthening supply chains, limited supplier capacity, and retailers' demands for early delivery, Sport Obermeyer undertook a variety of quick-response initiatives to shorten lead times. First, the company slashed the time it took to process orders and compute raw-material requirements by introducing computerized systems to support those activities. Second, because lead times for obtaining raw materials proved difficult to shorten, the company began to anticipate what materials it would require and pre-position them in a warehouse in the Far East. With materials in hand, Sport Obermeyer was able to begin manufacturing as soon as it received orders. Third, as delivery due dates approached, the company turned to air freight to expedite delivery from the Far East to its Denver distribution center. By 1990, those changes had reduced delivery lead times by more than one month.

In addition, Sport Obermeyer succeeded in persuading some of its most important retailer customers to place their orders sooner, thereby providing the company with valuable early information on the likely popularity of individual styles. Starting in 1990, the company accomplished this by inviting about 25 of its largest retailer customers to Aspen each February to give them a sneak preview of the new annual line and to solicit early orders. Every year since then, the orders resulting from this program, called Early Write, have accounted for about 20% of Sport Obermeyer's total sales.

Unfortunately, those efforts did not solve the problem of growing stockouts and markdowns. The company still had to base about half its production on demand forecasts, which was a big risk in the highly volatile fashion industry. Sport Obermeyer relied on an in-house "buying committee"—a group of company managers from a range of functional areas—to make a consensus forecast of the demand for each of the company's various products. But its track record was not particularly impressive. In the 1991–1992 season, for example, some women's parka styles outsold the original forecast by 200%, while sales of other styles amounted to less than 15% of the forecasted amount.

Sport Obermeyer's managers weighed the alternatives. Could they improve forecasting? Could they further reduce manufacturing lead times? Wasn't there some way to take greater advantage of the information generated by the Early Write program? Could they induce more retailers to place their orders early?

It was at that point that the four of us formed a research team to consider those questions. The accurate response approach evolved as a result. We realized that the problem was rooted in Sport Obermeyer's inability to predict what people would buy. A decision to produce a parka is essentially a gamble that the parka will sell. To help Sport Obermeyer avoid the highest-risk gambles, we needed a way to determine which products were safest to make before Early Write and which should be postponed until after the sales information gathered from Early Write became available. Taking the buying committee's original forecast as a starting point, we noticed that although some forecasts were indeed off the mark, about half were quite accurate, differing by less than 10% from actual sales. (See the first graph in Exhibit II.) Was there a way to tell which forecasts were likely to be accurate before we saw actual orders?

Exhibit II.

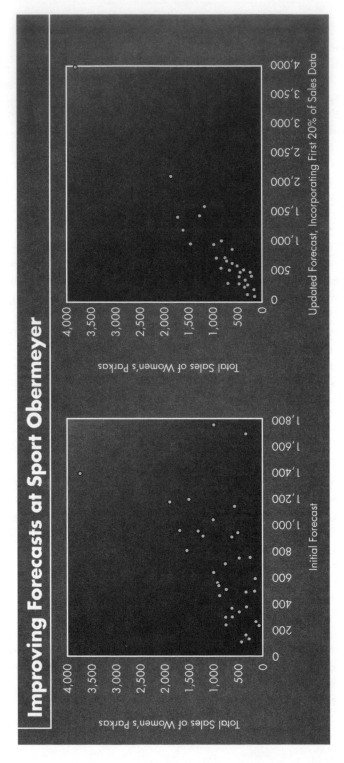

Exhibit II. (continued)

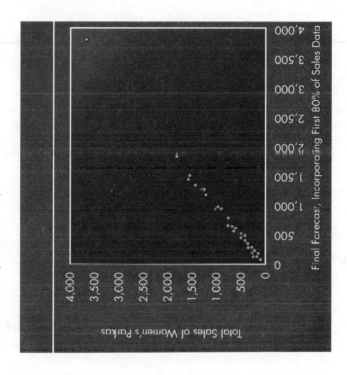

Total Sales of Women's Parkas

Final Forecast, Incorporating First 80% of Sales Data

Exhibit III.

How Sample Predictions Differ for Two Products								
Committee Members	Carolyn	Laura	Tom	Keny	Wally	Wendy	**Average**	**Standard Deviation**
Number of Pandora Parkas	1,200	1,150	1,250	1,300	1,100	1,200	**1,200**	**65**
Number of Entice Shells	1,500	700	1,200	300	2,075	1,425	**1,200**	**572**

To answer that question, we first examined the way the buying committee operated. The buying committee had traditionally provided a single consensus forecast for each style and color. We decided to ask each member of the committee to make an independent forecast for each style and color. At the beginning, committee members found that request somewhat unsettling. They were used to a collegial environment; they had been accustomed to arriving at the consensus forecast by holding an extensive discussion. Under the new system, individuals were responsible for their own forecasts.

But the change proved invaluable for two reasons. First, consensus forecasts rarely represent a true consensus. Dominant members of a group, such as senior executives, often unduly influence the outcome of a team forecast; they could not do this if each person had to submit his or her own forecasts. Second, and more important, the new process provided a way to determine statistically the probable accuracy of the committee's forecasts for each style.

Indeed, an interesting discovery emerged from the independent-forecasting process. Although the average forecasts for two parka styles could be the same, the dispersion of individual forecasts for the two styles could differ greatly. For example, everyone's forecast for the Pandora parka was close to the average, but the forecasts for the Entice shell were all over the map. (See Exhibit III.) It seemed plausible that the forecast for the Pandora was more likely to be right than the forecast for the Entice.

At the end of the 1992–1993 season, we were able to test our hypothesis that forecasts would tend to be more accurate when the buying committee's members had similar forecasts. The actual sales data showed that the variance in the individual forecasts was an almost perfect predictor of forecast accuracy. (For a detailed explanation of the forecasting process, see "Coping with Demand Uncertainty at Sport Obermeyer.")

Coping with Demand Uncertainty at Sport Obermeyer

Longtime industry player Klaus Obermeyer characterizes the skiwear market as extremely fickle. What possible use could formal statistical methods have in such an unpredictable setting? You'd be surprised. The trick lies in realizing that although demand for each product can be highly uncertain, the distribution of demand follows a discernible pattern.

At Sport Obermeyer, we found that demand data followed a normal distribution, which is defined by its mean (average) and its standard deviation (a measure of the dispersion, or "width," of the distribution and hence of the level of demand uncertainty).

The graph "Probable Sales of the Pandora Parka" shows a forecast distribution based on the demand predictions of the buying committee. The area under the curve between two points is equal to or greater than the probability of demand falling between those points. (For example, the shaded area represents the probability that demand exceeds 1,285 units.) If Sport Obermeyer were to have only one opportunity to produce Pandora parkas, we would use this curve in the following manner to find the production quantity that maximizes expected profitability by balancing the risks of overproduction and underproduction.

For the Pandora parka, Sport Obermeyer earns $14.50 in marginal profit for each unit sold and loses $5.00 for each unit produced and not sold. The company should keep producing parkas as long as it expects the gain from each parka to exceed the loss. Expected profits are maximized by producing up to the point where the expected marginal gain from producing a parka is roughly equal to the expected marginal loss from producing that parka. For the Pandora, that occurs when the company

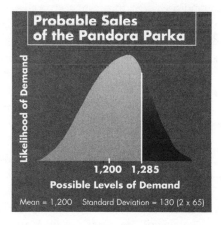

Probable Sales of the Pandora Parka

Likelihood of Demand

1,200 1,285

Possible Levels of Demand

Mean = 1,200   Standard Deviation = 130 (2 x 65)

produces 1,285 parkas, because the expected gain from producing the 1,285th parka is approximately equal to the expected loss from producing that parka. That is, the probability of selling the 1,285th parka (25.7%) multiplied by the profit if the company sells that parka ($14.50) is roughly equal to the probability of not selling it (74.3%) multiplied by what the company loses if it makes it and cannot sell it ($5.00).

This analysis illustrates two critical components of an accurate response program: assessing a probability distribution for demand, and estimating the costs of stockouts and markdowns. We have embedded this basic logic into a sophisticated algorithm that allows us to generate multistage, risk-based production schedules.[2]

To implement the approach described above, we had to estimate the mean and the standard deviation. For products with extensive historical demand data, those parameters can be estimated using statistical methods. However, with only a judgmental forecast available, we had to devise a different approach. We started by asking each member of Sport Obermeyer's buying committee to provide us with an individual forecast for each product.

We treated the average of the committee member's forecasts as the mean of the demand distribution. We estimated the standard deviation for each style to be twice the standard deviation of the buying committee's forecasts. We decided to scale by a factor of two because the average standard deviation of actual forecasting errors in preceding seasons was twice that of the buying committee's forecasts.

We believed that forecasts would tend to be more accurate for those styles for which the buying committee members had similar forecasts— that is, those whose forecasts had a low standard deviation. This hypothesis was confirmed with actual data from the 1992–1993 season. The close fit between actual and predicted forecasting errors gave us a solid basis for determining which products were safe to produce before additional sales data became available and which were not. Using this information along with detailed data about minimum lot sizes and other production constraints, we formulated an appropriate risk-based production sequence for Sport Obermeyer.

Just a quick-response and just-in-time programs cannot realize their full potential without corresponding changes in planning systems, neither should those changes in analytical approach exist in isolation. Improvements in supply chain speed and flexibility are essential to achieving the full potential of an accurate response program.[3]

Sport Obermeyer now had a way to estimate which styles were accurately forecast. But it still had to deal with those styles that had unpredictable demand. We made the critical—and startling—discovery that even though retailer demand is unpredictable enough to make accurate forecasting impossible, the overall buying patterns of Sport Obermeyer's retailers were remarkably similar. For example, by updating the buying committee's forecasts using just the first 20% of orders, the accuracy of forecasts improved dramatically. Naturally, as more orders were obtained, the forecast accuracy continued to improve. (See the second and third graphs of Exhibit II.) The challenge then became to devise a production-planning approach that would recognize and take advantage of that information.

The key to doing this was realizing that the production capacity Sport Obermeyer uses to make ski parkas actually changes in character as the season progresses. Early in the season, when the company has no orders, that capacity is nonreactive, in the sense that production decisions are based solely on predictions rather than on a reaction to actual market demand. As orders begin to filter in, starting with those generated by the Early Write program, that capacity becomes reactive. Now Sport Obermeyer can base production decisions on the signals it is receiving from the marketplace and on its more accurate forecasts.

It is important to fill nonreactive capacity with those styles for which demand forecasts are most likely to be accurate, so the precious reactive capacity can be devoted to making as many of the unpredictable styles as possible. This strategy, which we call *risk-based production sequencing*, allows Sport Obermeyer to be as responsive to the market as possible in the areas where the payoffs are the greatest.

Production planning at Sport Obermeyer is actually more complicated than we have presented; we have streamlined the process here to provide a general explanation of how accurate response works. In addition, we have omitted several case-specific factors. For example, in reality, the company must meet production minimums for each style. Also, for styles that have high enough sales levels relative to the minimums, it can use multiple production runs. That is, a style can be manufactured in two increments—the first using nonreactive capacity based on a portion of the predicted sales, the second reactively, based on information derived from actual sales. Further, the styles' different costs affect their riskiness: other things being equal, more costly styles carry greater financial risk.

We developed a complex computerized mathematical model to create an optimal production schedule that takes all these factors into account. The model identifies those products that should be produced nonreactively together with their optimal production levels. Then, after updating the initial forecast with early demand information, it determines the appropriate reactive production schedule. We implemented the model's recommendations and compared its decisions with past practice: using the model's recommendations reduced costs by about 2% of sales. Because profits in this industry average 3% of sales, the improvement increased profits by two-thirds.

The model can also be used to evaluate the cost impact of physical changes to the supply chain. For example, we used the model together with historical sales data from the 1992–1993 season to estimate how much stockout and markdown costs would drop as we increased the available amount of reactive capacity—that is, capacity committed in reaction to actual early demand information.

For Sport Obermeyer's women's parkas, stockout and markdown costs would be 10.2% of sales if none of the parkas could be produced reactively—that is, if all production commitments had to be made before any orders were received. At the other extreme, those costs would drop to 1.8% if all the parkas could be produced reactively—if all production commitments could be placed after a certain portion of orders came in. (See Exhibit IV.)

It is rarely possible to defer all production until after early demand information has been obtained; the important conclusion is that even a small amount of reactive capacity can have a dramatic impact on cost. In Sport Obermeyer's case, producing only 30% of the season's volume reactively provides nearly half of the potential cost reduction.

Guided by the model, Sport Obermeyer continued to make numerous refinements to its supply chain and product-redesign process, which collectively had a significant impact. Supply chain changes focused on keeping raw materials and factory-production capacity undifferentiated as long as possible. For example, in addition to warehousing raw materials, the company began to book factory capacity for the peak production periods well in advance but did not specify the exact styles to be manufactured until a later date. Sport Obermeyer assumed the risk of supplying the correct raw materials to the factories. In exchange, the factories allowed production commitments to be made later.

In addition to making supply chain changes, Sport Obermeyer has merged its design and production departments into one merchandising department and is thus broadening its strategy to encompass more production concerns. For example, the company has redesigned its parka line to reduce dramatically the variety of zippers used. Whereas it previously tended to match the color of both the zipper and its tape to the color of the garment, the company now uses black zippers in several lines as a fashion element introducing color contrast to the style. In this way, Sport Obermeyer has reduced the number of zippers

Exhibit IV.

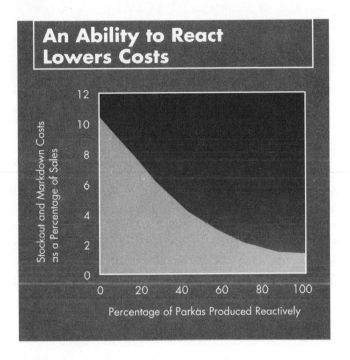

it requires more than fivefold. This change has been particularly valuable because of lengthy lead times caused by limited supply sources for high-quality zippers; the absence of a zipper of a certain length and color could hold up production of an entire style for months.

Sport Obermeyer is also encouraging designers to use the same kinds of raw materials in their patterns. For example, whereas each designer previously might have selected a different shade of red for a particular article of clothing, resulting in the company's having to work with five or six different shades, now the designers settle on two or three shades for any given design cycle. Sport Obermeyer has discovered that customers generally don't notice minute differences in color; they pay much more attention to a garment's overall appearance, quality of construction, and special features.

Achieving Accurate Response

When managers set out to assess the cost of stockouts and markdowns to see whether or not an accurate response program is warranted, they may be in for a surprise. The typical company lacks such information—mainly because tracking sales lost as a result of stockouts is difficult. But assessing lost sales is well worth the effort; even rudimentary estimates can be useful. For example, consider a product that sells evenly throughout a ten-week period. If supplies of that product run out at the end of the eighth week, it is logical to assume that the manufacturer and retailer could have sold 25% more than they had available.

Companies also can change their order-entry systems to capture orders that can't be filled because of insufficient inventory. Sport Obermeyer realized that orders during the retail selling season for products that were out of stock and hence could not be filled were not being entered into the computer. After it changed its system, it found that information invaluable for both improving forecasts and measuring the cost of insufficient inventory.

Some organizations have made ingenious changes that allow them to improve their estimates of how many sales they have lost because of stockouts. Dillard Department Stores' new policy regarding customer requests provides a good example. When a store is out of an article requested by a customer, the company will mail that item to the customer at no extra charge from another Dillard store. Dillard's original intent was solely to improve customer service and increase sales. However, the company has reaped an important side benefit. It now has a better understanding of true demand at each store, which allows it to do a better job of estimating lost sales and forecasting demand.

An important component of an accurate response program is to streamline the supply chain to reduce production and distribution lead times. Clearly, a reduction in cycle time offers the potential to reduce the cost of stockouts and markdowns by allowing production decisions to be deferred until more information and better forecasts become available. Yet realizing that potential also requires changes in forecasting and production planning.

Accurate response requires two changes in forecasting. The first is to be more resourceful in using demand indicators to improve forecasts. The second is to institute a system for tracking forecasting errors.

Sales data early in the season are an obvious source of information that can be used to revise and improve forecasts. But they are only one kind of indicator. If a company is imaginative, it can usually find or even create better ones. Take the case of National Bicycle, a subsidiary of Matsushita that manufactures bicycles in Japan under the Panasonic and National brand names.

Several years ago, National Bicycle found that sports bikes—ten-speed and mountain bikes—had become fashion items sold in part on the basis of bright, intricate color patterns that changed every year. National's inability to predict which color patterns would be hot each year was causing it to overproduce some colors and underproduce others, generating huge losses. To circumvent the forecasting problem, the company created a custom-order system by which customers were measured for their ideal frame dimensions and invited to choose their favorite color pattern from a wide selection. Their ideal bike was then created in the company's remarkably flexible plant in Kashiwara and delivered to their door two weeks later.

The program has become so popular that nearly half of National's sports bikes are now custom ordered. But surprisingly, the system also benefits the rest of National's operation. The company has found that the most popular colors for its custom-ordered bikes are an excellent indicator of which colors will be hot across the board for that season. It now uses that information to guide planning for its mass-produced bikes, which has greatly reduced losses due to overproduction and underproduction.

As an organization begins to improve its forecasts, it must also systematically track its errors. Most operations managers have an opinion of the accuracy of forecasts in their company, but too often that opinion takes the form of grousing about the latest blunder made by the marketing department. "They forecast we'd sell 2 million cans of mint-flavored dog food, so we made 2 million cans and now we have a 28-year supply sitting in our warehouse." Clearly, a more systematic approach is needed. Companies should note when a forecast was made, on what information it was based, and its level of detail (for example, was it on the aggregate or the SKU level?), and they should later compare it with actual demand.

For an existing product with at least one season of demand history, it may be possible to use past forecasting errors to predict future forecasting accuracy. Otherwise, we recommend the approach employed by Sport Obermeyer: convene a panel of experts to make independent forecasts, and use the variance in their predictions to measure the accuracy of the forecasts.

Using risk-based production sequencing requires plants to be flexible enough to switch between various seasonal products and to have access to required materials and components when they are needed. Achieving optimal flexibility may entail changes in equipment or require limiting risk-based production sequencing to product families that run on the same equipment. Ensuring access to the right supplies requires extensive discussions with suppliers to find a way to meet both parties' needs. For example, the suppliers' need for early commitment might be satisfied if the company specifies only the total volume requirements early. The company's need for flexibility might be satisfied if the suppliers allow it to postpone specifying the mix of supplies it needs until market trends become clear.

Finally, for all decisions about supply chain changes and production planning, it is important to adopt a framework rooted in a probabilistic model of demand. Contrary to what many believe, market uncertainty is a manageable risk.

Notes

1. This assertion is based in part on the study by Robert M. Frazier "Quick Response in Soft Lines," *Discount Merchandiser*, January 1986, p. 40.

2. For a description of the model, see Marshall L. Fisher and Ananth Raman, "The Value of Quick Response for Supplying Fashion Products: Analysis and Application," Department of Operations and Information Management Working Paper No. 92-10-03, The Wharton School, University of Pennsylvania, 1992.

3. For a description of such supply chain changes, see Janice H. Hammond, "Quick Response in Retail/Manufacturing Channels," in *Globalization, Technology, and Competition: The Fusion of Computers and Telecommunications in the 1990s*, ed. Stephen P. Bradley, Jerry A. Hausman, and Richard L. Nolan (Boston: Harvard Business School Press, 1993), p. 185.

PART

IV

Creating the New Manufacturing Organization

1
Manufacturing's Crisis: New Technologies, Obsolete Organizations

Robert H. Hayes and Ramchandran Jaikumar

Foreign-based competitors continue their assault on U.S. markets, exploiting their low wages or superior technological sophistication or both. Consumers are requiring ever-higher levels of quality and diversity, which has forced manufacturers to upgrade tolerances and designs, eliminate defects, and accelerate the rate of new product introduction. Meanwhile, just-in-time production systems are putting pressure on OEM suppliers to surpass their old standards of delivery and service. The challenges facing U.S. manufacturing companies are staggering.

Fortunately, manufacturing managers have new resources with which to respond to these challenges—a set of technologies that are collectively referred to as programmable automation. These include computer-aided design (CAD), computer-aided manufacturing (CAM), computer-aided engineering (CAE), flexible manufacturing systems (FMS), robotics, and computer-integrated manufacturing (CIM).

These advances promise to improve everything: cost, quality, flexibility, delivery, speed, design—everything. A recent study of FMS systems in 20 U.S. companies showed that they had reduced by more than 50% the amount of labor required to perform the same work, and reduced total product costs by as much as 75%. FMS installations have achieved significant reductions in the number of indirect workers and staff, in reject rates, and in time required to introduce products.

Still, most U.S. managers are having difficulty reaping these advantages. For years, manufacturers have acquired new equipment much in the way a family buys a new car. Drive out the old, drive in the new, enjoy the faster, smoother, more economical ride—and go on with life as before. With the new technology, however, "as before" can mean disaster. Executives are discovering that acquiring an FMS or any of the other advanced manufacturing systems is more like replacing that old car with a helicopter. If you fail to understand and prepare for the revolutionary capabilities of these systems, they will become as much an inconvenience as a benefit—and a lot more expensive.

Buy a helicopter and you can engage in new professional and recreational activities, live in some remote place, develop new work methods, get a new perspective on the lay of the land. If you don't do these things, you waste the small fortune you paid for the machine and for acquiring new skills and logistical support. In short, you don't buy a helicopter unless you're committed to getting the most out of it. You have to organize for it.

Managing Precision

The new manufacturing technologies can shock a business organization—as a helicopter would disrupt one's home life—because they require a quantum jump in a manufacturing organization's precision and integration. Automated machine tools can produce parts to more exacting specifications than can the most skilled human machinist, but to do so they need explicit, unambiguous instructions in the form of computer programs.

The new hardware provides added freedom, but it also makes possible more ways to succeed or fail. It therefore requires new skills on the part of managers—an integrative imagination, a passion for detail. To prevent process contamination, for example, it is no longer possible to rely on people who have a "feel" for their machines, or just to note on a blueprint that operators should "remove iron filings from the part." When using the new automated machine tools, everything must be stated with mathematical precision: Where is the blower that removes the filings, and what's the orientation of the part during operation of the blower?

Moreover, the tightness of the procedures that govern automated machine operation magnifies the harmful effects that faulty upstream processes have on downstream processes. Without machine operators physically handling parts, there is no one to realign them in a fixture, tweak cutting tools, or compensate for small machining or operational errors, and nobody to inspect parts for holes, cracks, or other materials defects. To replicate a machinist's talent for recognizing errors, engineers and supervisors of an automated system need either an elaborate data base incorporating, say, an expert system incorporating the implicit rules of the skilled machinist, or a scientific understanding of the technology itself. Process engineers must provide the system sensors to detect errors and programmed controllers to interpret the sensors' signals and initiate corrective actions or shut down the machine.

Indeed, production-control data will increasingly become useless to human operators in real time as batches of materials move down the line. It is the computer that analyzes the microstructure of processing from one microsecond to the next and that takes action against a badly made part. In the new manufacturing era, therefore, the manager's job is mainly taken up with making pieces fit together, both the equipment hardware and the programmed software. To maximize the capabilities of the new technologies, managers must learn to think more like computer programmers—people who break down production into a sequence of microsteps.

In this sense, a manager's task may be compared to a movie director's. Viewed continuously and from a certain distance, the film appears seamless. Apparently the director's only challenge is to inspire the actors. But stage directors who become film directors learn that gestures that look subtle on the stage seem rather gross in the cutting room. Once stage directors move to film, they have to think more like film editors. To control and integrate their product they have to understand the nuances of action, frame by frame.

Like film directors who master editing, manufacturing managers have to learn how to cut and splice small, discrete "frames" of information, then build them up in more elegant, internally consistent ways. A manager who doesn't understand one part of a factory process as well as the other parts finds it impossible to make the necessary trade-offs—between cost and smoothness, say, or speed and robustness. Managers need to develop procedures in advance, even before starting up a plant, to take into consideration all possible consequences from design to assembly.

Clearly, the new manufacturing hardware will work best in an organization geared for the tight integration of design, engineering, and plant control. The managers who preside over advanced manufacturing tasks must think more like cross-disciplinary generalists, people with a deep understanding of machine design, software engineering, and manufacturing processes. They must learn to direct highly educated people working in small, tightly knit groups. They must encourage corporate learning, harmonize the efforts of specialists. Why aren't more U.S. corporations making the changes necessary to put the new technology to work?

The real impediment lies not in the inherent demands of the hardware but in the managerial infrastructure that has become embedded in most U.S. companies over the past 50 years. This includes the attitudes, policies, systems, and habits of mind that are so ingrained and pervasive within companies that they are almost invisible to those within them. (It is said the last thing a fish discovers is water.)

Traditional managerial attitudes, manifested in top-down decision making, piecemeal changes, and a "bottom-line" mentality, are incompatible with the requirements and unique capabilities of advanced manufacturing systems. Until their attitudes change, companies will be slow to adopt the new technologies, and those that do will run a high risk of failure.

Such attitudes cannot change without profound reform in the modern corporation. At one level, reform means changes in cost accounting and performance measurement procedures, human resource management, and capital budgeting. At the next level, it means new organizational structures that can accommodate more interactive and cooperative working relationships. At a still higher level, reform means that top officers must cultivate new skills and managerial styles. It may well require a new generation of executives.

Corporate Divisions: My Gain, Your Loss

Underlying many of the problems in the modern manufacturing corporation is its organizational structure, which divides key people into separate functional responsibilities and measures their performance using different yardsticks (see Exhibit I). In a typical facility, the purchasing group acquires raw materials, and senior management measures the purchasing group's performance by examining the cost and quality of the materials it buys and the timeliness of its activity. Materials managers are measured by how quickly they deliver the finished goods and how large an inventory they keep. The production group usually is judged by the cost, quality, and timeliness of the conversion from raw materials into finished goods.

Similarly, the quality group is evaluated according to how well it prevents defective parts from entering the conversion process and defective goods from leaving it. The maintenance or manufacturing-engineering group, or both, is measured by the cost of maintaining and upgrading equipment and by mishaps like machine downtime.

A basic principle behind this design is that administrators' responsibilities equal their authority. That is, a group overseeing a certain job

Exhibit I.

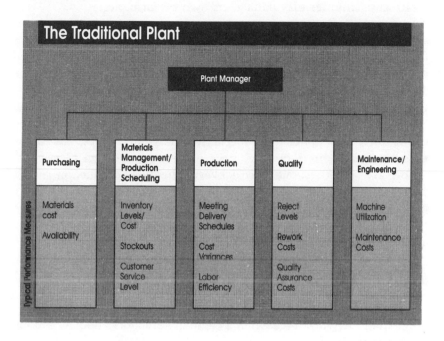

The Traditional Plant

		Plant Manager		
Purchasing	Materials Management/ Production Scheduling	Production	Quality	Maintenance/ Engineering
Materials cost Availability	Inventory Levels/ Cost Stockouts Customer Service Level	Meeting Delivery Schedules Cost Variances Labor Efficiency	Reject Levels Rework Costs Quality Assurance Costs	Machine Utilization Maintenance Costs

Typical Performance Measures

should be accountable for the steps it takes to carry it out. The performance of that task should be measurable, moreover. Since it would be unfair to measure the group's activities in dimensions that its management has little control over, customized performance measures have been developed. The narrower the task, the narrower the measure.

A factory divided into these functions and evaluated by these measures may operate quite well in a stable environment like that in which U.S. companies thrived for 30 years after World War II. Pressures on any one of these subgroups to make marginal improvements in performance—like improving quality, reducing inventory, shortening delivery times, and introducing new products at a faster rate—can be handled largely within itself. Where minor improvements are the goal, one group might ask another to cooperate by adjusting its behavior slightly, as long as such an adjustment does not much affect its own performance rating.

Problems do arise, however, when *major* improvements are called for simultaneously along several dimensions, as is the case with the new manufacturing. When they operate independently, subgroups simply cannot make dramatic improvements. Yet the help one sub-group gives another may damage its own performance.

In trying to slash inventories, for example, many companies have adopted some form of a just-in-time (JIT) system. Instead of accepting large quantities of purchased materials weekly or monthly, they demand daily or even more frequent deliveries of smaller quantities. But JIT works best if the company deals with only a few suppliers that, because of their flexibility or their location or both, can respond quickly. Yet the most responsive suppliers may be unable to match the prices of the low-cost suppliers who specialize in large quantities. The materials manager's gain, therefore, is the purchasing manager's loss.

To make sure they can meet delivery schedules, production supervisors often maintain backup inventories of parts and partially completed products. At first, reducing these inventories raises the chances that the production group will miss its schedules. People work at cross-purposes also when a company tries to improve quality, compress product development time, or introduce process control technology. When reject rates go down, quality managers look good, but production workers may look less productive purely in terms of output. So it's not surprising to see infighting among managers and resistance from the work force when a company embarks on an ambitious improvement program.

The efforts of financial officers to measure performance further confound the manufacturing organization. Accountants often lack the information necessary to show manufacturing how well (or how badly) it is doing.

When cost accounting was in its infancy, it was easy to allocate the fixed costs of production to particular work centers or products. The bulk of total production costs was variable costs, primarily direct labor and materials, for which elaborate measurement systems could be developed. Overhead costs, which comprised only 10% to 20% of the total, were then allocated to specific products and activities. Usually this was done by identifying (or simply asserting) a strong relationship between overhead and one or more variable cost—usually direct labor—and then distributing the overhead according to the amount of that variable cost incurred.

For instance, if supervision and factory support costs were small compared with direct labor, but there was a clear numerical relationship between the two—one supervisor for every ten workers, say—then one could ascertain a product's supervision costs by measuring the ratio between supervisory costs and direct labor hours *over all products.* The accountant then would multiply that "supervisory burden rate" by the number of direct labor hours consumed.

Today, however, the cost of direct labor in a typical high-technology company seldom exceeds 10% of total costs; increasingly it is under 5%, about the same as depreciation. Indirect factory costs—particularly materials control, quality assurance, maintenance and process engineering, and software development—have been growing rapidly. In many companies these now equal from five to ten times their direct labor costs. Therefore, viewing labor costs as a benchmark by which to distribute all other costs is misguided. Companies often devote three-quarters or more of their energy to measuring costs that are likely to account for less than 15% of the total.

By focusing attention on less important factors in today's production environment, traditional cost-accounting systems also distract managers from more critical issues. We know of one high-tech company whose overhead costs are almost nine times its direct hourly labor cost of $10. Managers in this company are eager to buy parts from vendors instead of making them. If they buy parts, they reduce their costs (including allocated costs) by $(1+9) \times \$10$, or $100, for each direct labor hour saved.

Overseeing an increasing number of vendors, however, requires extra staff. This company therefore found its direct labor costs falling while overhead costs rose—driving up its overhead allocation rate for the remaining products and encouraging managers to contract out even more. This may be an extreme case. But it is not atypical of many companies today driven in unanticipated directions by the apparently innocuous mandates of their accounting systems.

Irrational Incrementalism

To reduce the risk that comes with change, companies often seek piecemeal improvement via "islands of automation." Their approach to factory automation is similar to how most transportation companies build their route structures: they find two cities they can connect and serve at a profit, then gradually add cities and routes that are comparably profitable. Sometimes one part of the system grows faster than others, but eventually it usually can be linked profitably with the rest of the system. In the same way, factories are often modernized through a series of independent projects, each justifiable in its own dollar terms until, eventually, a way is found to link these individual islands of automation into a profitable whole.

Unfortunately, this approach is often not appropriate when moving toward computerized automation. No one component of a CIM network—a parts rationalization system, a CAD system, an FMS, a plant-floor data collection and information system, or a customer communication system—may be able to meet a company's profitability requirements. The desired returns materialize only when all these advances are in place.

For this reason, a CIM system should be built the way Federal Express built its famous hub-and-spoke system, which revolutionized the overnight-mail delivery business. No part of Federal Express's system could work effectively until all its parts were in place: the materials handling and sorting depot in Memphis; the planes to fly the route spokes radiating from there; and the pickup and delivery systems at each node. Building such a system requires a strategic vision, lots of money up front, and a tremendous amount of patience.

Paradoxically, even as this new hardware encourages more information sharing across the company, it enables different parts of the manufacturing organization to become more independent of one another. In fact, the new hardware encourages factories to break up into smaller units—plants-within-the-plant—of cells dedicated to making families of products. These minifactories tend to be tightly integrated, organizationally flat, almost entirely self-managing, and highly responsive to evolving market needs. The net result is reduced labor, reduced overhead, and increased capacity utilization. The factory that emerges from such changes is likely to be smaller—between a third and a fifth of the size of the traditional factories that generate similar volumes of products.

Incidentally, the new technology can also mean a revolution in relations between the company and the customer or—what is often the same thing—between OEM suppliers and procurement officers. Before the industrial revolution, people sought out craftsmen or small workshops to supply their garments, wagons, arms, and ornaments. Customers described what they wanted and the craftsmen gave them options for tailoring the product according to their wishes. The service was as important as the product.

Mass production profoundly changed the relationship between customer and producer. It shifted the emphasis of commerce away from service; products had to be designed to meet the generalized needs of large markets. With mass production, the designer, producer, and salesperson became three different people belonging to different parts of the organization. Similarly, the separation of customers from suppliers meant that customer preferences were revealed mainly through their purchasing decisions.

The new manufacturing technologies shift the focus from product features back to service, to customers. Correspondingly, they reestablish close ties between producers and suppliers. CAD and CAE allow small organizations to design prototypes faster and more economically than before. Components can be produced efficiently in relatively small batches, essentially to order, through CAM and FMS.

Command out of Control?

Some executives have argued that because the new manufacturing technologies are evolving so rapidly, they should hold off investing in them until the rate of technical progress slows. If they had similarly delayed buying a computer until computer technology had stabilized, they would be waiting still.

What those who resist the new technology fear, perhaps, is not its instability but its tendency to destabilize the chain of command. The interfunctionality engendered by the new manufacturing can mean much more informal cooperation at low levels in the organization—between engineers and market analysts, designers and manufacturers. This kind of teamwork is unnatural behavior for companies whose structures, staffing policies, and performance measures operate according to a command-and-control mentality.

Proponents of command and control expect senior management to make the major resource allocation decisions, with the help of staff and external experts whenever necessary. Their view of the line organization's role is simply to operate the established facilities, systems, and personnel according to senior management's targets.

Command-and-control managers assume that whatever specialties an organization lacks can be brought in from outside. They see management's primary task as the orderly assimilation, exploitation, and coordination of separate sources of expertise. Moreover, they thrive in hierarchical organizations in which the primary relationships between people are vertical. Decisions, rewards, and punishments flow down. Information flows back up.

None of these assumptions works well in the new manufacturing environment. Especially vulnerable are companies that have separated brute effort from intelligence by splitting them up—the engineering staff supplying the intelligence, presumably, the manufacturing-line organization, the effort. The advent of the new manufacturing technologies makes it necessary to recombine effort and intelligence, to make them more interactive. In one advanced company, a large engineering group has *become* the line organization—actually in charge of production and responsible for a factory's bottom line—while a small manufacturing group simply provides staff support, ensuring that the necessary material and information are available when needed.

As noted earlier, the companies that have mastered the new manufacturing technologies prize generalists. They strive to build close horizontal relationships throughout the company, so that product designers work directly with manufacturing process designers, vendor managers with production schedulers and quality controllers. Decisions are pushed down to operating level, and the experimentation taking place on the shop floor is no more controlled from above than that taking place in the R&D lab.

Moreover, these companies tend to dislike dependence on outside organizations or vendors for expertise. They respect the capabilities of others, but they want to develop their own people, equipment, and systems. Well-run companies like Lincoln Electric, Procter & Gamble, IBM, and Hewlett-Packard put great effort into recruiting, training, and retaining highly skilled people at the operating level.

The Biases of Capital Budgeting

Nowhere do the prejudices and inefficiencies of old, functionally separated manufacturing organizations show up more strikingly than in the capital-budgeting process. Imagine a company that is contemplating expanding its production capacity by buying standard equipment—another hundred looms, say, to supplement several thousand others that have been operating for several years. The cost of operating those looms is understood, the revenues expected from their operation are based on considerable market experience, and the capabilities needed to operate them are already in place. Buying looms is unlikely to require anything from the company beyond the money they cost, and their operation is unlikely to provide it with anything beyond the revenues they generate.

Now, suppose also that the company is considering spending an equal sum on an R&D project, perhaps on experiments with a new synthetic fiber, whose technical and commercial potential is promising but also highly uncertain. At the same time, the company is deciding whether or not it should expand its parking lot—just an added cost, but essential for its growing number of employees, suppliers, and customers.

These three investments clearly entail different demands on the organization. They generate very different business opportunities and create value in distinctive ways. The new looms merely replicate existing operations and provide an increment of capacity in a well-established business. The loom outlay fits the standard capital budgeting assumptions almost perfectly. But what about the R&D project and the parking lot? The former can create new knowledge, though it is hardly clear what this knowledge will be or how it could be employed. The R&D project's ultimate outcome may depend on future investments. The parking lot is valuable for carrying out the day-to-day work of the company, but it is just overhead. The returns from either investment are unpredictable. Neither has clearly identifiable future cash flows, and the degree of interaction with other projects and the nature of the risks incurred are almost impossible to estimate.

Most companies, of course, discern the differences among looms, pure R&D, and a parking lot. Unfortunately, they often fail to realize that most investment proposals fall somewhere between these three extremes and contain elements of each.

One metal products company faced a capacity shortage in its heat-treating operation. After a study by engineering staff and meetings with marketing and manufacturing and plant groups, the vice president of manufacturing directed the staff to draft a capital authorization request (CAR) for a new continuous-heat treating line. The line would combine two advanced technologies: a continuous-flow process and a computerized control system.

The CAR was based on a discounted cash flow analysis of the project using standard forms and computer programs under guidelines set by the corporate staff. But as the work proceeded, projections of sales volumes and profit margins seemed uncertain. The new line was designed to produce materials with higher strength and greater consistency, but it was doubtful whether customers would pay a premium for these qualities. So the CAR included conservative estimates from marketing, manufacturing, and engineering to calculate the project's annual cash flows.

Moreover, the equipment life was 20 years, but since marketing was willing to commit only to a four-year sales projection, the CAR simply extended the fourth year's sales and margin numbers through the remaining 16 years. It also excluded any benefits from the new line's increased operating flexibility, the novel products that it might facilitate, or the knowledge that the computerized systems would generate—i.e., "soft" benefits.

Here there was an obvious misfit between the standard capital-budgeting process and the new technology's power. The executive committee was trying to decide about the new processes as if it was buying something like a slightly more efficient loom whose costs and benefits were well known. In fact, it was buying table stakes in a new manufacturing technology—one that provided both traditional output and new capabilities.

In visits to dozens of U.S. factories, we have seen an astonishing number of 20-year-old or older machines in operation. Indeed, more than a third of U.S. machine tools fall into this category. Have these companies adopted a conscious strategy of competing with equipment that is obsolete, breaks down, and can't hold required tolerances?

After all, it takes 20 years to create a 20-year-old machine. Over that period, a number of investment proposals must have been studied, and well-meaning managers at various levels decided not to replace the equipment. For many companies, the cumulative effect of these decisions has been devastating. Such series of decisions—each no doubt justifiable but collectively suicidal—are an outgrowth less of a strategic plan than the normal functioning of the companies' capital-budgeting systems.

Once they recognize what is going on, many companies simply force new investment by short-circuiting their standard capital-budgeting process; for example, top management steps in to take responsibility for making decisions about major capital-equipment acquisitions. But this top-down approach keeps the organization's lower levels from understanding how strategic issues may affect them. It is also vulnerable to the preselection process that separates strategic from non-strategic investments. Unfortunately, most companies regard a manufacturing equipment choice as nonstrategic even though it may change the company's cost structure, improve its ability to introduce new products, and affect the way it interacts with its customers.

Moreover, a company does not learn to exploit the full potential of advanced equipment unless it is organized to do so. Too often, the operation of new manufacturing equipment is delegated to specialists, and equipment performance is tracked through the standard staffing, utilization, and downtime reports. New equipment is thus kept apart from the rest of the organization and has little impact on how engineers design new products, how the personnel office hires and trains people, how marketing deals with customers, or how controllers monitor the manufacturing organization's performance.

Physical Assets or Intellectual Assets

Radical changes in manufacturing technology—like the invention of the first machine tool, the development of interchangeable parts, or the moving assembly line—come along only once every generation or so. When one appears, there is little expertise that managers can draw on; long experience may provide little guidance for the immediate future.

The mistake most companies make is to treat new manufacturing equipment simply as *physical* assets. Programmable automation demands a much more interactive decision-making process and tight integration among corporate functions. It also demands attention to nonfinancial, long-term considerations, particularly its impact on the company's *intellectual* assets.

Again, the new manufacturing technology not only creates and processes materials, it also creates and processes information—information linked through computer networks and available to each workstation. If workers are trained and encouraged to use this information, the new hardware becomes a powerful means for enhancing knowledge—making nonexperts expert and experts more expert.

In the early 1980s, Deere & Company began rapidly modernizing its manufacturing facilities. It set up a "Computer-Aided Manufacturing Services" division, whose purpose was to develop a variety of software packages and to assist operating groups in implementing the new manufacturing technologies. As a result of these software development and internal consulting projects, the division developed considerable expertise in group technology, computerized process planning, flexible manufacturing systems, and computer-integrated manufacturing. By 1986, the group was confident enough to propose marketing its software and consulting skills externally. This new business has been quite successful, and it has opened up new markets for Deere's manufactured products.

Ideally, the manufacturing organization is made up of multidisciplinary engineering groups working with powerful computational tools and is evolving in new ways. Such *intelligent* organizations are ephemeral, formed when problems surface, disbanded when they are solved;

they often include suppliers and other people from the outside. The structure they assume is based on how the problem is posed. If it's noise in a motor, management would create a team of mechanical engineers; if it's faulty sensory feedback to a motor, a team of electrical engineers. Exploiting the potential of these dynamic coalitions becomes the new managerial challenge.

A company's ultimate success, therefore, depends on how effectively it can shift from measuring and controlling costs to choosing and managing projects that enhance its organizational capabilities. New measures of performance and new approaches to capital investment are needed in companies whose costs are mostly fixed, related not to the manufacture of certain products but to the creation of new capabilities. Continual improvement in production science is the ultimate measure of world-class manufacturers. They push at the margins of their expertise, trying on every front to be better than before. They strive to be dynamic, *learning* organizations.

Incidentally, not only does programmable automation make manufacturing support costs go up but the direct labor that remains becomes much less "variable." Worker skills are critical to a company's success; a layoff could mean permanent loss of that resource. At the same time, companies need to encourage cooperation among workers, to reinforce the value of long-term employment. People work best with people they know. The most important variable costs for an advanced manufacturing company may well be the costs of training and retraining people.

Just a few years ago, we used to hear this complaint from manufacturing managers: "Top management doesn't understand us. They don't understand the pressures we're under, the constraints we have to deal with, or the limited resources we can draw on. If only they would give us the authority and resources we need, we could achieve the goals they set for us."

Today it's top managers who are complaining: "Our manufacturing managers don't understand us. They don't understand the seriousness of the competitive situation we're facing or the magnitude of the improvements we must make if we're going to survive. We tell them, 'Let us know what your ideas are, and what new resources you need.' But all they come back with is more of the same. They don't seem to see that this new environment requires new approaches."

This change in the source of complaints reveals perhaps the most daunting problem of all. Over the past 30 years or so, top executives have tended to choose a certain kind of person to manage their manufacturing organizations. They assumed that if the manufacturing process was carefully set up, staffed, and equipped, all they needed to keep things running smoothly was a group of caretakers. Worse, they favored highly specialized caretakers, to the point where many factories today resemble the academic institutions that Ralph Waldo Emerson railed against 150 years ago, staffed by people who "strut about like so many walking monsters—a good finger, a good neck, a stomach, an elbow, but never a man."

Today, however, companies are beginning to realize that they need something more than caretakers and specialists. They need generalists—people with an architect's skill, who can pull out a fresh sheet of paper and design something new.

It is not easy, however, to convert caretakers into architects. It takes a long period of training, of trial and error—new expectations and new rewards. It probably will also require new people, people like the giants of the first half of this century who established most of the perfectly reasonable—but now failing—manufacturing infrastructure common today.

2
The Hidden Factory

Jeffrey G. Miller and Thomas E. Vollmann

While the world's attention is focused on the fight to increase productivity and develop new technologies, manufacturing managers—especially those in the electronics and mechanical equipment (machinery) industries—are quietly waging a different battle: the battle to conquer overhead costs. Indeed, our research shows that overhead costs rank behind only quality and getting new products out on schedule as a primary concern of manufacturing executives.

The reason for this concern is obvious: high manufacturing overhead has a dramatic effect on profit and competitiveness, and manufacturing managers believe themselves to be poorly equipped to manage these costs well. As one senior executive told us, "We've been brought up to manage in a world where burden rates [the ratios of overhead costs to direct labor costs] are 100% to 200% or so. But now some of our plants are running with burden rates of over 1,000%. We don't even know what that means!"

We are convinced that this renewed attention to overhead is not a cyclical phenomenon. No doubt, low capacity utilization accounted for some increase in awareness during the last recession; even so, awareness has remained high throughout the recovery. Overhead costs as a percentage of value added in American industry and as a percentage of overall manufacturing costs have been rising steadily for more than 100 years as the ratio of direct labor costs to value added has declined (see Exhibit I). Moreover, in today's environment, production managers have more direct leverage on improving productivity through cutting overhead than they do through pruning direct labor.

As America's factories step up the pace of automation, they find that

Exhibit I. **Components of value added**

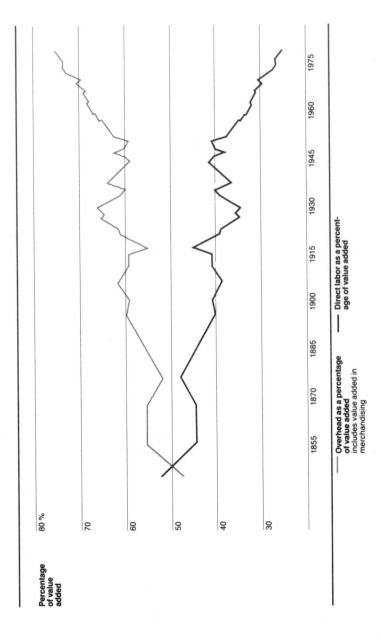

Percentage
of value
added

80 %

70

60

50

40

30

1855   1870   1885   1900   1915   1930   1945   1960   1975

—— **Overhead as a percentage
of value added**
includes value added in
merchandising

—— **Direct labor as a percentage of value added**

they are being hit twice: first, overhead costs grow in percentage terms as direct labor costs fall (everything has to add up to 100%); and second, overhead costs grow in real terms because of the increased support costs associated with maintaining and running automated equipment.

Exhibit II shows how overhead as a percentage of value added increases as a representative industry—electronics—moves down its product-process life cycle.[1] Highly customized and low-volume specialty businesses, such as those in the government systems segment of the industry, run job-shop-type operations with a relatively low ratio of overhead to direct labor. By contrast, in businesses producing high-volume standardized products in automated environments, as in the microcomputer segment of the industry, the ratio of overhead to direct labor cost is notably greater.

Our data suggest that across the spectrum of U.S. industry, manufacturing overhead averages 35% of production costs; the comparable figure for Japanese products is 26%, despite the fact that the Japanese have been rapidly automating. The differential is particularly large in the electronics and machinery industries, where American overhead accounts for 70% to 75% of value added, and Japan's for 50% to 60%. (See Appendix B for a description of the methods and data we used.)

A Focus on Transactions

For managers, the critical step in controlling overhead costs lies in developing a model that relates these costs to the forces behind them. Most production managers understand what it is that drives direct labor and materials costs, but they are much less aware of what drives overhead costs. True, we do have models that accountants use—as they do engineering standards and bills of material—to relate overhead costs to products produced. But these models do not so much *explain* overhead costs as *allocate* them.

Most of these efforts use the engineering standards and bills of material models that we do understand as the basis for allocating overhead costs that we do not understand. These efforts base overhead burden rates on direct labor, materials, or machine hours. The problem with this approach is that the driving force behind most overhead costs is not unit output or direct labor. Overhead costs do usually correlate with unit outputs, but that does not mean that unit outputs "cause" overhead costs. In fact, acting as though they were causally related

Exhibit II. Overhead as a percentage of value added in five segments of the electronics industry

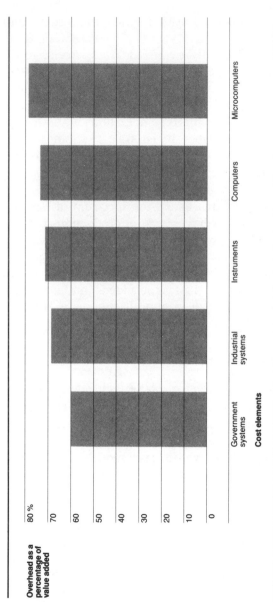

Overhead as a percentage of value added

80 %
70
60
50
40
30
20
10
0

Government systems   Industrial systems   Instruments   Computers   Microcomputers

Cost elements

Source:
Developed from data in the 1983 report of the American Electronics Association.

leads managers to concentrate on output measures or on direct labor rather than on the structural activities that determine overhead costs. (See Appendix A.)

Unit output drives direct labor and materials inputs on the actual shop floor that we all think of when we envision a factory. But in the "hidden factory," where the bulk of manufacturing overhead costs accumulates, the real driving force comes from transactions, not physical products. These transactions involve exchanges of the materials and/or information necessary to move production along but do not directly result in physical products. Rather, these transactions are responsible for aspects of the "augmented product," or "bundle of goods," that customers purchase—such aspects as on-time delivery, quality, variety, and improved design.

To see clearly how the hidden factory creates overhead costs, we must identify the basic types of transaction that are carried out there by the people whose wages and salaries account for the following costs:

Logistical transactions, which order, execute, and confirm the movement of materials from one location to another. These transactions are processed, tracked, and analyzed by many of the indirect workers on the shop floor as well as by people in receiving, expediting, shipping, data entry, data processing, and accounting. For the electronics industry, we estimate that processing such transactions accounts for 10% to 20% of total manufacturing overhead.

Balancing transactions, which ensure that the supplies of materials, labor, and capacity are equal to the demand. These result in the movement orders and authorizations that generate logistical transactions.

The people involved in processing such transactions include purchasing, materials planning, and control personnel (who convert master schedules and customer orders into materials requirements and purchase and shop orders) as well as human resource staff (who convert these demands into labor requirements). Also included are managers who process and authorize forecasts and who turn orders into production plans and master schedules. We estimate that these transactions also account for 10% to 20% of manufacturing overhead in electronics manufacturing.

Quality transactions, which extend far beyond what we usually think of as quality control, indirect engineering, and procurement to include the identification and communication of specifications, the certification that other transactions have taken place as they were supposed to, and the development and recording of relevant data. In the electronics industry, quality transactions add up to some 25% to 40% of manufacturing overhead.

Change transactions, which update basic manufacturing information systems to accommodate changes in engineering designs, schedules, routings, standards, materials specifications, and bills of material. These transactions involve the work of manufacturing, industrial, and quality engineers, along with a portion of the effort expended in purchasing, materials control, data entry, and data processing.

Change transactions can occur over and over again. The first time you design a product, for example, you transact a bill of materials; every time you process an engineering change order (ECO) for that product, you have to transact the bill again. The doing and undoing of logistical, balancing, and quality transactions that result from change transactions lead companies to incur overhead costs twice, three times, or more, depending on the stability of their manufacturing environments. Overall, change transactions represent 20% to 40% of overhead costs in electronics manufacturing.

Managing Overhead Transactions

If, as we believe, transactions are responsible for most overhead costs in the hidden factory, then the key to managing overheads is to control the transactions that drive them. By *managing transactions*, we mean thinking consciously and carefully about which transactions are appropriate and which are not and about how to do the important transactions most effectively. Manufacturers have rigorously applied this type of analysis to direct labor since the days of Frederick Taylor. Now that overhead costs far exceed direct labor costs, however, managers should redirect their analytical efforts.

TRANSACTION ANALYSIS

The design criteria used in developing most products and production processes rarely take overhead costs into account, let alone the transaction costs involved in alternative designs. It is possible, for example, to eliminate numerous transactions by designing short-cycle production processes without any work-in-process (WIP) inventory that would require logistical, balancing, or quality transactions. This is what the Japanese have done with their "just-in-time" philosophy of process design, which "pulls" work through the factory only as needed by operations downstream. This approach eliminates much of the need for elaborate and time-consuming WIP-tracking or shopfloor control systems.

One electronics product that was redesigned to meet competitive pressures provides a vivid example of what a low-transaction production system can do. Prior to the redesign, the product contained more than 700 parts, most of which had to be ordered from a supplier on a weekly basis and then placed in a materials inventory before being withdrawn in batches and taken to the final assembly area. The plant shipped each week's output to a finished goods inventory in the company's distribution system. A count of the number of monthly transactions required by this system is as follows:

Ordering transactions	=	700 parts x 4	=	2,800 transactions
Receiving transactions	=	700 x 4	=	2,800
Materials transactions (in and out of inventory)	=	700 x 4 x 2	=	5,600
Materials authorizations	=	700 x 4	=	2,800
Total transactions			=	14,000 per month

After careful study, management decided that:

1. Changes in product design and vendor specifications could reduce the part count from 700 to 200.
2. The factory could issue blanket orders instead of separate purchase orders for materials and could provide vendors with monthly shipping rates. The need for additional parts would be signaled by the return of an empty container of standard size.

3. A simple receiving and inspection procedure that calls for the packing slip to be sent directly to accounting on receipt of the container could replace the current complicated process. As a result, the company would need to send only one check per month to each vendor for goods actually received.

4. Delivering parts directly to the floor could eliminate the materials inventory, the necessity of putting materials away, the issuing of authorizations to withdraw them, and the work of pulling the materials out again.

5. A smoothed production flow would make quality problems immediately apparent and change management's focus from extensive record keeping to prevention and immediate correction.

This factory is now well on its way to implementing a production system with far fewer monthly transactions:

Ordering transactions	=	200 parts x 1	=	200 transactions per month
Receiving transactions	=	200 x 20 days x 2	=	8,000
Materials authorizations	=	0	=	0
Materials transactions	=	0	=	0
Total transactions			=	8,200

Needless to say, the overhead costs of this factory have plummeted, as have inventory costs. In some areas—receiving, for example—the number of transactions has actually increased, but a painstaking examination of the steps involved in carrying out transactions in the hidden factory has greatly simplified the flow of work and cut total transaction costs. Managers had only to study the transaction process of the hidden factory in the same way they have long examined the production process of the visible factory.

Another way to improve transaction-based overhead is to reduce the "granularity" of the data that are reported. Every manufacturing system embodies decisions about how finely and how frequently transaction data are to be reported. It makes no sense to process more data than needed or more often than needed.

One company, for example, found that its quality transaction system was collecting and keeping quality data on every possible activity—despite the very poor quality of its products. The quality department often complained that it never had time to analyze the data, which just sat in file cabinets and computer files, because it spent all its time collecting. By focusing on the few key areas where most of the quality problems existed, the department was able to improve quality dramatically while it reduced costs. It processed quality transactions more intensively in the key areas and much less intensively where things were running smoothly.

STABILITY

Perhaps the simplest way to reduce the number of transactions is to stabilize the manufacturing environment. Many American companies are now aggressively trying to implement Japanese just-in-time approaches, but visitors from Japan are often quite surprised at what they see here. In Japan, the first principle is stability, and great effort goes into engineering the process down to the finest detail and into training workers to follow instructions to the letter. Level loads, balanced work flows, and good housekeeping all help ensure that the unexpected does not destabilize the operations.

Every time an ECO is issued, a schedule breaks down, or a quality problem erupts, a wave of new transactions flows through a plant. The policy of "making it right the first time" applies to the processing of transactions just as it does to the making of products. Not only do these changes increase the number of transactions; they also have an important secondary effect. Instability in plant schedules and performance causes many plant managers to overstaff their work forces so that the plants can react to unexpected peak loads in transaction volume. As one veteran plant manager said, "You've got to keep shock troops in ready reserve to handle the problems that come up."

One reason for the low percentage of value added attributed to overhead in Japanese factories is that their plants are more stable than ours. Their way of handling ECOs is a case in point. Exhibit III shows the frequency with which Japanese and U.S. electronics plants authorize design changes. The Japanese process fewer ECOs than do their American counterparts (about two-thirds fewer) and authorize these changes much further in advance and thus allow for more stable, level transaction loads. With more planning, there are fewer errors.

Exhibit III.   The frequency of ECO authorizations in the U.S. and the Japanese electronics industries

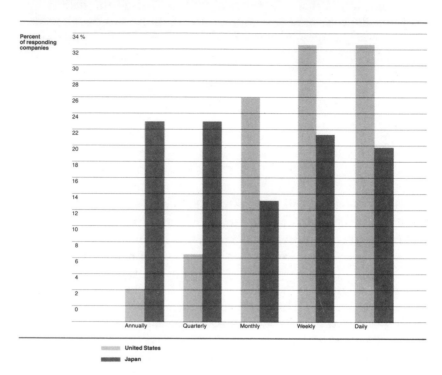

AUTOMATION

One of the most frequently discussed ways to reduce the overhead costs associated with the hidden factory is automation. Robots can have a role in sophisticated materials control systems that automate logistical transactions; lasers can read bar codes and eliminate the need for data entry operators to record movement transactions manually; computer-aided inspection can help reduce the costs of processing quality transactions; a smoothly running materials requirements planning system can make the processing of balancing transactions cheaper.

The cost of processing transactions manually can easily be ten times as great as processing them automatically. The issue is not only the cost of the transaction, however, but also the effectiveness of the transaction process. In addition to the costs of reading, distributing, filing, and retrieving, manual transactions often have a much more serious problem: they take too long. Response time is clearly a major issue in American manufacturing today, yet we know of companies that take 5 to 15 working days to turn a customer order into the proper form for manufacturing. A manual transaction based on retrieving information from a file cabinet, reading the document to understand the conditions, making the transaction, dispatching the results, and refiling can easily take 100 times longer than a comparable transaction done in a computer-supported environment.

Perhaps the most important means of automating transactions is using computer systems that are so well integrated that data need only be entered once. In virtually every large company, however, there is still a massive redundancy of transactions due to the existence of subsystems that cannot "talk" to one another. These problems exist both within manufacturing and between manufacturing and other functions.

Integrated systems offer more than efficiency; they can also improve accuracy and understanding. When the same data are kept in several places and separate organizational units independently calculate such facts as monthly shipments, the result is redundant records, redundant transaction processing, and general confusion. It is not unusual for managers to ask production, marketing, and finance to provide the unit shipment data for one product and to get three different answers.

Properly designed and integrated computer systems should lead to transactions being made only once—and to less confusion. Good systems adhere to the rule of encoding only new data: never design a transaction so that it requires data already in a computer to be reentered by hand. In far too many factories, we see people typing in data like part numbers while they look at computer-generated documents for the numbers.

Another type of data integration unites manufacturing databases with those of other functional areas. Most familiar is the link between engineering and manufacturing established by CAD/CAM systems, but there are others with equal or greater potential impact. One company, for example, is integrating its complex multiplant network with an equally complex order entry and customer service network so as to reduce overhead costs, increase delivery speed and effectiveness, and improve the accuracy of its order entry—configuration processes (a major source of quality problems). Another company is seeking to improve the efficiency of its large financial staff by linking its financial database with its manufacturing database and thereby to eliminate double entries and boost its ability to relate manufacturing plans to financial performance.

A Balanced Approach

There are, then, three general approaches to managing overhead costs more effectively: (1) analyzing which transactions are necessary and improving the methods used to carry them out, (2) increasing the stability of operations, and (3) relying on automation and systems integration. Of the three, U.S. manufacturers seem most enamored of the last.

Selectively applied, transaction automation and integration can be an important tool for reducing overall costs and for raising competitiveness in other dimensions as well. In too many instances, however, this tool has the reverse effect. Managers frequently justify this approach on the basis of substituting capital for labor, but they often forget that they are also replacing direct labor with overhead expense. As one operations manager has complained, "All that we succeeded in doing with our monstrous new computer system was to replace $10-an-hour workers with $30-to-$50-an-hour technicians whom we can't hire anyway because of their scarcity." According to another operations manager, "When we automated, direct labor expense was reduced, but total costs increased because of the increase in overheads."

In many of these instances, no one bothered to do a complete analysis of the impact on transaction volumes and costs as activities moved to middle management levels. Some companies even applied their old burden rates to the direct labor costs projected after automation.

A second and perhaps more serious problem occurs when manufacturers automate transactions that are not really necessary in the first place. One company that had recently built an advanced "factory of the future" later removed the automated guided vehicle system and a major portion of the automatic storage and retrieval systems that it had installed in order to reduce the cost of its internal logistical transactions. After installation the company found that it had simplified the transaction flow so much that no automation was necessary after all.

Another company, while evaluating a bar code system, recently discovered that its justification for the system disappeared when it eliminated the needless paperwork that had flowed among receiving, inspection, accounting, and production. The original projection had been for a two-year payback on the bar code system (based on the elimination of the clerical workers needed to produce the paperwork), but closer examination showed that most of that clerical reduction would come from just eliminating the unnecessary transactions.

The lesson, then, is to seek a balanced approach to managing overhead. Automation does not solve all problems; in fact, it may create some unless handled carefully.

As American managers face up to the task of controlling manufacturing overhead, they will have to go beyond process analysis in its usual sense and learn how to analyze transactional processes. Managers will also have to learn when and where to automate the transaction process, how to integrate it in manufacturing and across functions, and how and where to stabilize that process to its greatest strategic effect.

Finally, manufacturing managers will have to look beyond accounting conventions to analyze and categorize costs in a way that has functional meaning. We believe that the answer does not lie in inventing new accounting systems alone. This is a problem for the accountants to solve if they can; certainly it will help if they do. But no amount of bookkeeping magic will let manufacturing managers avoid one of the strategic necessities of the future: understanding how to manage the hidden factory.

Appendix A: Overhead Costs Defined

In principle, manufacturing overhead is easy to define: it includes all the direct and allocated costs of manufacture other than direct labor and purchased materials. Among these costs are:

Indirect labor, including the wages of hourly workers who do not directly contribute to the manufacture of a product but consisting mostly of labor dedicated to materials handling, maintenance, quality control, and inspection.

General and administrative expenses such as personnel administration, cost accounting, security, salaries for plant management, and direct labor supervision as well as corporate allocations for shared services and corporate staff.

Facilities and equipment costs such as insurance, depreciation of plant equipment, and tooling. These costs also include rents and other facilities-related expenses such as energy and utility costs. (Note that in process-based industries, energy costs may comprise the single largest component of overhead and total costs. Our data suggest that energy accounts for about 4% of the total manufacturing costs for a typical plant in the electronics or machinery industries.)

Engineering costs such as the salaries of manufacturing, industrial, and other engineers concerned with the design and maintenance of the production process itself.

Materials overhead costs, including those related to the procurement, movement (with the exception of those shop floor materials-handling costs relegated to the indirect labor category), and coordination of raw materials, components, subassemblies, and finished products. These costs also include the salaries of purchasing, production planning, receiving, stockroom, traffic, and manufacturing systems personnel.

This figure shows the average distribution of these cost categories in the four electronics plants we examined. None of these plants kept its overhead accounts in exactly the fashion we have described. Although their basic categories were the same, each had invented a somewhat different nomenclature and taxonomy for keeping track of these costs. To arrive at a relatively consistent—and comparable—set of numbers, we had to recast the costs at each of these plants.

Appendix B: Authors' Note On Research Methods

The research on which the data and conclusions in this article rest comes from two different sources. Most of the quantitative data come from the 1984 "North American Manufacturing Futures Survey," which we administer. Insights into overhead cost structures in the electronics industry—and the managerial problems and issues surrounding them—come from structured interviews and data analysis of four electronics factories in the United States and from subsequent follow-up visits to numerous other plants in the electronics and other industries in the United States and the Far East. The Boston University Manufacturing Roundtable sponsored both of these data-gathering efforts.

The Manufacturing Futures Project is an annual survey of the competitive strategies, concerns, recent activities, and plans that North American manufacturers are making to improve their operational effectiveness. In the 1984 survey, respondents included more than 200 senior manufacturing executives in as many different business units

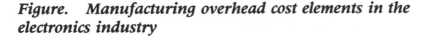

Figure. **Manufacturing overhead cost elements in the electronics industry**

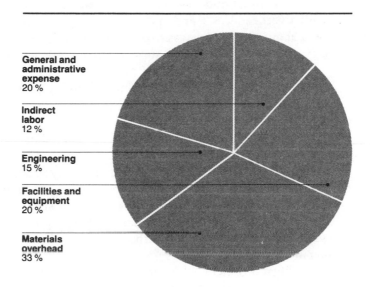

General and
administrative
expense
20 %

Indirect
labor
12 %

Engineering
15 %

Facilities and
equipment
20 %

Materials
overhead
33 %

(the typical title of the respondents was vice president of manufacturing). Participating business units came from a broad range of industries, which we categorized in five classes: electronics, consumer packaged goods, machinery, basic industries (chemicals, metals, paper), and other industrial goods. In 1984, the third consecutive year we administered the survey in North America, it was also administered to more than 200 business units in both Japan and Europe by our collaborators at Waseda University in Tokyo and at INSEAD in France.

The "Manufacturing Futures Survey" contains more than 50 multiple-part questions. A small number (those relating to managing overheads) formed the basis for the analysis in this article. For example, one survey question required respondents to indicate on a five-point scale the degree of their concern about 32 potential problem areas. The top five concerns were as follows (the number in parentheses indicates the mean scaled score given each potential concern across all respondents to the survey):

1. Producing to high quality standards (3.98).
2. Introducing new products on schedule (3.56).
3. High or rising overhead costs (3.55).

4. Low indirect labor productivity, including white-collar work (3.44).

5. Yield problems and rejects (3.28).

People in the electronics and machinery industries were the most concerned with overhead costs and indirect labor productivity, although concern about these areas was high in all five industry groups analyzed. To narrow the focus of our subsequent investigations, we decided to concentrate on the problems of managing overhead in the electronics industry. Our rationale was that this industry group had proved to be something of a bellwether for other industries during the history of the Manufacturing Futures Project.

Moreover, numerous plant visits convinced us that many of the problems in managing overhead in this fast-changing industry were reflected in other industries, especially in the machinery group. The very high levels of capital investment and energy consumption required in the basic and consumer goods industry groups substantially change the cost structure (and thus the nature of the problems of managing overhead), although we think that much of what we have to say is relevant for those groups.

Our fields investigations included extensive tours and interviews at four plants in the electronics industry—two focused on components manufacture and two on the assembly of high-volume equipment. Needless to say, we also spent considerable time discussing overhead costs with both accountants and managers from the plants.

To develop comparable data on overhead costs, we followed several conventions. First, we lumped all overhead costs into one pool. Second, we unbundled all costs so that they fell into mutually exclusive categories. For example, we put all depreciation and space costs in the "facilities" category, even though a particular company might follow the practice of allocating depreciation costs to organizational subunits like purchasing and rolling them up into a total purchasing cost (which we would put in the "materials overhead" category).

Notes

1. See Steven C. Wheelwright and Robert H. Hayes, "Link Manufacturing Process and Product Life Cycles," *Harvard Business Review*, January–February 1979, p. 133, and "The Dynamics of Process-Product Life Cycles," *Harvard Business Review*, March–April 1979, p. 127.

3
Yesterday's Accounting Undermines Production

Robert S. Kaplan

The present era of intense global competition is leading U.S. companies toward a renewed commitment to excellence in manufacturing. Attention to the quality of products and processes, the level of inventories, and the improvement of work-force policies has made manufacturing once again a key element in the strategies of companies intending to be world-class competitors. There remains, however, a major—and largely unnoticed—obstacle to the lasting success of this revolution in the organization and technology of manufacturing operations. Most companies still use the same cost accounting and management control systems that were developed decades ago for a competitive environment drastically different from that of today. Consider, for example, the following cases drawn from actual company experiences.

During Richard Thompson's two years as manager of the Industrial Products Division of the Acme Corporation, the division enjoyed such greatly improved profitability that he was promoted to more senior corporate responsibility. Thompson's replacement, however, found the division's manufacturing capability greatly eroded and a plunge in profitability inevitable.

Careful analysis of operations during Thompson's tenure revealed that:

Increased profitability had been largely caused by an unexpected jump in demand that permitted the division's facilities to operate near capacity.

Despite this expansion, the division's market share had decreased.

Costs had been reduced by not maintaining equipment, by operating it beyond rated capacity, by not investing in new equipment or product development, and by imposing stress on workers to the point of alienating them.

Many costs had been absorbed into a bloated inventory position.

Unit productivity had actually fallen.

By this time, however, Thompson was secure in his senior position and was still receiving credit for the high profits Industrial Products had earned under his direction.

The Carmel Corporation had made significant investments in labor-saving equipment. Yet with total costs, particularly overhead, still increasing, it was hard pressed to maintain market share with prices that fully recovered all of its costs. Carmel used a standard cost accounting system that allocated all nondirect costs on the basis of direct labor hours. The company had installed this procedure many years ago when direct labor accounted for more than 60% of total costs and machinery was both simple and inexpensive. Over the years, however, investment in sophisticated new machinery had greatly reduced the direct labor content of the company's products.

Staff costs rose as Carmel expanded its design and engineering staffs to develop specialized high-margin products. Because these new products required advanced materials, Carmel also expanded its purchase of semifinished components from suppliers. With direct labor (at an average wage of $12 per hour) plunging as a fraction of total costs, the accounting system was allocating the growing capital and overhead costs to a shrinking pool of direct labor hours.

The predictable result: a total cost per direct labor hour in excess of $60—and projections that it would soon rise to $80. Worse, efforts to offset these higher hourly rates by substituting capital and purchased materials for in-house production only compounded the problem. The accounting system was distracting management attention from the expansion of indirect costs.

Both these examples offer a pointed reminder that poorly designed or outdated accounting and control systems can distort the realities of manufacturing performance. Equally important, such systems can place out of reach most of the promised benefits from new CIM (computer-integrated manufacturing) processes. As information workers like design engineers and systems analysts replace traditional blue-collar workers in factories, accounting conventions that allocate overhead to direct labor hours will be at best irrelevant and more likely counterproductive to a company's manufacturing operations. And with the new manufacturing technology now available, variable costs will disappear except for purchases of materials and the energy required to operate equipment.

Not only will labor costs be mostly fixed; many of them will become sunk costs. The investment in software to operate and maintain computer-based manufacturing equipment must take place before any production starts, and of course that investment will be independent of the number of items produced using the software program. With the decreasing importance of variable labor costs, companies that allocate the fixed, sunk costs of equipment and information systems according to anticipated production volumes will distort the underlying economics of the new manufacturing environment.

In this environment, companies will need to concentrate on obtaining maximum effectiveness from their equipment and from their increasing investment in information workers and in what they produce. Controlling variable labor costs will become a lower priority. This major change in emphasis requires that managers learn new ways to think about and measure both product costs and product profitability.

Nonfinancial Aspects of Manufacturing Performance

It is unlikely, however, that any cost accounting system can adequately summarize a company's manufacturing operations. Today's accounting systems evolved from the scientific management movement in the early part of the twentieth century. They were instrumental in promoting the efficiency of mass production enterprises, particularly those producing relatively few standard products with a high direct labor content. Reliance on these systems in today's competitive environment, which is characterized by products with much lower direct labor content, will provide an inadequate picture of manufacturing efficiency and effectiveness.

Measurement systems for today's manufacturing operations must consider:

Quality. To excel as a world-class manufacturer, a company must be totally committed to quality—that is, each component, subassembly, and finished good should be produced in conformity to specifications. Such a commitment to quality entails major changes in the way companies design products, work with suppliers, train employees, and operate and maintain equipment. But this commitment must also extend to a company's measurement systems. Data on the percentage of defects, frequency of breakdowns, percentage of finished goods completed without any rework required, and on the incidence and frequency of defects discovered by customers should be a vital part of any company's quality-enhancement program. Otherwise, the impact of variations in quality will show up in cost and market share data too late and at too aggregate a level to be of help to management. Direct quality indicators should be reported frequently at all levels of a manufacturing organization.

Inventory. A second nonfinancial indicator of manufacturing performance is inventory. American managers are well versed in optimizing inventory levels according to the economic order quantity (EOQ) model, which balances the cost of additional setup time with the cost of carrying inventory. They are less familiar with the effort, common among Japanese producers, to eliminate setup times and to implement just-in-time inventory control systems, which together reduce drastically overall levels of work-in-process (WIP) inventory.[1]

Many of the savings in reduced working capital, factory storage, and materials handling from cutting WIP will eventually be reflected in lower total manufacturing costs. But many of the savings that arise from transactions *not* taken—less borrowing to finance inventory, for example, or less need to expand factory floor space—will not be reflected in these costs. Therefore, such direct measures as average batch sizes, WIP, and inventory of purchased items will provide much more accurate and timely information on a company's manufacturing performance than will the behavior of average manufacturing costs.

Productivity. Direct measures of productivity are a third important set of nonfinancial indicators. Even in companies publicly committed to productivity improvements, accurate measurement of productivity is often impossible because accounting systems are designed to capture dollar-based transactions only. Without precise data on units produced, labor hours used, materials processed, energy consumed, and capital employed, administrators must deflate dollar amounts by aggregate price indices to obtain approximate physical measures of productivity. But errors in approximation often arise that can easily mask any period-to-period changes in real productivity.

Alternatively, managers rely on partial productivity measures, such as value added per employee or output per direct labor hour, which attribute all productivity changes to labor. These measures tend to overlook gains from the more efficient use of capital, energy, and managerial effort and so encourage the substitution of capital, indirect labor, energy, and processed materials for direct labor. But as direct labor costs decline relative to total manufacturing costs, it becomes more—not less—important to focus on total factor productivity.

Nor can managers finesse these measurement problems by looking only at aggregate data on profitability. In the short run, product profitability may be caused more by relative price changes and holding gains not recognized by historical cost-based systems than by structural improvements in the production process. A temporary expansion of demand can, for example, enable a company to boost its prices faster than its growth in costs. In the long run, however, the higher wages paid by U.S. companies will lead to competitive difficulties—unless offset by higher productivity. During the 1960s and 1970s, many U.S. companies earned a comfortable profit and did not notice that their productivity had begun to stagnate or even decline. They are noticing now.

Innovation. Some companies choose to compete not by efficiently producing mature products that have general customer acceptance and stable designs but by introducing a constant stream of new products. Customers buy the products of these innovative companies because of the value of their unique characteristics, not because the products are cheaper than those of competitors. For innovating companies, the key to success is high performance products, timely delivery, and product customization. Attempts to impose cost minimization and efficiency criteria—especially early in the product development process—will be counterproductive.

Cost accounting systems, however, rarely distinguish between products that compete on the basis of cost and those that compete on the basis of unique characteristics valued by purchasers. Thus, it is difficult to manufacture new products in facilities that also manufacture mature products since plant managers, evaluated by an accounting system that stresses efficiency and productivity, find it disruptive to make products for which both the designs and the process technology are still evolving. Companies that cannot afford the luxury of a separate facility for new product manufacturing must learn to de-emphasize traditional cost measurements during the start-up phase of new products and to monitor directly their performance, quality, and timely delivery.

Work force. Another limitation of traditional cost accounting systems is their inability to measure the skills, training, and morale of the work force. As much recent experience attests, if employees do not share a company's goals, the company cannot survive as a first-rate competitor. Hence, the morale, attitudes, skill, and education of employees can be as valuable to a company as its tangible assets.

Some companies, noting the importance of their human resources, conduct periodic surveys of employee attitudes and morale. They also monitor educational and skill levels, promotion and training, and the absenteeism and turnover of people under each manager's supervision. These people-based measures are weighted heavily when managers' performance is evaluated. Meeting profit or cost budgets does not lead to a positive job rating if it is accompanied by any deterioration in these people-based measures.

In summary, the financial measures generated by traditional cost accounting systems provide an inadequate summary of a company's manufacturing operations. Today's global competition requires that nonfinancial measures—on quality, inventory levels, productivity, flexibility, deliverability, and employees—also be used in the evaluation of a company's manufacturing performance. Companies that achieve satisfactory financial performance but show stagnant or deteriorating performance on nonfinancial indicators are unlikely to become—or long remain—world-class competitors.

Improving Control Systems

Improving manufacturing performance requires more of accounting systems than the timely provision of relevant financial and nonfinancial data. Fundamental changes in management control systems are also needed. In particular, there is a need to rethink the way companies use summary financial measures like ROI to coordinate, motivate, and evaluate their decentralized operating units.

The ROI measure was developed earlier in this century to help in the management of the new multi-activity corporations that were then forming. ROI was used as an indicator of the efficiency of diverse operating departments, as a means for evaluating requests for new capital investment, and as an overall measure of the financial performance of the entire company.

Through the use of ROI control, early twentieth century corporations achieved a specialization of managerial talent. Managers of functional departments (manufacturing, sales, finance, and purchasing) could become specialists and pursue strategies for their departments that increased the ROI of the entire company. Senior managers, freed from day-to-day operating responsibility, could focus on coordinating the company's diverse activities and developing its long-term strategies.

In practice, decentralization via ROI control permitted senior executives to be physically and organizationally separated from their manufacturing operations. For many years, this separation was a valuable and necessary feature that enabled corporations to expand into many diverse lines of business. Recently, however, problems with running corporations "by the numbers"—that is, with excessive reliance on ROI measures but without detailed knowledge of divisions' operations and technology—have become uncomfortably apparent.

INFLATION AND ROI

The financial executives who pioneered in the application of ROI measures were not concerned with the distortions introduced by inflation. After World War II, however, as ROI-based control systems came into widespread use, continuous price increases gave a steady upward bias to ROI.

When fixed assets and inventory are not restated for price level changes after acquisition, net income is overstated and investment is understated. Thus managers who retain older, mostly depreciated assets report much higher ROIs than managers who invest in new assets. Such apparent differences in profitability, of course, have nothing to do with actual differences in the rates of return of the two classes of assets.

FINANCIAL ACCOUNTING MENTALITY

Such distortions of economic performance are but one manifestation of a broader problem: the use in a company's internal reporting and evaluation systems of accounting practices and conventions developed for external reporting. This is, for the most part, a recent phenomenon and is more common in the United States than in other parts of the world.

In Europe, many companies have one department to collect and analyze data for internal operations and another to prepare external reports. Some companies, like Philips in the Netherlands, even report to stockholders on the basis used to evaluate internal operations. By contrast, contemporary practice in the United States is to use for internal purposes conventions either developed for external reporting or mandated by such external reporting authorities as the Financial Accounting Standards Board and the SEC.

INTEREST EXPENSE.　For example, many American corporations regularly allocate corporate expenses—say, interest costs—to divisions and profit centers according to some arbitrary measure of a unit's assets or working capital. Now, it is sensible to charge divisions for capital employed. It is not sensible, however, to use a pro rata share of the interest expense reported on external financial statements as the appropriate internal cost of capital. Such a procedure implies that a company financed entirely through equity would allocate no capital charges to divisions since it has no recorded interest expense.

Consider, at the other extreme, an autonomous division engaged in real estate whose assets are mostly debt financed. The financial accounting mentality would have this division bear a higher interest charge against earnings than would divisions financed more heavily by equity. But does anyone believe that the cost of debt capital is higher than that of equity capital?

Divisions should be charged for their investment in net controllable assets through a divisional cost of capital, perhaps adjusted to allow lower charges for working capital than for higher-risk fixed assets. Few companies use such a method today, perhaps because the divisional capital charges will "overabsorb" a company's actual interest expense. But considering actual interest expense as a company's only cost of invested capital is more a limitation of contemporary financial reporting than it is a criticism of charging divisions for the full cost of their investments.

PENSION COSTS.　Financial accounting practices can also lead to bad cost accounting in the allocation of pension costs. For example, prior service costs are sunk costs. They represent an obligation of a company for the past service of its employees. No current or future action of the company can affect this obligation. The amortization of prior service costs must, however, be recognized as a current expense in the company's financial statements. Therefore, many companies allocate prior service costs to divisions.

One company allocated these costs in proportion to pension benefits accrued. A plant with an older work force received almost all of its division's prior service costs, but several newer plants with much younger workers bore almost none. This arbitrary allocation produced a $4 per labor hour cost penalty on the older plant. As a result, the company was shifting work from the older plant to the newer ones. In addition, the older plant was losing market share as it raised prices in an attempt to earn a satisfactory margin over its high labor costs. Put simply, the company became a victim of its financial accounting mentality: first it allocated a noncontrollable, sunk cost to its plants and then it relied on this arbitrarily allocated cost for pricing and product sourcing decisions.

OTHER DISTORTIONS. Distortions created by the financial accounting mentality intrude on many other internal measurements. How often, for instance, do executives, when measuring a division's investment base for an ROI calculation, include leased assets only when, according to FASB regulations, they must be capitalized on the external financial statements? Are development and start-up expenses, including software development, considered part of the investment in a computer-integrated manufacturing process, or are these investments in intangibles expensed as incurred because, according to SFAS 2, this treatment is mandated for external reporting? Do companies translate operations in foreign countries according to their economic exposure overseas, or do they use whatever translation method the FASB happens to be mandating at the time?

The point, of course, is that companies seeking to compete effectively must devise cost accounting systems that reflect their investment decisions and cost structures. Internal accounting practices should be driven by corporate strategy, not by FASB and SEC requirements for external reporting. Surely, the cost of record keeping in an electronic age is sufficiently low that aggregating transaction data differently for external and internal purposes cannot be a burdensome task.

FINANCIAL ENTREPRENEURSHIP

Another set of difficulties with ROI-based measurements stems from the ability of executives to generate greater profits from financial activities than from managing their assets better. Sixty years ago managers knew that higher profits and ROI came from efficient production, aggressive marketing, and a continual flow of product and process improvements. During the past 20 years, however, as it has become more difficult to increase profits through selling, production, and R&D,

some companies have looked to accounting and financial activities to generate earnings.

At first, these activities—switching from accelerated to straight-line depreciation, for example—did little harm. Occasionally they proved costly, as when companies opted to pay unnecessary taxes by delaying or refusing a switch to LIFO because of its adverse impact on reported profits. Today, however, the romance with these devices is in full swing: mergers and acquisitions, divestitures and spinoffs, debt swaps and discounted debt repurchases, debt defeasance, sale-leaseback arrangements, and leveraged buyouts.

Some of these activities may create value for shareholders (current research is still attempting to sort out the net effect of these financial activities). Still, it is hard to imagine that a focus on creating wealth through the rearrangement of ownership claims rather than on managing tangible and intangible assets more effectively will help companies survive as world-class competitors. Ultimately, wealth must be created by the imaginative and intelligent management of assets, not by devising novel financing and ownership arrangements for those assets.

INTANGIBLE ASSETS

The final and most damaging problem with ROI-based measures is the incentive they give managers to reduce expenditures on discretionary and intangible investments. When sluggish sales or growing costs make profit targets hard to achieve, managers often try to prop up short-term earnings by cutting expenditures on R&D, promotion, distribution, quality improvement, applications engineering, human resources, and customer relations—all of which are, of course, vital to a company's long-term performance. The immediate effect of such reductions is to boost reported profitability—but at the risk of sacrificing the company's competitive position.

The opportunity for a company to increase reported income by forgoing intangible investments illustrates a fundamental flaw in the financial accounting model. This flaw compromises the role of short-term profits as a valid and reliable indicator of a company's economic health. A company's economic value is not merely the sum of the values of its tangible assets, whether measured at historic cost, replacement cost, or current market prices. It also includes the value of intangible assets: its stock of products and processes, employee talent and morale, customer loyalty, reliable suppliers, efficient distribution network, and the like.

Suppose this stock of intangible assets could be valued each period. Then, when the company decreased its expenditures on these assets, their subsequent decline in value would lower the company's reported income. We do not, however, have methods to value objectively intangible assets. Therefore, reported earnings cannot show a company's decline in value when it depletes its stock of intangible assets. It is this defect in the financial accounting model that makes the quarterly or annual income number an inadequate summary of the change in value of the company during the period.

The Task at Hand

Present cost accounting and management control systems rest on concepts developed almost a century ago when the nature of competition and the demands for internal information were very different from what they are today. When companies now make arbitrary allocations of corporate expenses to divisions and products, accounting systems may provide even less valid cost data than did the cost accumulation systems in use 50 years ago. In general, though, an accounting model derived for the efficient production of a few standardized products with high direct labor content will not be appropriate for an automated production environment where the factors critical to success are quality, flexibility, and the efficient use of expensive information workers and capital.

General managers must be alert to the inadequacies of their present measurement systems. It is doubtful whether any company can be successfully run by the numbers, but certainly the numbers being generated by today's systems provide little basis for managerial decisions and control. Managers require both improved financial numbers and nonfinancial indicators of manufacturing performance. Because no measurement system, however well designed, can capture all the relevant information, any operational system must be supplemented by direct observation in the field. The separation of senior management from operations that the ROI formula made possible 80 years ago will have to be partially repealed. Successful senior managers must be knowledgeable about the current organization and technology of their operations.

For their part, accounting and financial executives must redirect their energies—and their thinking—from external reporting to the more effective management of their companies' tangible and intangible assets. Internal management accounting systems need renovation. Yesterday's internal costing and control practices cannot be allowed to exist in isolation from a company's manufacturing environment—not, that is, if the company wishes to flourish as a world-class competitor.

Note

1. See for example, Jinichiro Nakane and Robert W. Hall, "Management Specs for Stockless Production," *Harvard Business Review*, May–June 1983, p. 84; Larry P. Ritzman, Barry E. King, and Lee J. Krajewski, "Manufacturing Performance—Pulling the Right Levers," *Harvard Business Review*, March–April 1984, p. 143; and Hal F. Mather, "The Case for Skimpy Inventories," *Harvard Business Review*, January–February 1984, p. 40.

4
The Human Costs of Manufacturing Reform

Janice A. Klein

If there is anything more powerful than an idea whose time has come, it is one that is the product of wishful thinking. Ask any manager or management consultant what the related essentials of manufacturing reform are, and the answer will likely come back: a just-in-time approach to eliminating waste, rigorous statistical process control to improve quality, and increased employee participation and self-management. One manager I know was emphatic: "JIT, SPC, and worker involvement in production management are like the three legs of a milking stool. Each is critical. If any one of the three breaks or is missing, the others will fall down."

He was an operations manager, eager to tap his workers' knowledge. He also anticipated their enthusiasm. It seemed obvious to him that increased participation was precisely what workers wanted or would quickly come to want. Implicit in that view is the belief that reformed manufacturing is more consistent with the moral ideal of "autonomy" than traditional manufacturing is.

Is it? That depends on what one means, precisely, by "participation": employee involvement, self-management, and teams. In the United States and Europe, most designers of employee participation programs think of teams as a way of *empowering* the work force. Companies involve workers in manufacturing reform by allowing team members a good deal of autonomy in managing daily activities—in scheduling the work and determining the procedures to carry it out.

In Japan, in contrast, where JIT and SPC have been used most extensively, employees are routinely organized into teams, but their involvement in workplace reform is typically restricted to suggestions for process improvement through structured quality control circles or *kaizen* groups. Individual Japanese workers have unprecedented responsibility. Yet it is hard to think of them exercising genuine autonomy, that is, in the sense of independent self-management.

To be sure, managers can—and must—involve workers in workplace decisions. But the attack on waste, it must be understood, inevitably means more and more strictures on a worker's time and action. Our conventional Western notions of worker self-management on the factory floor are often sadly incompatible with them.

The Engine Plant

Nothing brought this point home to me more graphically than the case of an engine plant I've studied. Over ten years ago, a large engine company designed a greenfield site; high among its priorities were worker morale and participation. The organizational design included self-managing work teams, many provisions for multiskilled workers, a reasonably flat—not hierarchical—management structure, and an explicit commitment to a "factory culture" based on growth, trust, equity, and excellence. Workers met schedules they themselves helped to set, laid out their work space to suit themselves, and performed assembly tasks in the manner they thought best. Meanwhile, inventory buffers provided time for workers to participate in management decisions. The plant soon became a model for the corporation, outperforming its traditional manufacturing operations not only in improved quality and safety but also in reduced overhead.

In the early days, the plant was not under severe cost or delivery pressures; the primary focus was on producing a top-quality product in an enriching work environment. But with the oil embargo, a recession in the automobile industry, and intensified foreign competition, the corporation found it necessary to reduce its manufacturing costs drastically. Top management believed that JIT and SPC would improve the company's competitiveness and quality and decided to introduce these approaches throughout the corporation's facilities.

The plant workers, who were by now accustomed to taking the initiative, quickly responded by forming a number of groups to plan the implementation process. One group began by scanning literature, attending seminars, and visiting other companies that had implemented JIT and SPC. A second focused on the plant's work flow, taking on the challenge of improving fixtures and tooling to reduce setups on individual work stations. (It videotaped the operations of all the teams, whose members then viewed the tapes and brainstormed to find ways of reducing "non-value-added" work.) After documenting all preliminary ideas, the team estimated savings from each policy and identified short-, medium-, and long-term goals. A third group ultimately carried out implementation: it planned the redesign of the shop and set the implementation schedule.

This is when the problems started. Management had expected smooth sailing because of the work force's flexibility. As one manager recalled: "When we decided to introduce JIT and SPC, we talked with others who had already implemented them to learn from their experiences. They all said you get increased commitment from employees. And they did not have as highly flexible work situations as we did." But as JIT and SPC began to take hold, employees began to complain that the plant's basic principle of employee involvement was being undermined.

In fact, workers were losing much of their freedom with the regimentation necessitated by JIT and SPC. Particularly vexing was the elimination of buffer inventory between, and within, work teams. Many workers and team managers began to voice concern: "We're losing our team identity and individual freedom with JIT." "Management is reverting to the traditional control mentality." "The shift in the plant is from a human focus toward more business basics for survival."

In retrospect, it is hard to believe that none of us saw this coming. True, under JIT and SPC, employees become more self-managing than in a command-and-control factory. They investigate process improvements and monitor quality themselves; they consequently enjoy immediate, impartial feedback regarding their own performance. (Managers don't have to tell them how they're doing. They help design the system, and *it* tells them how they're doing.) They also gain a better understanding of all elements of the manufacturing process.

On the other hand, the reform process that ushers in JIT and SPC is meant to *eliminate all variations within production* and therefore requires strict adherence to rigid methods and procedures. With JIT, workers meet set cycle times; with SPC, they must follow prescribed problem-solving methods. In their pure forms, then, JIT and SPC can turn workers into extensions of a system no less demanding than a busy assembly line. They can push workers to the wall.

Let us look more closely at what is lost.

Loss of individual autonomy. In a continuous-process operation, the coupling of worker and machine is limited by *machine* cycle time.

Operators typically have a significant period to monitor dials or gauges, which may allow them a certain amount of slack time. Similarly, lengthy machine cycles often provide operators sufficient time to perform "vertical" tasks (administrative or other duties traditionally performed by supervisors or staff personnel) or to assemble for a team meeting.

In a nonautomated or barely automated assembly line, the limiting factor is *operator* cycle time. With JIT, buffers are reduced—as is slack and idle time. As a result, employees have less time, if any, for vertical tasks or team meetings. Operators in job shops, who are expected to run multiple machines, can conceivably have even less time than workers in assembly line operations.

Although JIT advocates argue that abolishing wasteful operations leads to more meaningful, effective work, there are in fact a number of reasons for higher stress levels among line operators under JIT. Under the Toyota Production System, for example, workers adhere to rigid cycle times and are expected to adjust immediately to changes as demand fluctuates.

At Toyota, a multiskilled operator attends to as many as 16 machines at once. The operator first picks up one unit brought from the preceding process and sets it on the first machine. At the same time, he (or she) detaches another piece already processed by this machine and puts it on a chute in front of the next machine. Then, while walking to the second machine, he pushes a switch to start the first machine. After performing a similar sequence on all 16 machines, the operator returns to the initial process. "This is done in exactly the cycle time necessary, perhaps five minutes, so one unit of a finished gear will be completed in five minutes."[1]

According to one informed observer, line operators at Toyota have claimed that the JIT pace led to "more major accidents (resulting in a loss of four or more days at work) than in other Japanese automakers and an unusually high number of suicides among the blue-collar work force." Officials deny such claims but do admit that they encountered startup problems: lack of skills in adjusting to different types of equipment and resistance to running multiple machines.[2] Incidentally, less severe but similar problems occurred at the engine plant, where there was an increase in the number of medical restrictions for working on the assembly line under JIT.

At the engine plant, finally, the inflexible pace of the line impaired motivation. As one manager commented: "Everyone is affected. If I were a person who liked to build a lot of engines and could work fast, the line used to be fun. It felt good, I accomplished a lot, and got a lot of satisfaction from it. Today, I am slowed down and bored. Or take a slow person, one who wasn't pushed at all by the old system. He would now have an awful lot of stress because he's really pacing the line. The entire day is very stressful."

Loss of team autonomy. Under JIT, individual team activities must be tightly coordinated with other teams in the production pipeline. The loss of inventory buffers means that team meetings cannot simply be held whenever the need arises. Even coffee breaks must be coordinated across teams. As a result, individual team autonomy is replaced by carefully structured patterns of collaboration. Which is why team members at the engine plant complained that they had less freedom in solving problems; they felt limited in making process improvements because they believed they could only make changes that didn't affect other teams.

In addition, JIT drastically alters performance measurements. In traditional line flows, team members are typically given monthly stretch goals, as opposed to daily quotas. Under JIT, performance is measured against cycle goals. "It is not a 30-day time span, it is a 3-minute time span," noted one manager. Another put it this way: "It used to be that you had a monthly goal and you really shot for it. If you were down, you would have the business manager and the team manager—everyone working on the line—try to make the monthly goal. Now they have targets every day. It used to be that you could loaf a little bit, and other days you knew you were under the gun. Now you're under the gun all the time."

Loss of autonomy over methods. When the engine plant first started, teams had a great deal of autonomy in the improvement process. They had the freedom, within certain guidelines, to make changes on a trial basis; they were encouraged to be free-lancers, to take risks. As one team manager noted: "I was told in strong terms during the first several years I was here that I wasn't to do anything just because 'that's the way it's done.' I was told to do things the smartest way I could." Under JIT and SPC, this "entrepreneurial" spirit was limited; ideas are still encouraged but have to be tested under SPC guidelines.

Clearly, managers shouldn't give license to experiment where, in departing from established procedures, workers might jeopardize product integrity. But displacing worker trial and error with more scientific methods may have a negative psychological effect. Employees complained that SPC's structured experimentation restricted their freedom to make process changes. They perceived a loss of trust. As one manager noted: "It used to be that workers trusted us to listen to their ideas. Now we are troubleshooting more analytically and saying 'no' to workers more often than not. We say that their ideas don't fit SPC procedures. They say their ideas used to be worth something—now they are not."

Finally, SPC's process-capability studies may require operator certification programs. This is demoralizing for veteran workers. One worker responded to the certification process this way: "I can run every machine on this line, and I have done it on weekends, holidays, whenever. Now you say that I have to pass this road test to do it."

From Autonomy to Collaboration

What is to be done? Obviously, worker participation programs were never a carte blanche issued to operators to run production processes the way they wanted. The programs recognized axioms like concern for the customer, for the next team on the line, and for the schedule. Indeed, under JIT and SPC, tasks are more tightly coupled than ever before.

The key to protecting workers' self-esteem, then, is setting up a process for greater collaboration between teams—a time-consuming process, to be sure, but worth it in the long run. At NUMMI, the GM-Toyota joint venture, collaboration is now the name of the game. Whenever there is a cycle-time change (like when the plant went from a 54-second to a 68-second cycle time to accommodate slackening market demands), the teams have two to four weeks to plan changes in work station assignments. Teams have significant latitude in determining task sequences and work methods at each station; the team leaders (UAW working leaders) and group leaders (first-line supervisors) essentially become industrial engineers.

The objective is to balance the work load across all stations. This eliminates "cake jobs" and ensures that team members who rotate between stations within their teams can perform their tasks following standard procedures. When, for example, one team believes it would be better to reassign a particular task to another team—thereby changing the assembly sequence—all teams involved must reach a consensus.

Likewise, when a team member has a suggestion for improving a standardized job, a collaborative process begins again. The team member explains the idea to the team leader on that shift. If the team leader agrees that the idea has merit, the two try to sell it to their group leader. If the group leader likes it, then the three of them present it to the group leader and team leader on the other shift. Once there is a consensus at this level, the team members on both shifts are asked for input. If there is a problem, both shifts meet to try to gain consensus.

If there is agreement, the idea is ready for implementation. One shift will first try it out for approximately one week. During this period, the team leader, group leader, and quality assurance personnel evaluate the change, making modifications where necessary. If the idea works, it's instituted across shifts.

Again, process may appear tedious, but both managers and team members agree that the system has mitigated the frustrations that workers are apt to feel in such an interdependent system. It pushes joint responsibility and ownership for goals and objectives down to the teams and encourages their members, who cannot be wholly responsible for problem solving and designing work methods, to at least feel like participants. Needless to say, this is a far cry from the previous traditional management style at GM plants, where engineers dictated the work methods.

The only decision at NUMMI that might be considered completely at the discretion of individual workers is the pulling of the "andon," or line stop cord. However, even this initiates a collaborative process: when the cord is pulled, the team leader and the group leader quickly converge on the troubled work station to help solve the problem.

Tektronix also chose to emphasize the need for collaboration, but in a less structured way. For the assembly of one of Tektronix's portable oscilloscopes, a team of 35 assemblers and technicians broke into four subgroups: three feeder groups channeling work via a kanban system to a final assembly group. Individuals were free to change the procedure at their own work station, provided it did not affect any other work station. The revised procedure sheet informed anyone filling in at that station of any changes. (If a change affected the product in any way, the suggestion had to be reviewed with a team engineer.)

If any team member at Tektronix wanted to make a change that affected other members of the subgroup, for example, a change in the sequence of operations, the team member had to gain consensus from the group before making the change. If the change affected the entire team, however, the suggestion had to be raised at a weekly team meeting, where members would make a collaborative decision.

Here are other specific suggestions to mitigate the harsh effects of JIT and SPC:

Rethink zero inventory. In moving toward JIT, reducing inventory to an absolute zero level may not be the most economical or the wisest thing to do, at least not if it invites the system to break down.

The ultimate goal of JIT should be process control, not merely reducing inventory levels. NUMMI maintains a low level of "standard in-process stock" to balance the line and assure efficiency of the process. A minimum level of inventory may be justified to allow for team discussions or to alleviate individual employee stress. At the Saab-Valmet plant in Finland, for instance, buffers don't go below 20 minutes worth of work, because, as one of the managers put it, "Scandinavian respect for the workers' quality of life requires that the worker have the ability to work quickly for a few minutes in order to take a small personal break without stopping the line."[3]

Emphasize flow, not pace. Although JIT eliminates workers' ability to control their own work pace, using a kanban system allows workers to answer to each other rather than to a computer printout or supervisors. On the whole, kanban allows for more person-to-person initiative and communication. It therefore leads to a perception of increased worker control over the flow of production—though the reality may be otherwise. At Tektronix, for example, one team suggested increasing the kanban size to smooth production flow and still actually maintained daily output. If, however, too small a number of kanban squares allows for no buffer stock, the "human" system may prove even more stressful than any computerized one.

Focus on task design, not execution. Although there are limits on team freedom with respect to task execution, there is still room for teams to be involved in task design. Teams can still have significant say regarding initial tooling and task sequence. Indeed, given the short product life cycles in many industries, production processes tend to be very dynamic; new products mean many new opportunities for employees to contribute to the work method. Of course, the excitement may wear off if the job becomes routinized over several months. It's important to allow for continual reassessment of the process.

Give workers the right to move and choose. As long as teams coordinate their activities with other teams, there is nothing to suggest that management must establish the times of breaks or "indirect" tasks. One might even argue that JIT and SPC give workers more opportunity to move around—to rotate between jobs or fill in wherever a problem arises. Such movement, of course, is not wholly discretionary. Workers must move where they are needed. Nevertheless, the sheer relief of changing tasks can make workers feel freer.

Furthermore, JIT and SPC do not restrict team autonomy with respect to assigning individual members to various tasks or determining job rotations. In some processes, team members may also be able to establish their own work hours, in accordance with a set flextime plan. At Tektronix, the first assemblers to arrive will fill their kanbans; if the assemblers in the following work stations have not arrived, the first assemblers will then rotate to the next station, working down the line until others arrive.

Teams can have significant autonomy in laying out the job. The technology will, in part, dictate the parameters. However, in many cases a team could simply be given the square footage available and a blank piece of paper to design its space.

Allow for workplace management of quality and resources. JIT helps to uncover the "rocks"—the bottlenecks and wasted motion—and SPC provides a tool for improving quality. Team members should be encouraged to reject incoming nonconforming materials and halt outgoing shipments of poor-quality goods. Teams can also continue to control quality through peer evaluations in performance ratings.

Moreover, work teams typically have access to and responsibility for securing the resources they need for their production goals. They may monitor and disperse resources within budget constraints, make staffing decisions, train new team members, and obtain assistance from support personnel. JIT and SPC in no way limit overall team autonomy in these areas, only the timing of these activities.

Managers experienced with JIT and SPC establish set times when teams and team members can perform such activities. Moreover, vertical tasks can be rotated among individual team members when production pressures require workers full-time on the line. Team meetings can be held during shift overlaps or when the line is shut down.

All such ideas require revising traditional performance measurement systems. Companies recognize the need to schedule downtime for preventative maintenance of machines. But preventative maintenance for people is just as critical. Employees need periodic relief—more frequently than a scheduled ten-minute break every two-hours—

especially as cycle times shorten. NUMMI plans for the line to be down 5% of the time as a result of line stops.

Managing Expectations

If employees have never been given the latitude associated with self-managing work teams, their expectations tend to be lower. Hence many of the problems encountered by the engine manufacturer will not surface right away when JIT and SPC are introduced. But managers in high-commitment work systems particularly have to modify their workers' expectations without appearing to be reversing philosophy. This takes time. Time to teach, time to try to reach a consensus among workers that the changes associated with JIT and SPC are necessary.

As one manager at the engine manufacturer noted, "The teams feel like something was done to them, not with them. It is like having to get married, rather than wanting to get married." In the long run, a patient courtship will pay off.

And aside from time, there is timing. If, for example, worker participation programs are implemented *after* JIT, there will be less confusion: workers will then not be invited to imagine greater freedom just when the new process takes freedom away. Even if some workers participate in the design of the system, this doesn't necessarily mean the plant will be operated by worker teams from the start. Besides, it is the task of managers, as always, to prepare the ground. They ought not to promise workers autonomy when they mean them to deliver an unprecedented degree of cooperation.

Notes

1. Yasuhiro Monden, *Toyota Production System: Practical Approach to Production Management* (Atlanta, Ga.: Industrial Engineering and Management Press, 1983), pp. 69–70.
2. Michael A. Cusumano, *The Japanese Automobile Industry: Technology and Management at Nissan and Toyota* (Cambridge: Harvard University Press, 1985), p. 305.
3. Suzanne de Treville, "Disruption, Learning, and System Improvement in Just-in-Time Manufacturing," unpublished dissertation, Harvard Business School, 1987.

V

Strategic Manufacturing: Competing through Superior Capabilities

1
Strategic Planning—Forward in Reverse?

Robert H. Hayes

Since I began to study American industry almost 30 years ago, there has been a revolution in the science and practice of management and, especially, in the attraction of bright, professionally trained managers to the work of strategic planning. Yet as corporate staffs have flourished and as the notion of strategy has come to dominate business education and practice, our factories have steadily lost ground to those in other countries where strategy receives far less emphasis and the "professionalization" of management is far less advanced.

Over the years, I have prowled through hundreds of American factories and talked at length with innumerable line managers. Of late, I have been increasingly troubled by a recurring theme in the explanations they give for their companies' competitive difficulties. Again and again they argue that many of those difficulties—particularly in their manufacturing organizations—stem from their companies' strategic planning processes. Their complaint, however, is not about the misfunctioning of strategic planning but about the harmful aspects of its *proper* functioning.

In explaining why they continue to use old, often obsolete equipment and systems in their factories, some of these managers assert that their corporate strategic plans call for major investments elsewhere: in acquisitions, new lines of business, new plants in new locations, or simply the subsidization of other parts of their organizations. Their job, they say, is to "manage for cash," not to upgrade the capabilities of their existing plants. Others complain that their companies' strategic plans force on them new products and equipment that require capabilities their organizations do not have (or, worse, no longer have).

Still others report that they must assimilate acquired companies that "do not fit" or must grow faster than is prudent or even possible. With money being thrown at them faster than they can absorb it, much of it is poorly spent.

These comments do not come from ineffective managers who are looking for excuses. Nor are their companies unsophisticated in the art of strategic planning. Most of them have been at it for a long time and are widely regarded as experts. How, then, are we to make sense of the fact that, although the United States has poured more resources—both in total and on a per company basis—into strategic planning over the past 20 years than has any other country in the world, a growing number of our industries and companies today find themselves more vulnerable strategically than when they started? Not only do they fall short of goals, but they also lag behind competitors, largely of foreign origin, that place much less emphasis on strategic planning.[1]

Consider, for example, the experience of one company that, for a dozen years, emphasized the expansion of its market and the achievement of "low-cost-producer" status while allowing its R&D budget to fall to just over half its previous level (in constant dollars). The company has now come to realize that the high-volume, low-cost end of its business has moved irretrievably offshore and that its only hope for survival lies in rapid product innovation. There is, however, little innovative spark left in the organization, and neither increases in the R&D budget nor additions of new people appear to have had much impact. In desperation, the company is contemplating a merger with another company that has a better record of product innovation, but it is finding stiff resistance to its advances because of its reputation as a "researchers' graveyard."

Or consider the experience of another company that has a reputation for having modern production facilities and for being in the forefront of product technology in its fast-changing industry. As soon as it tests out the process for making a new product, management builds a new factory dedicated to that product. Unfortunately, once in place, this new facility tends to ossify because management also believes that the product life cycle in its industry is so short that continual investment in process improvement is uneconomic. As a result, the company has recently found itself losing market position to competitors that have pushed ahead in process technology. Although loath to cede business to those who came later, it has so far been unable to muster the ability (or, some say, the commitment) to keep up with its challengers' processing capabilities. Worse, management is realizing that the next generation of new products will require many of the manufacturing skills that it has neglected and its competitors have forced themselves to master.

How can these well-run companies that impose on themselves the rigorous discipline—and employ the sophisticated techniques—of modern strategic planning end up worse off than when they started? Is this a statistical accident or is there something about the process itself that is bad for corporate health? In this article, I will argue that, under certain circumstances, the methodology of formal strategic planning and, even worse, the organizational attitudes and relationships that it often cultivates can impair a company's ability to compete. Moreover, the circumstances under which this occurs is true for much of U.S. industry today.

To understand the damaging effects of that methodology, we must take a hard look at the logic that shapes it. The traditional strategic planning process rests on an "ends-ways-means" model: establish corporate objectives (ends); given those objectives, develop a strategy (ways) for attaining them; then marshal the resources (means) necessary to implement this strategy.

There are two familiar lines of argument for keeping these three elements of the planning process (ends, ways, means) in their current order. First, ends should precede ways because managers must know what their objectives are before deciding how to go about attaining them. A generation of MBA students has had pounded into their heads the story of Lewis Carroll's logician, the Cheshire Cat in *Alice in Wonderland*. When Alice comes upon the Cat and asks, "Would you tell me, please, which way I ought to go from here?" the Cat responds, "That depends . . . on where you want to get to." Alice answers, "I really don't much care where," and the Cat tells her, "Then it doesn't matter which way you go!"

The second argument has a different basis: to maximize efficiency, the choice of strategy should precede the assembling of the resources for carrying it out. Because each strategy is likely to require a different mix of resources, developing resources before choosing one of them exposes a company to the risk that it will be short of some resources and have too much of others.

What is wrong with this model? Let me raise questions about four of its aspects: (1) the ends that companies usually select, (2) the ways they try to attain those ends, (3) the means through which they carry out those ways, and (4) the logic that strings these elements together in the ends-ways-means order.

Choosing Ends

Most companies select goals that are too short term. It is almost impossible for a company to create a truly sustainable competitive advantage—one that is highly difficult for its competitors to copy—in just five to ten years (the time frame that most companies use). Goals that can be achieved within five years are usually either too easy or based on buying and selling something. Anything that a company can buy or sell, however, is probably available for purchase or sale by its competitors as well.

A series of short-term goals also encourages episodic thinking. When attention focuses on meeting immediate objectives, organizations often find the successive hurdles they have set for themselves increasingly difficult to surmount. Finally, the accumulated weight of deferred changes and seemingly innocuous compromises becomes too great, and managers trip badly on a hurdle that seemed no higher than the rest.

In most of the companies that I have observed, the goals are not only short term but also highly quantitative, focusing on rates of growth in profitability, return on investment, and market share. Unfortunately, quantitative goals follow Gresham's Law: they tend to drive out nonquantitative goals. It is easy for an organization tied to quantitative goals to believe (or to act as if it believes) that anything that is not quantitative is not important.

In practice, the danger is that hard numbers will encourage managers to forget that different kinds of goals have different values at different levels in an organization. Goals like return on investment have great meaning and value for senior managers, who understand the need to allocate capital efficiently and who are themselves evaluated on their ability to do so. ROI has almost no meaning for production workers, however, whose only contact with investment decisions is indirect: roofs that leak, old equipment that does not hold tolerances, new equipment that creates more problems than it solves. What does have meaning for these workers is quality (getting the work done correctly), timing (meeting delivery schedules), the working environment, and the satisfaction that comes from doing a good job as part of an appreciative organization. Objectives that have little meaning for large segments of an organization cannot be shared and cannot weld it together. Nor, for that matter, can episodic goals ("last year's emphasis was on quality, but this year's emphasis is on productivity"), which succeed only in diffusing commitment.

Developing Ways

Short-term goals also work to back companies into a mode of thinking that is based on forecasts (What do we think is going to happen?) rather than on visions (What do we want to happen?). Unfortunately, even though the usual five- to ten-year time periods are too short to achieve truly strategic objectives, they are much too long to obtain accurate forecasts.

Consider, for example, the forecasts made more than a decade ago of a stable, slow-moving enterprise: the U.S. economy. In 1970, when a number of eminent economists tried to predict how the economy would fare during "the sizzling seventies," their consensus was that inflation would continue at about 2.5%, productivity growth would average about 3%, and real growth in GNP would approach 4.5%. Instead, inflation averaged 8%, productivity growth only 1.3%, and real GNP a bit over 3%. As a result, the average American in 1980 enjoyed an income nearly 15% less than that predicted ten years before.

In the early 1970s, many U.S. corporations based their strategies on comparable forecasts of economic growth, as well as on their own forecasts of the much less predictable behavior of particular markets and competitors. Should we be surprised that most of their forecasts were totally off the mark, as were the elaborate strategies to which they gave rise? I suspect that the surge in domestic merger and acquisition activity in the late 1970s reflected in part the growing frustration of American managers who realized they could not reach the forecast-driven goals they had set for their companies and themselves through internal activities alone.

Inevitably, quantitative goals and reliance on long-term forecasts, combined with too-short planning horizons, lead corporate strategists to spend most of their time worrying about structural, rather than behavioral, means for achieving their objectives. After all, they reason, specific, measurable results come through "hard," measurable efforts: investments in new plants and equipment, the introduction of new products, the redesign of organization charts, and so on. This leads them to neglect less easily measured factors like performance evaluation and reward systems, work-force policies, information systems, and management selection and development policies. As the recent interest in "corporate culture" suggests, however, real strategic advantage comes from changing the way a company behaves, a task far more difficult and time-consuming than simply making a few structural decisions.

Another problem with today's strategic planning processes is that they reduce a company's flexibility. Like all organizational processes, strategic planning is subject to the first law of bureaucracy: if you give a smart, ambitious person a job to do, no matter how meaningless, he or she will try to make it bigger and more important. Jack Welch learned this lesson soon after he became chairman and CEO at General Electric. According to Welch, "Once written, the strategic document can take on a life of its own, and it may not lend itself to flexibility. . . . An organization can begin to focus on form rather than substance."[2] He also described to a group of Harvard MBA students how GE's strategic plans had become less and less useful as they got bigger and bigger, as more and more hours went into preparing them, and as planners embellished them with increasingly sophisticated graphics and fancy covers.

William Bricker, chairman and CEO of Diamond Shamrock, has much the same reaction: "Why has our vision been narrowed? Why has our flexibility been constricted? To my mind there is one central reason: our strategies have become too rigid. . . . A detailed strategy [is] like a road map . . . [telling] us every turn we must take to get to our goal. . . . The entrepreneur, on the other hand, views strategic planning not as a road map but as a compass . . . and is always looking for the new road."[3] This is a provocative analogy: when you are lost on a highway, a road map is very useful; but when you are lost in a swamp whose topography is constantly changing, a road map is of little help. A simple compass—which indicates the general direction to be taken and allows you to use your own ingenuity in overcoming various difficulties—is much more valuable.

STRATEGIC LEAPS OR SMALL STEPS?

The difficulties that highly visible U.S. industries are now experiencing surprise and puzzle many Americans. Why is the nation that put a man on the moon and invented genetic engineering unable to produce a consumer videocassette recorder (all those sold by U.S. companies are imported, even though a U.S. company produced the first commercial videotape machine 30 years ago) or even a better small car than Toyota? One possible reason, of course, is that we *can* put a man on the moon. The very skills and psychology that enable us to conceive and carry out something like the Apollo project may hamper

Exhibit I. Competitive progress

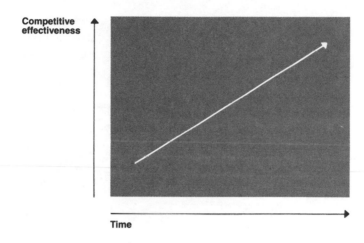

us when we are in a competitive environment that bases success more on a series of small steps than on a few dramatic breakthroughs.

Consider the graph in Exhibit I, where the horizontal axis measures the passage of time and the vertical, competitive effectiveness (lower cost, better quality, more features, faster delivery). In a free market, a company's competitive effectiveness should improve over time—that is, it will move from a position in the lower left of the graph to a position in the upper right. Now, how does a company accomplish this movement?

One approach, shown in Exhibit II, is through a series of strategic leaps, a few giant upward steps at critical moments. These leaps may take a variety of forms: a product redesign, a large-scale factory modernization or expansion, a move to another location that promises great improvement in wage rates or labor relations, an acquisition of a supplier of a critical material or component, or adoption of a new manufacturing technology. Between taking these giant steps, managers seek only incidental improvements in competitiveness, as the company digests the last step and contemplates the next.

At the opposite extreme, as shown in Exhibit III, a company may try to progress through a series of small steps whose cumulative impact will be just as great. Rather than rely on a series of discontinuities, such a company continuously strives to bolster its competitive position through a variety of incremental improvements.

Exhibit. II.   *Progress through strategic leaps*

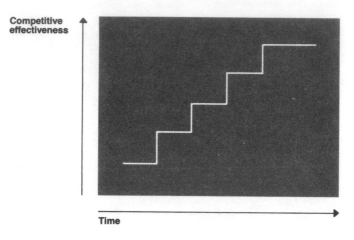

Which approach is best? Both can get you to the same point, but each places different demands on an organization and exposes it to very different risks.

Strategic leaps. Each step in Exhibit II is highly visible and usually requires a major expenditure of funds. Thus the timing of the change becomes important. A decline in profits, a potential acquisition, a sudden surge of orders that pushes the organization to the limit of its resources—any such development can delay the project or put it on hold. Further, managers at all levels in an organization must get involved in analyzing and approving the decision to take the step. Extensive staff involvement is also essential, as is the expertise of many specialists—financial analysts, strategic planners, legal experts, scientists, outside consultants, and public relations personnel—who often have more allegiance to their own "professions" than to the company itself.

Because each step is so big and so visible, whoever proposes the change takes on an enormous risk in return for the chance to reap huge rewards. Success creates heroes; failure brings severe consequences. The people who rise to the top in such organizations usually fall into one of two camps: they are either "lucky gamblers," who were involved in two or three successful leaps, or "corporate kibitzers," who managed to avoid entanglement in any disasters.

Such companies regard the corporate staff as an elite group and treat

Exhibit III. *Progress through incremental improvements*

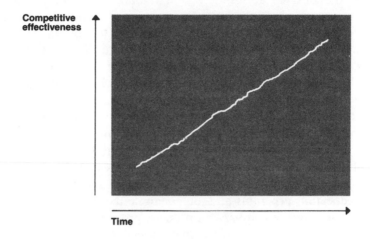

Competitive
effectiveness

Time

assignments of line managers to staff positions as promotions. At lower levels in the organization, however, there is little need for outstanding, highly trained people. The task of people at these levels is simply to operate the structure that top management and its staff of experts have created. It does not seem necessary in such companies to put much time and effort into training and upgrading factory workers or managers because the next strategic leap may make their newly developed skills obsolete. Nor do personnel policies that reward employee longevity seem particularly desirable because they reduce the company's flexibility—its ability, say, to pull up stakes and move to a new location, to sell the business, or to implement a significant reduction in employment as part of an automation program.

In similar fashion, a reliance on strategic leaps makes it unnecessary for workers or lower level managers to have a detailed understanding of how their own operations affect—and are affected by—other parts of the organization. The same logic robs employee suggestion programs of their usefulness, for workers cannot possibly understand how the changes they may propose fit into the company's overall strategy, much less the leap it is contemplating next.

Small steps. If, however, a company follows an incremental approach to improvement, few of the steps it takes are highly visible or risky. Because major capital authorization requests are seldom necessary, there is little need for much staff assistance or outside advice.

Rather than put massive resources into the development of elaborate plans in the rarefied atmosphere of a remote headquarters, such a company expects the bulk of its improvements to bubble up, in an entrepreneurial fashion, from lower levels in the organization. Its corporate staff is much smaller and less powerful than that of a strategic leap organization. Its main role is to offer support services. In effect, the organization charts of these companies look more like tables than pyramids.

This incremental approach requires immense low-level expertise— not expertise of a low level, but expertise at low levels. Developing this kind of expertise takes a long time. Executives need to expend great effort on recruiting people who are both loyal and trainable, and on continuously improving their capabilities once hired—through both formal education programs and job assignments that provide a broad understanding of the company's products, processes, and competitive environment. In turn, top management needs to augment this understanding and keep it up to date by disseminating information about current financial results, market behavior, and competitors' activities.

Having made so extensive an investment in low-level expertise, a company will do its best to retain the people who have it. Long-time employees have another advantage: over time, through their multiple job assignments, they develop relationships with people in different parts of the organization. These relationships make it easier to implement the small changes that require communication and cooperation among several different groups.

Incremental projects generally require so little capital that managers can often fund them out of a plant's annual operating budget. It stands to reason that plant managers will support such efforts if they are intimately familiar with the production systems and people involved and are committed to the plant's long-term success because they expect to stay in their jobs for a long time. Such projects are also more likely to thrive if workers, plant engineers, and lower level managers participate in developing them—through suggestion programs, quality circles, and the like—and if they identify the company's long-term success with their own.

This kind of company does not believe that many of its problems can be solved by top management. The information and expertise needed for dealing with them reside lower down in the organization, and the problems themselves are continuously evolving. Therefore, top management's role is less to spot and solve problems than to create an organization that can spot and solve its own problems.

THE TORTOISE AND THE HARE

Up to this point, I have been describing, rather abstractly, two contrasting "pure" strategies. In practice, of course, few companies choose approaches so extreme; most strategies fall somewhere along the spectrum between them. U.S. companies do, however, tend to adopt approaches toward the strategic leap end; those of our two most powerful international competitors, Germany and Japan, tend to seek incremental improvements within an existing structure and technology. They are the tortoise; we are the hare.

In the fable, as we may recall with some apprehension, the tortoise won the race. Are we to share the hare's fate? To answer that question, let us examine the risks and rewards of each approach.

The central risk of following the incremental approach is that a company will be "leapfrogged" and left behind by a competitor that abandons its traditional technology, location, or corporate strategy and adopts a new and more successful one. The folklore of American business is full of such examples: the replacement of piston engines by jet engines, of vacuum tubes by transistors, of ditto machines by xerography, of New England textile companies by those that moved south. The list goes on and on.

Conversely, the central risk of following the strategic leap approach is that a breakthrough may not always be available exactly when it is needed. After seizing a major competitive advantage, a company may see its lead nibbled away by competitors that gradually adapt themselves to the new technology or strategy and then push it beyond its initial limits. This is the time to make another leap, but what if the company's technicians and strategists reach into their hats and find nothing there?

One obvious response to this predicament is to use an incremental approach, like that of the competition, until a breakthrough does become available. Doing so, however, is not easy for a company that has organized itself around the expectation of repeated breakthroughs. As I have argued, the kind of organization adept at making strategic leaps bears little resemblance to one that takes the incremental approach. Entrepreneurship from below cannot be "ordered" by managers from above—particularly when, as is usually the case, top-down, staff-dominated planning and control systems have caused most of the entrepreneurs to leave.

Unfortunately, the reverse is not true. As our Japanese and German competitors are demonstrating all too well, companies that adopt an incremental approach *can* eventually accommodate themselves to a new technology. As a rule, they are not as fast but, if given the time, they can do it. In other words, the ability to progress through incremental change does not preclude, although it may slow down, a company's ability to master discontinuous change. In fact, an organization that is used to continuous small changes and that has balanced strategic expertise at the top with operating expertise and entrepreneurship at the bottom is probably better prepared for a big leap than is an organization that has gone for several years without any change at all.

Assembling Means

The third element (after ends and ways) in the strategic planning paradigm is the selection and assembling of the resources necessary to implement the chosen strategy. Although a strategy will usually require many different types of resources, strategic planning in most corporations devotes most of its attention to just one: financial wherewithal. There are two reasons for this.

First, since managers usually state their ultimate objectives in financial terms, it is natural for them to state required resources in financial terms as well. Second, resources get used most efficiently when management provides only those that are absolutely necessary. Understandably, companies try to maintain their resources in as liquid (that is, financial) a form as possible for as long as possible, for doing so gives them maximum flexibility to convert liquid resources into the desired form at just the moment they are needed.

Such a practice works well if reasonably efficient markets exist for important assets like market position, worker or manager skills, and technological capabilities. Many companies have come to realize, however, that technology, market position, and organizational skills are not as transferable as they had expected. As a result, those that try to buy them often run into the infrastructure problems I described earlier.

Informed businesspeople, who understand well the danger of trying to place a modern steel mill in a less developed country like Bangladesh, have sometimes been willing to try to implant advanced new technologies in organizations that are unprepared to receive them. In most cases, these organizations respond by starving the new technology of understanding and resources—just as the human body tries to reject a heart transplant that is essential to its survival. No matter how brilliant its technological underpinnings, a new product will fail if the company's manufacturing organization is unable to make that product efficiently or if the company's sales force is unable to sell it effectively. Such capabilities cannot be bought from the outside. They must be grown from within, and growing them takes time.

The Logic of Ends-Ways-Means

When managers in strategic planning demand that ends should precede ways and both should precede means, they make certain assumptions about the environment and the nature of competition. First, they assume that the world of competition is predictable and that clear paths can be charted across it much like a highway system across a road map. Equally important, they assume that reasonable objectives, arrived at by thoughtful people, can be achieved through purposeful activity and that progress toward those objectives is both measurable and controllable.

The managerial logic of ends-ways-means also attributes a certain stability to the company itself. There is an expectation that the company's values and needs will not change over the planning horizon and that the objectives it sets will seem as desirable up close as they do from afar. Managers can, therefore, concern themselves with "static optimization"—that is, with making a few key decisions and then holding to them. There is a further expectation that, once these objectives and the strategies for achieving them are in place, managers can assemble the necessary resources in the required time frame and convert them into the appropriate form.

Underlying all these assumptions is the belief that responsibility for organizational success rests primarily on the shoulders of top management. This "command-and-control" mentality allocates all major decisions to top management, which imposes them on the organization and monitors them through elaborate planning, budgeting, and control systems. In many ways this logic is similar to that which underlies modern conventional warfare: generals set the strategy, provide the resources, establish the detailed plan of action, and continuously monitor the progress of engagements as they occur.

Does this logic make sense? Earlier I questioned the notion that means should follow ways on the ground that important resources—technology, skills, and effective working relationships—cannot always be purchased when needed. Now I also question whether managers should decide on ends before selecting ways.

Taken to an extreme, these questions could turn into a general attack on logic as applied to business planning. Such attacks are more and more common these days, from *In Search of Excellence*'s claim that "detached, analytical justification for all decisions . . . has arguably led us seriously astray" to the *Washington Post*'s insistence that "preoccupation with logic has helped to improve and reform the world, but it has also put professionals dangerously out of touch with the gritty everyday world." My point is not to disparage the relevance of all logic to planning but to suggest that there may be alternative logics worth exploring. One of them, in fact, is to turn the ends-ways-means paradigm on its head: means-ways-ends.

How might such a logic work? First, it suggests that a company should begin by investing in the development of its capabilities along a broad front (means). It should train workers and managers in a variety of jobs; educate them about the general competitive situation and the actions of specific competitors; teach them how to identify problems, how to develop solutions for them, and how to persuade others to follow their recommendations. It should acquire and experiment with new technologies and techniques so that workers and managers gain experience with them and come to understand their capabilities and constraints. It should focus R&D activity on fewer lines but spread it more widely throughout the organization. Managers should have cross-functional assignments so that they develop a broad understanding of the company's markets, technologies, and factories.

Second, as these capabilities develop and as technological and market opportunities appear, the company should encourage managers well down in the organization to exploit matches wherever they occur (ways). Top management's job, then, is to facilitate this kind of entrepreneurial activity, provide it with resources from other parts of the company, and, where feasible, encourage cooperative activities. In short, the logic here is, Do not develop plans and then seek capabilities; instead, build capabilities and then encourage the development of plans for exploiting them. Do not try to develop optimal strategies on the assumption of a static environment; instead, seek continuous improvement in a dynamic environment.

The guiding force throughout such disparate activities will not come from a set of directions or controls. To the contrary, it will come from a balance between integration, which arises out of a sense of organizational unity and camaraderie, an instinctive banding together in the face of common enemies, and direction, which arises out of a set of shared values rooted in a long-term vision of the kind of company that its people want it to become—in short, group cohesion and a compass. A compass, remember, is not an end; it only provides a sense of direction, a means to a variety of possible ends.

Under what circumstances might such a means-ways-ends logic be effective? When the competitive world is like a swamp that is shifting in unpredictable ways, particular objectives are likely to lose their attractiveness over time. Even so, a common vision can keep people moving ahead, moving around unforeseen obstacles and beyond immediate (largely because they are visible) objectives.

Is Guerrilla Warfare Always Better?

An organization that takes a means-ways-ends approach to strategic planning assumes everybody is responsible for its prosperity. Its success rests on its ability to exploit opportunities as they arise, on its ingenuity, on its capacity to learn, on its determination and persistence.

There is an obvious analogy here with guerrilla warfare. It would, of course, be wrong to suggest that strategic planning based on a strategic leap approach is always less effective than that based on an incremental approach. Even in guerrilla warfare, someone must decide where to fight and which goals to seek. Someone must select and train leaders and rally soldiers to the cause. On occasion, conventional pitched battles are perfectly appropriate.

Sometimes companies must change their objectives; they may decide to enter a new business or abandon an old one. These decisions seldom bubble up from the bottom. Instead, they flow down from the top. The trick, of course, to managing such discontinuities without alienating the organization or undermining its capabilities is to employ a patient, consensus-seeking decision process in which all parties have an opportunity to be heard. More important, everyone must regard a necessary leap as the exception, not the rule. Once a guerrilla army decides that the only person with any real authority is the supreme leader, its field commanders lose their credibility.

Therefore, I suspect that the Japanese and German companies that are currently studying the American approach to strategic planning do not intend to make it a way of life. They intend simply to graft it onto their existing systems so they can be better prepared for dealing with the discontinuities that sometimes confront them. What they may not appreciate is how seductive such an approach can be for top management. When the balance of power begins to shift, when the "counters" gain ascendency over the "doers," the best doers may seek to become counters. Or they go elsewhere, where they can do it *their* way.

Further, in most mature industries, the development of markets and technology is not discontinuous but moves forward in a steady, almost predictable manner. Even in high-technology industries like semiconductors and computers, for example, progress during the past decade has taken place within technological frameworks that were essentially in place more than 15 years ago. The opportunities for dramatic breakthroughs and strategic "end runs" have diminished as sophisticated multinational companies have identified most of the untapped markets and have uncovered most of the unexploited pools of low-cost labor in the world. They are running out of islands to move to.

Seen in this light, the present struggle between U.S. companies and their foreign competitors can be likened to a battle between a bunch of hares, trained in conventional warfare and equipped with road maps, and an unknown number of tortoises, equipped with compasses and an expertise in guerrilla warfare. Unfortunately, the battle is taking place in a swamp and not on a well-defined highway system.

The logic of ends-ways-means that got the hares into this situation is unlikely to get them out. They will need to explore a new logic, possibly a reverse logic, and be willing to question the basis of formal strategic planning as it is practiced today. Perhaps they should return to the approaches they used to follow—when they spent less time developing strategies but their industrial capabilities were the envy of the world.

Notes

1. A number of studies suggest there is either no relationship between planning and various measures of organizational performance or a negative one. See, for example, P.H. Grinyer and D. Norburn, "Planning for Existing Markets: Perceptions of Executives and Financial Performance," *Journal of the Royal Statistical Society* (A) 138, pt. 1 (1975), p. 70; Ernest A. Kallman and H. Jack Shapiro, "The Motor Freight Industry—A Case Against Planning," *Long Range Planning*, February 1978, p. 81; Ronald J. Kudla, "The Effects of Strategic Planning on Common Stock Returns," *Academy of Management Journal*, March 1980, p. 5; Milton Leontiades and Ahmet Tezel, "Planning Perceptions and Planning Results," *Strategic Management Journal*, January–March 1980, p. 65; Leslie W. Rue and Robert M. Fulmer, "Is Long-Range Planning Profitable?" *Academy of Management Proceedings* (1973), p. 66.

2. "Managing Change," keynote address, Dedication Convocation, Fuqua School of Business, Duke University, April 21, 1983.

3. "Entrepreneurs Needed," *Oil and Gas Digest*, November 15, 1982.

2
Beyond World-Class: The New Manufacturing Strategy

Robert H. Hayes and Gary P. Pisano

During the 1980s, U.S. manufacturing companies rediscovered the power that comes from superior manufacturing and initiated a variety of activities to improve their competitiveness. Many announced that their "manufacturing strategy" was to become "world-class"—as good, along various measures, as the best companies in their industries. In pursuing this goal, they typically adopted one or more of a growing number of improvement programs, such as TQM (Total Quality Management), JIT (Just-in-Time) production, and DFM (Design for Manufacturability), not to mention lean manufacturing, reengineering, benchmarking, and the ubiquitous team approach.

While some of these improvement efforts have been successful, the majority, according to recent surveys, have not. Even some of the Japanese companies that pioneered these approaches appear to be having second thoughts. These conflicting results have led to frustration, confusion, and a growing debate about whether the difficulties with these efforts are the result of poor management or of flaws in the programs themselves.

This debate is misdirected. The problem is not with the programs nor with the way they are implemented. The problem is that simply *improving* manufacturing—by, for example, adopting JIT, TQM, or some other three-letter acronym—is *not* a strategy for using manufacturing to achieve competitive advantage. Neither is aspiring to lean manufacturing, continuous improvement, or world-class status.

In today's turbulent competitive environment, a company more than ever needs a strategy that specifies the kind of competitive advantage that it is seeking in its marketplace and articulates how that advantage is to be achieved. If managers pin their competitive hopes on the implementation of a few best-practice approaches, they implicitly abandon the central concept of a strategy in favor of a generic approach to competitive success. How can a company expect to achieve any sort of competitive advantage if its only goal is to be "as good as" its toughest competitors?

We propose a new explanation for the problems that many companies have experienced with improvement programs. Our view reflects the current shift in thinking not only about manufacturing but also about the essence of competitive strategy itself. And it integrates manufacturing strategy with the notions of both core competences and learning organizations.

The crux of the issue is that most companies focus on the *form* of their organizational assets—for example, the mechanics of JIT and TQM—rather than on their *substance*, the skills and capabilities that enable a factory to excel and make it possible for various improvement programs to achieve their desired results. The consequence of this outlook is that managers have tended to view such programs as solutions to specific problems rather than as stepping-stones *in an intended direction*.

Looking at manufacturing strategy as an intended direction has ramifications for almost every aspect of running a corporation because it implies that the key to long-term success is being able *to do certain things* better than your competitors can. Such superior organizational capabilities provide a competitive advantage that is much more sustainable than one based on something you can build or buy. You may be able to buy access to a certain technology, for example, but you cannot buy the ability to produce it efficiently, sell it effectively, or advance it over time. The road to competitive success is not paved with advanced equipment, the transfer of production to a low-wage area, or improving quality by adopting a TQM system. These are all programs that your competitors can copy relatively easily.

In a stable environment, competitive strategy is about staking out a position, and manufacturing strategy focuses on getting better at the things necessary to defend that position. In turbulent environments, however, the goal of strategy becomes *strategic flexibility*. Being world-class is not enough; a company also has to have the capability to switch gears—from, for example, rapid product development to low cost—relatively quickly and with minimal resources. The job of manufacturing is to provide that capability.

If managers consider the capabilities they want to develop or preserve, they may make very different decisions about closing a plant or exiting a business, about "make versus buy" decisions, about alliances and acquisitions, about whether to automate an operation or move it to a low-wage area, about training and management career paths. (See "A New Approach to Investment.") Considering desired future capabilities can also help managers think through whether JIT or any of the other new "best practices" is the best vehicle for building the capabilities that will be central to their company's long-term success.

A New Approach to Investment

Traditionally, companies have viewed investments in new facilities, technology, and R&D as the primary means to enhance their existing manufacturing capabilities. But according to the new approach to manufacturing strategy, managers should think about investments more in terms of their capacity to build new capabilities. Rarely, if ever, is a strategically worthwhile capability created through a one-shot investment. Capabilities that provide enduring sources of competitive advantage are usually built over time through a series of investments in facilities, human capital, and knowledge.

The idea of investments as crucial steps in the capability-building process conflicts with an assumption that often underlies capital-budgeting decisions: that investments can be reversed or delayed. According to traditional capital budgeting, an asset that is sold can often be bought back, and an investment can often be deferred with no penalty other than that contained in the time value of money. This may be true for certain types of assets, such as a new plant. But a company's capabilities are more than its physical assets. In fact, they are largely embodied in the collective skills and knowledge of its people and the organizational procedures that shape the way employees interact. Like muscles, capabilities embodied in human capital atrophy with disuse—and deterioration can be irreversible.

Consider a company that is contemplating closing a plant. Accounting standards require that it recognize the loss in book value resulting from that closure. But what about the loss of the specialized capabilities embedded in the plant—things like skills in precision machining, a highly motivated work force, and detailed knowledge of customer needs? If demand picks up again, the company can go out and buy a plant and equipment, but replacing the human capital that took years to build will be much more difficult.

The traditional financial models used to evaluate capital investments also ignore the fact that investments can create opportunities for learning. These opportunities are a lot like financial options: they have value, and that value increases as the future becomes more unpredictable. If a company cannot predict whether future customers will emphasize high performance or low cost, an option that would allow the company to achieve either one as the situation evolves has a very high value.

Consider a company that needs to expand capacity. One way might be to add a production line that is identical to existing lines. A second might be to invest in an R&D effort directed at improving productivity. Certainly the latter is more risky, but it also provides an opportunity to gain a deeper understanding of the production process. This new knowledge, in turn, might create opportunities for future investments, such as a new design for production equipment or the development of substitute materials. It might also open up new competitive options. Discovering a way to reduce setup times, for example, may increase capacity without additional investment. Alternatively, it could allow the company to produce smaller lot sizes without any loss in capacity. Neither of these would be options if the company expanded by adding another line just like its existing ones.

Some history is needed to help explain the forces behind this new strategic framework for manufacturing.

Until the early 1980s, most managers in the United States thought about manufacturing in terms of a paradigm whose roots went back over 100 years. The American system of manufacturing, with its emphasis on mass markets, standard designs, and high-volume production using interchangeable parts, revolutionized manufacturing in the mid-1800s. Modified and elaborated by the principles of scientific management as promulgated by Frederick Taylor and his disciples as well as by such great industrialists as Isaac Singer, Andrew Carnegie, and Henry Ford, this new paradigm helped the United States become an industrial powerhouse by the 1920s.

The following ideas were accepted as dogma: that work was most efficiently done when divided up and assigned to specialists; that managers and staff experts should do the thinking so that workers could concentrate on "doing"; that every process was characterized by a certain amount of variation, hence an irreducible rate of defects; and that communication in an organization should be tightly controlled and should proceed through a hierarchical chain of command. Manufacturing should emphasize long runs, utilize equipment designed for each process stage whose capacities are matched as closely as possible, and use inventories to buffer different stages both from each other and from the erratic behavior of suppliers and customers. Work should be organized and conducted systematically, in a logical sequence, and under tight supervision.

In 1969, Wickham Skinner challenged Taylor's assertion that there was one best way to manufacture in his now-classic HBR article, "Manufacturing—Missing Link in Corporate Strategy" (May–June). The kernel of his argument was that: (a) companies have different strengths and weaknesses and can choose to differentiate themselves from their competitors in different ways; (b) similarly, different production systems, the composite of decisions in a number of key decision areas, have different operating characteristics; and therefore, rather than adopting an industry-standard production system, (c) the "task" for a company's manufacturing organization is to configure a production system that, through a series of interrelated and internally consistent choices, reflects the priorities and trade-offs implicit in its competitive situation and strategy.

Despite the emergence of a totally different world order for industrial competition, this basic framework has proven to be remarkably robust. A number of common practices used today trace their roots to it. For example, the concept of a "focused factory" follows naturally from the idea that no single organization can do all things equally well. Consider a company that markets one product line sold in a market where purchasing decisions are driven largely by price and another to people who are willing to pay a premium for high quality and customized features. Since no one plant can be expected to provide all these characteristics equally well, the focused factory concept argues for splitting the production of the two lines into separate factories or subunits within the same plant.

Another offshoot is the idea of matching product and market evolution with manufacturing process characteristics. The product-process life cycle suggests that as a product matures, the relative importance of competitive priorities will shift, and these shifts have important implications for manufacturing. For example, in its early stages, a product often competes on the basis of special features or innovative designs. This calls for a production process that is very flexible with respect to market shifts and design changes. Such an operation might employ highly skilled workers, general-purpose tooling, and little automation; moreover, it should be located close to R&D and, to reduce the risk of obsolescence, produce small batches. As the product matures, the market typically evolves toward a small number of high-volume products that compete with each other largely on the basis of price. To this end, factories ought to be highly automated, located in areas where labor or material costs are low, employ less skilled workers, and, in order to minimize changeover costs, schedule production around long runs.

Skinner's framework for manufacturing strategy is based on the notion of strategic fit: a company's manufacturing system should reflect its competitive position and strategy. Focus provides both a means to achieve this fit and a discipline for maintaining it in the face of a barrage of opportunities. And the product-process life cycle helps guide the adjustments in strategy and systems that will likely be required in a changing world.

It soon became clear, however, that this framework is incomplete. It doesn't explain, for example, why two appliance makers may adopt similar competitive strategies and choose similar production processes, but one may end up being far more successful than the other.

Japanese companies began in the late 1970s to assault world markets in a number of industries with increasing ferocity. Their secret weapon turned out to be sheer manufacturing virtuosity. Most were producing products similar to those offered by Western companies and marketing them in similar ways. What made these products attractive was not only their cost but also their low incidence of defects, their reliability, and their durability.

For a while, it appeared that Japan's manufacturing superiority could be attributed to the traditional precepts of manufacturing strategy. By and large, the Japanese adopted consistent policies in their pursuit of high efficiency and quality. They also operated focused factories; in fact, their emphasis on "repetitive manufacturing," "just-in-time" production, and smooth work flows led them to be almost obsessive in their pursuit of long runs of standard products. And their emphasis on continuous improvement appeared, at least initially to those looking for familiar reference points, to mirror the U.S. fascination with learning curves.

But as our eyes slowly grew accustomed to the many nuances of Japanese culture and began to pick out the details of their management practices, certain paradoxes became evident. During the 1980s, a new paradigm of manufacturing that challenged both the American system of manufacturing and some of the basic tenets of manufacturing strategy began to emerge.

Are trade-offs really necessary? Manufacturing strategists had long argued that different production systems exhibited different operating characteristics: some were good at low cost, some at high quality, and some at fast response times. In designing a production system, therefore, managers had to decide which was most important. And if there were conflicts among different objectives, they had to make tough choices based on a careful analysis of the trade-offs. But many Japanese factories practicing lean manufacturing appeared to surpass their U.S. counterparts on several dimensions: they achieved lower cost, higher quality, faster product introductions, and greater flexibility, all at the same time.

In *The Machine That Changed the World*, the widely read book on the auto industry, authors James Womack, Daniel Jones, and Daniel Roos describe how, in contrast to mass production, lean production "is 'lean' because it uses less of everything . . . half the human effort in the factory, half the factory space, half the investment in tools, half the engineering hours to develop a new product in half the time. Also it requires keeping far less than half the needed inventory on-site, resulting in fewer defects, and produces a greater and ever-growing variety of products."[1]

Lean manufacturing has apparently eliminated the trade-offs among productivity, investment, and variety. (See "Allegheny Ludlum: Minimizing Manufacturing Trade-Offs.")

Allegheny Ludlum: Minimizing Manufacturing Trade-Offs

The Allegheny Ludlum Corporation is one U.S. company that has been pursuing a strategy of minimizing the trade-offs inherent in manufacturing by expanding its capabilities through a variety of tailored programs. The specialty steelmaker, which has had a consistently high return on equity in the last 13 years (a period during which many steelmakers lost money), has managed to achieve a substantial degree of flexibility (in terms of customizing individual orders) and low costs.

Allegheny's success cannot be explained by its adherence to the traditional concept of manufacturing strategy or to lean manufacturing, but by the way it has successfully integrated both. Like other companies that have embraced lean manufacturing, Allegheny emphasizes product variety, continuous efforts to reduce manufacturing costs, teamwork, and delegated decision making.

But some of Allegheny's approaches contradict conventional lean-manu-facturing practices. Although the company employs the cross-functional teams favored in lean manufacturing, it maintains a primarily functional structure. And while lean manufacturing stresses "horizontal" problem solving (dealing with problems at lower levels in the organization), Allegheny's top management is very involved with all aspects of the business. Daily reports on productivity, utilization, yield, rejects, and variances flow vertically to its CEO, who uses the information to institute immediate corrective actions.

The steelmaker has made a commitment to invest in, improve, and capture (through models) its knowledge about process technology. To encourage plants to undertake technically risky experiments, the company charges their cost to a separate corporate account rather than to the plants themselves.

One such endeavor developed capabilities that enabled Allegheny to double the capacity of its melt shop without any physical expansion. This involved several projects. One focused on finding lower cost raw materials, while others concentrated on increasing batch sizes, reducing the time required between batches, and cutting the time between the completion of the melt and further processing. These projects involved experimentation on the shop floor, with the active involvement of first-line supervisors, and contributions from other departments. For example, R&D developed computer programs to increase control over the melting process. This increase in capacity gave Allegheny the option of expanding its total output of commodity steels (at a lower cost than competitors), making more customized orders, or some combination of both. When there is uncertainty about the demand for each type of product, having this option is obviously valuable.

Like companies engaged in lean manufacturing, Allegheny engages in vigorous and continuous manufacturing improvement. Unlike improvements in many of these companies, these improvements take place within a strategic framework that recognizes that the key to achieving competitive advantage is deciding which capabilities to build.

Information for this example was obtained from the HBS case "Allegheny Ludlum Steel Corporation" (9-686-087) by Artemis March under the supervision of Professor David Garvin and the HBS case "Allegheny Ludlum: Research and Engineering Resource Allocation" (9-692-027) by Geoffrey Gill under the supervision of Professor Dorothy Leonard-Barton.

Do factories have to be focused? Although Japanese factories initially appeared to restrict product variety and encourage uninterrupted work flows, many elite Japanese companies embarked on an orgy of product proliferation during the 1980s. Sony, for example, introduced over 300 versions of its basic Walkman (disclaiming the need for market research, it simply introduced a new model and saw how it sold), and Seiko was renowned for its ability to introduce a new watch model every working day. Didn't this product proliferation refute the idea of focus? The emergence of new flexible manufacturing systems, which apparently made it possible for factories to produce a broad range of products with little loss in efficiency, also seemed to undercut the need for focused factories.

Is strategic fit enough? Although the traditional manufacturing strategy framework provided a vision of the contribution that a company's manufacturing organization could make to its competitive success, it left vague certain key issues. For example, while it was clear that once a company settled on a competitive strategy, its manufacturing organization should develop the specific capabilities required to implement that strategy, it was less clear how much freedom manufacturing should have to develop competences that went beyond the strategy's immediate requirements. And there was little discussion of the criteria that should be used to guide the selection of capabilities to be acquired.

Moreover, while many Japanese companies had built exceptional manufacturing capabilities, they did not appear to have an enduring approach to competition. Instead, the form of their attack changed, sometimes with bewildering speed, from low cost to high precision to flexibility to innovativeness. And through such changes, they were sometimes able to transform the nature of competition within an industry.

Japanese companies had apparently found an approach to manufacturing uniformly superior to the "Taylor system," which was characterized by an emphasis on speed and flexibility rather than volume and cost. According to this lean approach, people should be broadly trained rather than specialized. Staff is "overhead," and overhead is bad. Rejects are unacceptable. Communication should take place informally and horizontally among line workers rather than through prescribed hierarchical paths. Equipment should be general purpose, possibly using some form of programmable automation, and organized in cells that produce a group of similar products rather than specialized by process stage. Production throughput time is more important than labor or equipment utilization. Inventory, like rejects, is "waste." Supplier relationships should be long-term and cooperative. Activities associated with product development should be done concurrently, not sequentially, and should be carried out by cross-functional teams.

The Japanese approach has brought us full circle from the days of Frederick Taylor: speed and flexibility have replaced cost and hierarchy, but once again, we have settled on "one best way" to compete. The question, then, is what role is left for manufacturing strategy? What's the point of worrying about whether you should emphasize cost or flexibility when your competitors have adopted approaches to manufacturing that allow them to beat you on both?

In the relatively stable environment of the 1960s and early 1970s, the name of the game in strategy was to find an attractive industry position (offer the lowest cost or the highest quality) and build a competitive fortress around it. A good manufacturing strategy was one that defended a company's position through a narrowly focused set of capabilities.

When, however, the terms of competition shifted from low cost to high quality to flexibility to innovativeness, companies found that both their competitive strategy and their manufacturing strategy quickly became outdated. Centralizing production in a highly automated facility may look like a brilliant decision when customers place a premium on low price. But as the marketplace shifts and competitors adjust to provide higher quality and faster response times, while keeping their costs *reasonably* low, a centralized facility can quickly become a corporate millstone.

On the other hand, companies that choose product innovation rather than low cost as the way to compete could have the opposite problem. For example, Compaq prospered in the 1980s by being one of the fastest developers of new products in the personal computer industry. But it ran into trouble in the 1990s, when customers placed greater importance on low cost and fast response in customizing products, incrementally improving features and delivery. After great organizational turmoil, Compaq was able to realign its operations to reduce its costs and, more recently, has begun to make further changes in hopes of providing a customer responsiveness that matches rival Dell Computer's.

Unfortunately, neither the traditional approach to manufacturing strategy nor the lean-manufacturing paradigm pay much attention to bolstering an organization's strategic flexibility. In fact, both of these approaches often hinder flexibility. The early approach to manufacturing strategy led top managers to focus their companies' operations around specific competitive priorities that tended to make them vulnerable to strategic shifts. And lean manufacturing drives companies to become similar to one another.

The problem is not with lean manufacturing itself nor with any of its component practices like concurrent engineering, JIT, or TQM. The problem is the way companies apply these practices to their own problems. Companies tend to embark on such programs to correct particular weaknesses in their operations. But managers typically define their problems in terms of starting points and end points: "We need to reduce our variable cost by $1 per unit," or, "We need to reduce our defect level to 200 parts per million." And they seek solutions through the adoption of specific practices: "We're going to implement a JIT system in order to become more responsive," or, "We need a TQM program to improve our quality."

It is hard to imagine any manufacturing-improvement process progressing very far without specifying certain changes in practices and measurable goals. But thinking in terms of time periods and framing the solutions as the adoption of specific practices can lead to two types of problems. The first is equating an improvement in manufacturing capabilities with a manufacturing strategy. The second is failing to recognize that new practices build new capabilities that can form the basis of a new manufacturing strategy—if they are recognized and exploited.

After embarking on a major manufacturing-improvement effort, companies may find that just when they appear to have solved the problem (for example, reduced the quality gap between themselves and their competitors), they encounter new problems that require new approaches, some of which seem to contradict those just put in place. Once quality has improved, for instance, companies may find they may need to compress product-development times or reduce delivered costs.

Some would argue that such changes in priorities simply reflect the need for continuous improvement. After all, one can never expect to stop making improvements. Unfortunately for those involved—the managers, first-line supervisors, and shop-floor employees—such efforts are more like continuous frustration. Despite the seemingly successful implementation of one new set of practices after another, the company always seems to be trying to catch up with its competitors.

Whistler, a U.S. consumer electronics company, faced a choice in the late 1980s when it was rapidly losing market share to Asian competitors: either improve domestic operations to achieve cost parity or move offshore, as its U.S. competitors had done. Whistler chose the former and succeeded in reducing its manufacturing costs to Asian levels over two years. Unfortunately, by the time the company achieved this, Asian competitors were taking market share by introducing a barrage of new products.

Whistler's problem was not that its improvement program was flawed or poorly implemented; it had succeeded in reducing costs dramatically. But in doing so, it had distracted management attention from new product development while Asian competitors had been able to become more innovative *and* maintain relatively low costs.

Without realizing it, Whistler's manufacturing-improvement efforts had actually resulted in a shift in its manufacturing strategy from being the first to introduce innovative products to achieving cost parity. Had the company viewed its problem in this light, it might have chosen a different path. Rather than simply trying to change its operations to become more cost competitive, but less innovative, it might have looked for ways to *change the trade-off* between cost and innovativeness.

By viewing different improvement programs as targeted solutions to specific competitive problems, managers overlook the true power of these programs: their ability to build new capabilities. Thus, a key role for a company's manufacturing strategy is to guide the selection of improvement programs.

Consider a plant that establishes the long-term goal of drastically reducing its lead times and inventories. It can proceed toward this goal in either of two directions. One might be the immediate adoption of a JIT pull system. If the plant lacks the skills that make JIT work (for example, low setup times and defect rates), this approach might be very costly. Adopting this system will, however, create strong incentives to reduce setup times and defect rates, as well as to develop other JIT-related skills and induce an ethic of continuous improvement. Over time, a true JIT system might emerge.

An alternative approach would be to begin with a manufacturing resources planning (MRP) system, a computerized production-scheduling system based on forecasts of future demand and production lead times, as well as on real-time data from the shop floor. The initial results might not be close to JIT. Lead times, in fact, might even temporarily increase, since MRP systems tend to be rather clumsy in handling schedule changes and rush orders. On the other hand, MRP exerts pressure to improve shop-floor discipline and develop better data, which facilitates better production scheduling and the transition to computer integrated manufacturing. Once MRP control has been established, the lead times in the system can be steadily whittled away until it approaches a pure JIT system.

Both approaches may eventually allow the company to respond quickly to customer demands with low inventories. However, they cultivate different capabilities over time. Adopting an MRP-type system fosters skills in using computers and managing databases, neither of which are central to a JIT approach. Pull systems, on the other hand, encourage skills in factory-floor problem solving, incremental process improvement, and fast response. Each approach, in short, leaves the organization with a different set of skills and thus a different set of strategic options in the future. A decision about which approach to pursue should not be made without considering which set of capabilities will be most valuable to the company.

Thinking about TQM, JIT, and other manufacturing-improvement programs not as *ends* in themselves, but in terms of the capabilities they both require and create drives one to think differently about solutions. Within a static framework, solutions to problems are regarded as one-shot deals. In a dynamic setting, however, solutions are viewed as part of a longer term *path* of improvement. Individual practices are adopted not just to solve an immediate problem but also to build new skills that open up new opportunities. From this perspective, manufacturing strategy is not just about aligning operations to current competitive priorities but also about selecting and creating the operating capabilities a company will need in the future. (See "Hitachi-Seiki: Building Capabilities.")

Hitachi-Seiki: Building Capabilities

Many Japanese companies have realized that by expanding the range of their manufacturing capabilities, they increase their strategic options. Even so, few have created strategies that spell out exactly which capabilities they should develop to enhance their strategic flexibility. Hitachi-Seiki seems to be one of the exceptions. A relatively obscure manufacturer of machine tools in the 1950s, by the mid-1980s, the company had become one of the world's leading suppliers of flexible manufacturing systems, computer-controlled equipment that can perform a variable sequence of machining tasks.

As early as 1952, when the first numerically controlled machine tool was developed at MIT, Hitachi-Seiki set for itself the extremely ambitious goal of developing the capabilities required to become a leader in computerized automation. It began by embarking on basic research in automated production, some of which was done in collaboration with other Japanese manufacturers through a consortium organized by the Ministry of International Trade and Industry. After the consortium disbanded and despite the fact that the many problems with the new technology led most companies to stick with traditional manufacturing processes, Hitachi-Seiki continued to build its knowledge base.

Recognizing early on that successful automation would require the integration of mechanical design (the traditional machine tool technology) and electronics, the company began hiring electrical engineers. And in 1967, it set up a new engineering discipline, which it called "mechatronics."

The company's earliest efforts in flexible manufacturing systems failed. Its first system, developed in 1972, had only slightly better productivity than conventional machinery and was plagued by reliability and coordination problems. Yet developing that system built capabilities for future projects. For example, it brought together for the first time some of the company's top engineers from different disciplines to write software. They encountered difficulties in coordinating their efforts. But through this early experience, Hitachi-Seiki was able to cultivate engineers with broad skills and perspectives.

The company's second project incorporated some of the lessons learned from the first. While the results were slightly better, it also fell short of its goals, and its productivity was still not high enough to generate an adequate return on investment. But the company again learned critical lessons. One was that viewing flexible manufacturing as a set of purely technical problems that could be solved with technical expertise was a mistake. Instead, the company needed to take a systems approach to development that combined manufacturing and engieering perspectives.

For its third project, Hitachi-Seiki created a development team that brought together a variety of functions, including manufacturing, machine design, software engineering, and tool design. The project leader was trained as a mechanical engineer but had experience in tool design and manufacturing.

The team had learned from the prior projects that it would be difficult to develop one system that could achieve all the desired performance targets. These included automatic tool changing, flexible fixtures that could hold materials of different sizes, and the ability to operate untended. So the team members decided to develop three systems and created separate teams to tackle each. All three systems were finished in record time and met their financial and performance targets.

The lesson of the Hitachi-Seiki story is not simply "If at first you don't succeed, try, try again." The company had a long-term goal but lacked the capabilities to achieve it. Early projects were vehicles for building these capabilities. With each project, the company expanded its knowledge of technical matters (i.e., computer software) and organizational issues (i.e., how to integrate disciplines to solve problems). And with each successive project, engineers who began as specialists gradually became generalists.

After developing the company's first commercially successful flexible manufacturing system, many of the project team members were transferred to the Customer Service Department, where they designed and built systems for customers. This leveraged the skills they had developed and broadened their understanding of customer needs. It also ensured that a new group of engineers would begin to learn how to develop flexible manufacturing systems.

Information for this example was obtained from the HBS case "Hitachi-Seiki" (Abridged: 9-690-067) by Robert Hayes.

This change in perspective has tremendous implications for basic corporate decisions. Let us look at two examples.

Focused Factories. Advocates of the traditional approach to manufacturing strategy and lean manufacturing consider the idea of focus differently. The idea that factories should be focused on a narrow set of tasks or objectives continues to gain acceptance in the United States, even though it is not always clear whether a given facility should focus around products, processes, or regions. Advocates of lean manufacturing, in contrast, regard focus as an outdated concept, reflecting America's long fixation with mass production.

Despite their apparent differences, both fail to recognize that how a manufacturing system is organized affects not only its current performance but also, over time, the things it can do easily or with difficulty. Whether and how a plant should be focused depends on the capabilities it wants to build.

A plant's skills can be thought of as the set of tasks it regards as routine. Whether or not a given task is routine depends on experience and capabilities. For example, high-precision assembly may, over time, become routine for one plant but still be considered very difficult by a less experienced plant. This explains why so many poorly performing plants have been transformed by adopting the focus concept. Their poor performance reflected a lack of operating skills, and focus provided a mechanism for channeling managerial attention and resources toward mastering those skills. As an organization gains operating experience, difficult tasks become routine, and it can take on additional complexity with little performance penalty.

Vertical Integration and Sourcing. Lean manufacturing favors outsourcing and long-term relationships with suppliers. U.S. companies, on the other hand, have traditionally viewed sourcing decisions in terms of financial trade-offs and resource constraints. Again, both views downplay the dynamics of such decisions.

Consider a company that is trying to decide whether to make a component or buy it from an outside supplier. Typically, such decisions are made by analyzing the relevant production and organizational costs of the two alternatives. That kind of analysis becomes suspect, however, if one thinks not in terms of parts that get incorporated into products, but in terms of those capabilities that are closely linked and mutually reinforcing as opposed to those that can be separated. If a potential supplier possesses capabilities that are essential to a company's competitive success, the company must either work to assimilate those capabilities or develop very close, partnership-like relations with that supplier.

A decision to outsource an activity may completely alter the calculus for future decisions. Like people, organizations can forget how to do things. As skills atrophy through disuse, bringing activities back in-house at some future point becomes less feasible. So, like the decision about focused factories, outsourcing requires an evaluation of learning potential. Bringing in-house some activity with which the company has little expertise may be inefficient and less "lean" in the short term but absolutely essential over the long term because it builds critical skills that the company currently lacks.

Manufacturing strategy can no longer confine itself to guiding short-term choices between conflicting priorities like cost, quality, and flexibility. Nor can managers limit themselves to choosing which faddish improvement technique to adopt or which company to emulate. Long-term success requires that a company continually seek new ways to differentiate itself from its competitors. The companies that are able to transform their manufacturing organizations into sources of competitive advantage are those that can harness various improvement programs to the broader goal of selecting and developing unique operating capabilities. How can a company create such a strategy?

First, it must start with the idea that the primary way manufacturing adds value to an enterprise is by enabling it to do certain things better than its competitors can. Which things and how they are better will be different for individual companies, and for the same company at individual points in its evolution. Every company occasionally falls behind its competitors in some area, but for the long term, it must identify one or two areas—for instance, flexibility and innovativeness—in which it will try to be in the forefront most of the time.

Obviously, these capabilities should be ones that customers value; even better, they should be ones that are hard for competitors to duplicate. Customers may value low cost, for example, but as many consumer electronics companies learned during the 1970s and 1980s, achieving low cost by going offshore does not provide a sustainable advantage because competitors can do the same. Competitors can also license a new technology or hire those who participated in developing it. Great manufacturing strategies are built on unique skills and capabilities, not on investments in buildings, equipment, or specific individuals.

Second, a company must develop a plan for building the capabilities it wants to acquire. This is where the question of which manufacturing-improvement approaches to use and in which order comes in. A company may decide to use teams, but only after it has cultivated the capabilities that will allow teams to be effective: credibility and trust between functional groups and a cadre of effective team leaders.

Before adopting any program, managers should ask themselves, "What specific capabilities will this program create for my organization, and are these capabilities valuable in competitive terms?" Providing clear answers to such questions is usually easier if managers focus on only a few, carefully selected improvement activities. And the ones chosen will probably have to be modified to meet the company's needs. Neither capabilities nor improvement programs come in one size fits all.

In today's world, where nothing is predictable and unfamiliar competitors emerge from unexpected directions at the worst possible time, a company should think of itself as a collection of evolving capabilities, not just as a collection of products and businesses, which provide the flexibility needed to embark in new directions. Corporate strategy must provide a framework for guiding the selection, development, and exploitation of these capabilities. Since many of the capabilities with the greatest competitive value reside in a company's manufacturing organization, corporate strategy must become much more explicit about, and reliant on, manufacturing considerations than in the past.

Note

1. James Womack, Daniel Jones, and Daniel Roos, *The Machine That Changed the World* (New York: Macmillan, 1990), p. 13.

About the Contributors

Norman Berg is a professor of general management and chairman of the Owner/President Management Program at the Harvard Business School. His research interests include the strategic and organizational problems resulting from diversification and the international competitive challenges facing American industry. He is co-author of *Policy Formulation and Administration* and author of *General Management: An Analytic Approach,* and has written a number of articles and studies related to diversification.

Andrew C. Boynton is an associate professor at the Kenan-Flagler Business School, University of North Carolina at Chapel Hill. He has published numerous books and articles on topics ranging from information technology management to requirements for flexible organizational designs. His latest research is on process design and transformation.

Richard B. Chase is the Justin B. Dart Term Professor of Operations Management and director of the Center for Operations Management Education and Research at the School of Business Administration, University of Southern California. Specializing in issues of service strategy and value-added service in manufacturing, he consults regularly to businesses and industry groups worldwide and has served as an examiner for the Malcolm Baldrige National Quality Award. Dr. Chase is co-author of a leading textbook in operations management and has published articles on service management in a wide variety of journals.

Kim B. Clark is the Harry E. Figgie, Jr., Professor of Business Administration at the Harvard Business School, where he serves as chair of the technology and operations management area and heads the Science and Technology Interest Group. Specializing in issues of product development and technology, and operations strategy, he is a frequent contributor to the *Harvard Business Review* and other management journals, and is the co-author with Steven Wheelwright of *Revolutionizing Product Development, Managing New Product and Process Development*, and *Leading Product Development*. He is also the co-author with Takahiro Fujimoto of *Product Development Performance* (Harvard Business School Press), which received the 1992 Nikkei Culture Award for Economic Publications.

Don Clausing is the Bernard M. Gordon Adjunct Professor of Engineering Innovation and Practice at the Massachusetts Institute of Technology, where he has integrated the principles of quality function development, low-cost quality engineering, and other international practices designed to improve product development and manufacturing. Formerly principal engineer at Xerox, Dr. Clausing served on the MIT Commission of Industrial Productivity and the Defense Science Board, and is the author of *Total Quality Development*.

Peter F. Drucker has been writing about management since he published *The Future of Industrial Man* —his second book—in 1943. Since 1971 he has been a professor of social science and management at The Claremont Graduate School in Claremont, California. His latest book is *Post-Capitalist Society*, published in 1993.

Marshall L. Fisher is the Stephen J. Heyman Professor and co-director of the Center for Manufacturing and Logistics Research at The Wharton School, University of Pennsylvania. Dr. Fisher has published widely on both practical and theoretical aspects of logistics, and has been a consultant to Fortune 500 companies on more than 30 logistics restructuring projects. His current research and consulting focuses on supply chain coordination and developing the operational capabilities required to support a customer responsive strategy. Dr. Fisher's activities have been recognized by numerous awards; most recently, he was elected a member of the National Academy of Engineering.

David A. Garvin is the Robert and Jane Cizik Professor of Business Administration at the Harvard Business School, where he teaches in the MBA and Advanced Management programs and has led seminars on teaching by the case method. He is a frequent contributor to the *Harvard Business Review* and received the McKinsey Award for best article of 1983. His recent books include *Operations Strategy: Text and Cases* and *Education for Judgment* (co-editor).

Janice H. Hammond is associate professor at the Harvard Business School and co-founder of the Harvard University Center for Textile and Apparel Research. Her research interests include the effect of coordination on the performance of manufacturing and retail channels.

Robert H. Hayes holds the Philip Caldwell Professorship in Business Administration at the Harvard Business School, where he teaches courses in operations management and serves as senior associate dean, director of faculty planning. His current research focuses on manufacturing competitiveness, technological development, and the integration of design with manufacturing. A frequent contributor to the *Harvard Business Review*, Dr. Hayes has received the McKinsey Award for best article on three occasions. His books include *Restoring Our Competitive Edge: Competing Through Manufacturing*, co-authored with Steven Wheelwright, *Dynamic Manufacturing: Creating the Learning Organization*, co-authored with Steven Wheelwright and Kim Clark, and *The Uneasy Alliance: Managing the Productivity-Technology Dilemma*, co-edited with Kim Clark and Christopher Lorenz, Harvard Business School Press.

Ramchandran Jaikumar is the Daewoo Professor of Business Administration at the Harvard Business School, where his research centers on computer-integrated manufacturing. He is currently working on building more intelligence into manufacturing control systems in order to significantly improve quality and reliability and reduce disruptions. He has published widely in academic and professional journals and has contributed to several books. He has been an advisor to the Congressional Office of Technology Assessment and to the U.S. Senate Subcommittee on Science and Technology.

Joseph M. Juran is founder and chairman emeritus of Juran Institute, Inc. Since 1924, his work has centered on managing for quality and he has made extensive contributions to the subject in books, papers, video tapes, training courses, lectures, and a global consulting practice.

Robert S. Kaplan is the Arthur Lowes Dickinson Professor of Accounting at the Harvard Business School. Author of more than 90 papers in accounting and management journals, he received the McKinsey Award for outstanding article in the *Harvard Business Review* in 1984. His current research focuses on developing new management accounting systems for the rapidly changing environment of manufacturing and service organizations. He is co-author of *Relevance Lost: The Rise and Fall of Management Accounting*—winner of the Wildman Medal in 1988—and editor of *Measures for Manufacturing Excellence* (Harvard Business School Press). He is also featured in a Harvard Business School Management Productions video series, "Measuring Corporate Performance," which explores the use in actual companies of two techniques—activity-based costing and the balanced scorecard—he has helped develop.

Uday Karmarkar is the Times Mirror Professor of Management Strategy and Policy and director of the Center for Technology Management at the Anderson Graduate School of Management, UCLA. His research interests include manufacturing management, health care management, industrial marketing, and operations and technology strategy for manufacturing and service firms. Dr. Karmarkar has published in a wide variety of management and industry journals and has conducted consulting and research projects and executive education programs in the United States, Europe, and Asia.

Janice A. Klein is a visiting associate professor at the Sloan School of Management at the Massachusetts Institute of Technology. Previously, she was an assistant professor at the Harvard Business School.

Constantinos C. Markides is associate professor of strategic and international management and director of the Accelerated Development Program at the London Business School. His research interests include international competitiveness, corporate restructuring, and the management of international acquisitions. He is author of numerous articles and the forthcoming *Diversification, Refocusing and Economic Performance* and *Breaking the Rules: Putting Innovation Back into Strategy.*

Jeffrey G. Miller is professor of operations management at the Boston University School of Management and director of Boston University's Manufacturing Roundtable. He is co-author of two texts on operations management and numerous articles and case studies on production, logistics, materials management, and operations strategy. Formerly at Dow Chemical, Dr. Miller has led executive education programs and consulted to companies worldwide.

Walter R. Obermeyer is a principal of Sport Obermeyer Ltd. and regional vice president of Heritage Trust and Asset Management, Inc., a Colorado trust and asset management firm.

B. Joseph Pine II is the founder and president of Strategic Horizons, Inc., a management consulting firm based in Ridgefield, Connecticut. He was formerly a program manager of management research with the IBM Consulting Group, where he was responsible for research into leading-edge management consulting practices and executive education after holding several technical and managerial positions within IBM. He has received numerous awards for his achievements, including IBM's Outstanding Innovation Award. He is author of *Mass Customization* (Harvard Business School Press).

Gary P. Pisano is an associate professor at the Harvard Business School in the technology and operations management area, where he specializes in manufacturing strategy and the development of new process technology. His articles on these topics have appeared in the *Harvard Business Review, Research Policy,* and *Administrative Science Quarterly.* He is currently conducting research on process development and manufacturing strategy in the global pharmaceutical industry and he is writing a case book on manufacturing and operations strategy with Robert Hayes and David Upton.

Ananth Raman is an assistant professor at the Harvard Business School in the technology and operations management area. His research focuses on supply chain coordination for products with uncertain demand. His findings have been published in a variety of management and industry journals.

Wickham Skinner is the James E. Robison Professor of Business Administration Emeritus at the Harvard Business School. His current research interests include manufacturing policy and corporate strategy, management of human resources, and corporate revitalization. He has conducted research, consulting, and education programs on manufacturing strategy worldwide and has served as director of a wide variety of companies in the United States and Canada. He has published numerous books and articles and received the McKinsey Award for best article in the *Harvard Business Review* (1986).

Genichi Taguchi is executive director of the American Supplier Institute. He has developed various kinds of methodology, known as Taguchi Methods, in quality engineering, business, and management fields. He has received numerous awards for his contributions to engineering, product design, and manufacturing, including the Deming Prize and the Blue Ribbon Award from the Emperor of Japan.

Bart Victor is an associate professor of management at the Kenan-Flagler Business School, University of North Carolina at Chapel Hill. Specializing in organizational cultures and business ethics, he is the author of numerous research publications on managing conflict, business ethics, and organizational design.

Thomas E. Vollmann is professor of manufacturing management and director of the Manufacturing 2000 Project at the International Institute for Management Development. He is author or co-author of nine books and has published more than 75 articles. His research has been primarily in operations management, manufacturing planning and control systems, manufacturing performance measurement systems, and total quality management; his current focus is on benchmarking and manufacturing restructuring. Dr. Vollmann has served as consultant to many firms on issues of manufacturing and information systems.

Steven C. Wheelwright is the Class of 1949 Professor of Business Administration at the Harvard Business School, having previously been the Kleiner, Perkins, Caufield and Byers Professor of Management at Stanford University's Graduate School of Business, where he directed the strategic management program. His research and writing focuses on product and process development, manufacturing strategy, and competing through manufacturing, in relation to commercializing new product and manufacturing process technologies. Dr. Wheelwright is the author or co-author of numerous articles and 13 books, including *Revolutionizing Product Development, Managing New Product and Process Development,* and *Leading Product Development,* with Kim Clark; *Restoring Our Competitive Edge,* with Robert Hayes; and *Dynamic Manufacturing,* with professors Clark and Hayes.

INDEX